Pakistan's Security Dynamics and Nuclear Weapons

Pakistan's Security Dynamics and Nuclear Weapons

Edited by
Shalini Chawla
Rajiv Nayan

Foreword by
Ambassador Sujan R. Chinoy

KNOWLEDGE WORLD
KW Publishers Pvt Ltd
New Delhi

INDIAN PUGWASH SOCIETY

INDIAN PUGWASH SOCIETY

Indian Pugwash Society
No. 1, Development Enclave, Delhi Cantt.
New Delhi-110 010
Phone: +91-11-26717983
Website: www.pugwashindia.com

ISBN 978-93-91490-65-2 Hardback
ISBN 978-93-91490-77-5 ebook

Published in India by Kalpana Shukla

KW Publishers Pvt Ltd
4676/21, First Floor, Ansari Road
Daryaganj, New Delhi 110 002
Phone: +91 11 43528107
Marketing: kw@kwpub.in
Editorial: production@kwpub.in
Website: www.kwpub.in

Printed and bound in India

A Tribute

Shakti Sinha (1957-2021)

Shri Shakti Sinha's contribution to this volume, fittingly on the subject, which has always been close to his heart, was possibly his last scholarly work. He submitted his chapter on "Pakistan's Afghanistan Dilemma" just a day before his passing.

Shri Shakti Sinha was not simply an able bureaucrat with an exceptional outlook and public duty, but a creative thinker and a thoughtful policy analyst. Having served on a UN mission to Afghanistan, Shri Sinha's abiding interest in the country was legendary and established him as a foremost commentator on Pakistan and Afghan affairs.

Contents

Section 2
THE ARMED FORCES

Section 3
THE NUCLEAR DIMENSIONS

Foreword

Pakistan remains a major strategic concern for India for its unrelenting efforts to weaken India by all means. It has perennially sought parity with India through its "willing-to-eat-grass-but-will-make-bomb" strategy. It has used terror as an instrument in its proxy-war with India and wasted its diplomatic energy in attempt to vilify India at the international level.

All this is often attributed to an exaggerated sense of fear of India, carefully nurtured by the power elite in Pakistan, which has been disseminated among the people across generations through manipulation of facts of history and misinterpretation of Indian policies. This fear is existential and leads Pakistanis to believe that India is out to dismantle Pakistan and reverse partition. The military of Pakistan, which has directly ruled the country for 33 years out of 75 years of its sovereign existence, derives its legitimacy from such conjured up fear and continues to control the process of democracy. Through misuse of the media and other means of communication, the military has successfully emasculated and maligned the political leadership in Pakistan, which has affected the quality of representative and democratic politics in the country and precluded the possibility of any constructive engagement with India over the years.

Pakistan has unleashed four direct wars with India in addition to its unceasing proxy war through the terror machine it has raised since the 1990s. In fact, its subversive strategy vis-à-vis India is as old as the Lashkar invasion it had orchestrated in Kashmir in 1947. Some Pakistani analysts, including a retired air marshal of the Pakistani Air Force, have acknowledged the fact it was Pakistan which had initiated all the four wars (in 1947, 1965, 1971 and 1999) and ended up suffering huge reverses. The Kargil War of 1999 showcased Pakistan's familiar strategy of using non-states actors to provoke India and start an interstate war.

Pakistani calculations to use nuclear blackmail and intensify terror operations inside India with impunity has been deftly countered by India in recent years. The military strategists in Islamabad had imagined that the threat of nuclear conflict would deter any escalatory response from India. However, India has successfully used both surgical strikes and full-scale military operations (Operation Balakot of February 2019) in the face of brazen attacks by non-state actors acting at the behest of the Pakistan Army and sent a strong message to Pakistan. Nevertheless, as continuing terrorist incidents in Kashmir indicate Pakistan's policy of sponsoring and fuelling terrorism in India has not abated.

Against this backdrop, it becomes pertinent for strategic analysts in India to continually monitor developments in Pakistan with a focus on its policies and strategies vis-à-vis India. Its military preparedness, strategic alliances with external powers, approach towards the neighbourhood, internal faultlines as well as its nuclear efforts require critical analysis and evaluation.

The volume at hand, titled *Pakistan's Security Dynamics and Nuclear Weapons*, edited by Dr Rajiv Nayan and Dr Shalini Chawla, is a welcome effort in this regard. The editors have invited leading experts on Pakistan to contribute to this volume and dwell on critical aspects of Pakistani security, politics and economy. The ongoing economic crisis, Pakistan's involvement in regional extremism and terrorism, its internal security problems emanating from its mishandling of the Baloch insurgency and its approach to Afghanistan have been deftly covered by various authors who have the required expertise on these themes. The chapter on the Indus Water Treaty invites the attention of the readers to an important issue, which has been misrepresented in the discourse in Pakistan in recent years. All the three arms of the Pakistan military, the Army, Navy and Air Force, have been studied in a comprehensive manner in the second section. The third section of the book deals with Pakistan's nuclear policy, which has a critical bearing on its policies vis-à-vis India. In this section, experts focus on Pakistan's grand strategy, its efforts to ensure full spectrum deterrence, missile build-up, nuclear proliferation and the debate on tactical nuclear weapons (TNWs).

I am confident that such well-rounded dissection of Pakistan and incisive analyses will go a long way in providing analysts, policymakers and the wider public in India with critical information about a country that remains an outliner in South Asia March towards peace, stability and progress.

New Delhi
20 June 2022

Amb. Sujan R. Chinoy
Director General
Manohar Parrikar Institute for
Defence Studies and Analyses

List of Tables and Figures

Tables

Figures

Editors and Contributors

Editors

Dr. **Shalini Chawla** is Distinguished Fellow at the Centre for Air Power Studies (CAPS), New Delhi. She joined CAPS in 2006 and has published more than 100 research articles/chapters in national and international journals/books on a wide range of issues relating to Pakistan and Afghanistan. She lectures regularly at various universities, think tanks and leading institutions of the Indian armed forces and Indian Foreign Service. She is actively engaged in India's Track 1.5 initiatives. She received a Commendation and Badge from the Chief of Air Staff in October 2020 for displaying great dedication, professional ability and praiseworthy contribution to the service. She has authored/co-edited five books titled *Pakistan's Military and Its Strategy* (2009), *Nuclear Pakistan* (2012), *India's Sentinel* (ed.) (2014), *Strategic Advantage of Air Power* (ed.) (2019) and *The 1971 Indo-Pak Air War: Reflections and Projections* (ed.) (2021).

Dr. **Rajiv Nayan** is Senior Research Associate at the Manohar Parrikar Institute for Defence Studies and Analyses, New Delhi. Rajiv was a Visiting Research Fellow at Japan Institute of International Affairs, Tokyo, where he published his monograph *Non-Proliferation Issues in South Asia*. He was also Senior Researcher at Peace Research Institute, Oslo, a Senior Visiting Research Fellow at King's College, London and a Visiting Fulbright Scholar at the Center on International Cooperation, New York University. He has authored a book titled *Global Strategic Trade Management: How India Adjusts its Export Control System for Accommodation in the Global System* (2019) and edited a volume titled *The Nuclear Non-Proliferation Treaty and India* (2012).

Contributors

Ms. **Aarushi Vikram** was a research intern in the ALACUN Centre at Manohar Parrikar Institute for Defence Studies and Analyses in 2019. She holds Double MA in International Politics, Gender and Development with a primary research interest in Terrorism and Conflict. Her works include a dissertation thesis titled, "Differing Consequences of War: Why does the Status and Contributions of Women in Conflict Differ in Different Nations?" (2018); "AMISOM Amidst the Dangers of Al-Shabaab" (2019); "James Hamill, Africa's Lost Leader: South Africa's Continental Role Since Apartheid (2020). She is presently working at Uniform Rights and Justice Assured (URJA), an NGO providing legal counsel and information to underprivileged women.

Air Vice Marshal **Amit Aneja** is a veteran fighter pilot recipient of three presidential awards for distinguished service. He holds an MPhil in Defense and Strategic Studies and is a graduate of Air Command and Staff College, USA and of National Institute of Defense Studies, Japan. He is a keen observer of National Security Policy Process and geopolitics. He is an avid golfer.

Mr. **Arjun Anand** interned with the Manohar Parrikar Institute for Defence Studies and Analyses in 2019. He worked with the Centre for Nuclear Arms and Control and contributed to the Centre's policy research and advocacy projects. Arjun holds a master's degree in public policy from the National Law School of India University and a Bachelor of Arts (Honours) in Political Science from Sri Venkateswara College, University of Delhi. His other works include a dissertation thesis titled "Unlocking Slumbai: Raising the Economic Potential of Urban Slum Inhabitants Through Land-titling in Mumbai" (2020) and "A Discourse on Dissent".

Lieutenant General **DS Hooda,** PVSM, UYSM, AVSM, VSM & Bar, ADC (Retd) served in the Indian Army for forty years. He retired as the Army Commander of Northern Command where he was responsible for operations along the Line of Control with

Pakistan and the Line of Actual Control with China in Ladakh. He also commanded the counterinsurgency operations in Kashmir. Lt Gen Hooda is a co-founder of the Council for Strategic and Defense Research, a New Delhi based think tank, and a Senior Fellow at the Delhi Policy Group.

Mr. **Jayadeva Ranade** is a former Additional Secretary, Cabinet Secretariat, Government of India and is presently president of the Centre for China Analysis and Strategy. He is a former Member of the National Security Advisory Board (NSAB). He has specialised for over 40 years in analysing developments relating to China, Tibet and East Asia and is the author of four books with *Xi Jinping: China's Third New Era* published in February 2022.

Dr. **Manpreet Sethi is** Distinguished Fellow at the Centre for Air Power Studies, New Delhi, heads its programme on nuclear security. Recipient of K Subrahmanyam award (2014) and Commendation by Chief of Air Staff (2020). Receiving her doctorate in 1997, she has worked on nuclear energy, strategy, arms control & disarmament. She is author/co-author/editor of eight books and over 120 papers. She lectures regularly at National Defence College and other establishments of Indian Armed Forces, Police, Foreign Services and Universities. Dr. Sethi regularly participates at policy conferences, Track II initiatives and UNIDIR. She was Member, Prime Minister's Informal Group on Disarmament in 2012. She is on Board of Directors of Asia Pacific Leadership Network (APLN), and Co-chair, Women in Nuclear-India.

Professor **Rajaram Nagappa**, is a honorary Visiting Professor at National Institute of Advanced Studies (NIAS). He joined NIAS on 1st February 2007. Most significant research contributions include, analysis of Pakistan's ballistic missile production capacity. He has specialised in aerospace propulsion and has worked extensively to design and develop solid propellant rockets. His interests are in missile technology and space weaponisation. He has served in the Vikram Sarabhai Space Centre, ISRO as its Associate Director, and later was Pandalai Memorial Chair Professor at Anna University, Chennai. He is a recipient of the Astronautical Society of India Award, Distinguished Alumnus Award of the Madras Institute of Technology, DRDO's Agni Award for Excellence in Self Reliance, Certificate of Appreciation of the International Astronautical Federation and the Honorary Fellowship of the High Energy Materials Society of India.

Ms. **Riya Sinha** is a foreign policy researcher based in New Delhi. Her research focuses on analysing regional connectivity in South Asia, particularly in the area of economic integration. She has also conducted various studies on connectivity between India and Pakistan such as building sector-specific value chains, cross-border trade, regulations and infrastructure, and tariff and non-tariff barriers.

Dr. **Shakti Sinha** was the Honorary Director of the Vadodara-based think tank, the Atal Bihari Institute of Policy Research & International Studies (MS University) and the Honorary Director of the Delhi School of Public Policy & Governance, an Institute of Eminence established by the Delhi University. He was a Distinguished Fellow at the India Foundation, New Delhi. Earlier, he was the Director of the Nehru Memorial Museum and Library, New Delhi. His book *Vajpayee: The Years That Changed India* (2020) is critically acclaimed and continues to be read with great interest. He also edited seven books, the most recent one being an authoritative account of Sardar Patel, the thinker and doer.

Lieutenant General **Syed Ata Hasnain,** PVSM, UYSM, AVSM, SM, VSM** (Retd) served 40 years in the Army spending much of his command and field tenures at the LoC and LAC in J&K. He commanded the Indian Army's elite formations, the Brigade at Uri, Dagger Division at Baramula and XV Corps at Srinagar. He continues to pursue the study of the dynamics of J&K and is currently the Chancellor of the Central University of Kashmir. He is also a Member of the National Disaster Management Authority of India. He writes frequently for mainstream media and is a regular television commentator on Afghanistan, Pakistan, China and issues connected with India's National Security.

Mr. **Tilak Devasher** is an author of three widely acclaimed books on Pakistan: *Pakistan: Courting the Abyss* (2016); *Pakistan: At the Helm* (2018); and *Pakistan: The Balochistan Conundrum* (2019). Tilak Devasher retired as Special Secretary, Cabinet Secretariat, Government of India in October 2014. He is Member at National Security Advisory Board (NSAB), Consultant at Vivekananda International Foundation, Emeritus Resource Faculty at Rashtriya Raksha University and Distinguished Fellow at United Services Institution of India. He is currently working on his fourth book on Pakistan.

Dr. **Uttam Sinha** is a leading commentator on trans-boundary water issues, climate change, and the Arctic region. After a brief stint in the print media and a doctoral degree from Jawaharlal Nehru University, he joined the Institute for Defence Studies and Analyses in 2001 (now renamed as Manohar Parrikar-IDSA) where he heads the non-traditional security centre and is the Managing Editor of *Strategic Analysis* published by Routledge, the Institute's flagship journal. He is a recipient of many fellowships and leadership programmes including senior fellow at the Nehru Memorial Museum and Library (2018-2020). He is the author of the recent published book *Indus Basin Interrupted: A History of Territory and Politics from Alexander to Nehru* (2021) and the co-edited volume *Modi 2.0: A Resolve to Secure India* (2021).

Dr. **Vijay Sakhuja** is former Director, National Maritime Foundation, New Delhi. He is currently associated with a number of think tanks in India and overseas. He has published over 40 books, edited volumes and monographs on international relations, Indo-Pacific and Indian Ocean affairs, maritime security, the Arctic, Blue Economy, and Industry 4.0 technologies. He is currently pursuing issues concerning 'energy transitions' in the maritime domain.

1. Introduction

Shalini Chawla and *Rajiv Nayan*

At present, Pakistan is well known as a problem state in the international system. Considered the epicentre of the global jihad movement and international terrorism yet projecting its geopolitical significance in the great game played in the region and the world, Pakistan has been weaving a paradoxical security narrative. Strangely, despite the frequent discovery of its hands in harbouring global terror machination, it finds takers of its narrative of victimhood in the international community. Quite notably, this narrative is constructed by its military and Imams, and unfortunately, democracy merely becomes a façade to emit the signal provided by the army and the madrasas. One of the American observers rightly noted: "What cannot be disputed, however, is that the country lies in a dangerous part of the world, and its internal politics are violent and volatile. The government often tries to pursue multiple agendas and to reconcile competing interests."[1]

Ironically, this paradox is underlined not merely by international leaders but also occasionally by Pakistani officials. One of the American Presidents once remarked: "If there is a major attack on an Asian, European or African city it's likely to have ties to al Qaeda's leadership in Pakistan."[2] Quite significantly, one of the Pakistani Prime Ministers, Benazir Bhutto, too, underlined the stark reality by stating: "I seek to lead a democratic Pakistan which is free from the yoke of military dictatorship and that will cease to be a haven, the very petri dish of international terrorism." Elsewhere she told, "The military wants a system that protects its policies and privileges." Despite the acknowledgement of a dangerous Pakistan, the nation has been engaged by all the top leaders of the democracies and dictatorships.

To hide its insidious acts and agenda, Pakistan has been playing the victim card. The patron of the terrorist organisations such as Al-Qaeda and Lashkar-e-Taiba, strives to convey to the world that in fact, it joined a coalition of countries willing to fight terrorism. However, contradictions of the Pakistani security state expose its true face time and again. The power dynamic within the country continues to be dominated by the military lobby and the democratic regime is 'conscious' of its 'limitations'. Pakistan made its official security policy India-centric but it troubled other countries like Afghanistan. Its overemphasis on security state led to the stress within. Pakistan imploded and the worst outcome was the formation of Bangladesh in 1971.

Noticeably, Pakistan presents a very interesting set of contradictions: the strategic decision-making is completely dominated by men in khaki, but the state continues to function as a democratic state; portrays itself as a victim of terrorism, but continues to use terrorism as a foreign policy tool against India and Afghanistan; its territorial boundaries are engaged in full-blooded insurgency from as early as 1940s, but the state continues to support and conduct insurgency in its neighbourhood; strategically needs Afghanistan to be on its side, but supports the instruments of civil war in Kabul; has promoted its threat perceptions and deems India as an existential threat, but is responsible for waging four wars against India. Pakistan's challenge to peace and stability in the region resulted in four wars. It forced India to fight the first India-Pakistan War just after its independence. The architect of activities such as Operation Gibraltar to infiltrate the Indian Territory and Operation Grand Slam vows to defend its own territory from aggression.

The Pakistani leadership has been consistent in its strategy (against India) of maintaining the centrality of covert war (guerilla war through terrorism). India has faced Pakistan's covert war and its varied dimensions for six decades now and Islamabad has shown no signs to alter its strategic calculus, although tactics and intensity may undergo changes in the near future. Pakistan's objective is to disturb the status quo which is anyway, currently, in its favour as it is sitting occupying a large part of Jammu and Kashmir and Ladakh; at the same time, it also wants to occupy more and more of India's territory. And for its aggressive designs, quite curiously, Pakistan blames India by propagating that India is not reconciled to the partition of Pakistan and wants to undo the partition. Pakistan tries to draw legitimacy to its wrong deeds through this kind of propaganda.

Pakistan has been seeking arms and other military assistance from outside apparently to secure itself. Soon after its formation, Pakistan looked towards the Western bloc to fix its security. It joined the Southeast Asia Treaty Organisation (SEATO) and the Central Treaty Organisation (CENTO) in 1955. As its defence industry was weak, and remained so, to an extent, even now, it acquired armaments, mainly from the West. In return, it allowed the West to set up a military base for multiple military activities. Islamabad's strategically advantageous geostrategic location brought in the US alliance easily and also allowed an exponential evolution of its all-weather friendship with China. It hardly tried to build its own defence industry but did succeed in setting up a few defence institutions.

Pakistan that declared itself a nuclear weapon state in 1998 had a long ambition of acquiring nuclear weapons, though the 1998 Indian declaration was the most trivial justification offered by apologists of the Pakistani bomb. Even the pledge of Zulfiqar Ali Bhutto to eat grass but build the nuclear bomb does not provide the correct picture of the beginning of the Pakistani nuclear ambition. Pakistan had started dreaming for nuclear weapons and ballistic missiles, possibly just after its creation. For the purpose, it did set up the institutional framework, including scientific institutions and laboratories. Time to time, it used major and minor technological and political developments in India to justify its nuclear quest. However, the rudimentary scientific, technological, industrial and financial base prevented it from developing nuclear weapons. As a result, from the very beginning, it experimented and innovated its nuclear route. The most well-known route was the use of the clandestine proliferation network.

The international security community has frequently been publishing on the Pakistani nuclear puzzle. The Pakistani security rationale has remained one of the dimensions of the Pakistani puzzle. In this context, the narrative of threat perceptions became an integral part of Pakistan's strategic posturing for the outside world and domestically to justify its unreasonable inclination towards defence and nuclear build-up. The argument of survival of a small state against conventionally superior adversary is an old narrative but is being used by Pakistan for decades now. Interestingly, the bomb for the survival of Pakistan has become a serious question of international security because of its struggling with raging insurgencies, growing extremism, and inconsistent economic growth. Admittedly, Pakistan has still managed to 'sustain' itself. For more than a decade, the international community has put pressure on Pakistan for securing its nuclear arsenal. But Pakistan has been managing international community and continuing to expand its nuclear arsenal with China's assistance.

With all the existing domestic, economic and security challenges, which are detrimental to nations' growth, the stable factor has been Pakistan's military build-up—conventionally and very importantly, nuclear expansion. Conventional military modernisation accelerated post 9/11 (with US military assistance and Chinese support) and the nuclear build up (primarily with Chinese assistance) has been significant, placing the arsenal as the world's most rapidly expanding arsenal amongst the nuclear actors. Saudi Arabia's financial and other links add further complexity to the dynamics of Pakistan's nuclear weapons.

Similarly, its acquisition of nuclear weapons will continue to be rationalised as a deterrent to Indian conventional military superiority and to provide an umbrella to pursue a proxy war through terrorism. In the given context, it is important to undertake a study on Pakistan's security dimensions to allow India to evaluate its options against Pakistan. Pakistan's nuclear weapons in particular and its security in general have been the subject matter of the study of not only Pakistani authors based in and outside Pakistan but also several non-Pakistani scholars and writers.

An appraisal of literature indicates broadly four categories of writings on Pakistani nuclear weapons. First and the predominant category[3] of writings is fixated to the unrealistic South Asia paradigm. Most of these writings do not go beyond India-Pakistan binary even when it uses the framework of South Asia. This category has writings from the West and the West-funded and influenced individuals and institutions. Some Pakistani writings tactically use this paradigm to shield Pakistani nuclear weapons. Achieving strategic stability is projected as the panacea for all the problems of the region. Following it logically, it may be inferred that Pakistan's security is also integrated with strategic stability of South Asia. These writings either ignore the India-Pakistan nuclear risk reduction measures or confidence building measures taken after and even before the 1998 nuclear tests or pay passing reference to them.

Even before becoming the nuclear weapons states in 1998, India and Pakistan signed an agreement that both countries would not attack each other's nuclear facilities. On 1 January, both the countries exchange a list of their nuclear installations. Quite obviously, the idea behind the annual exchange of the list of the facilities is that there would be no attack on these facilities. The exchange of list continued even when the two countries had very tense relationship, but more importantly, the two countries complied with the letter and spirit of the agreement for not attacking each other's nuclear facilities. India and Pakistan have also signed joint documents and made several statements that both the countries have developed command and control arrangements to avoid relating to nuclear weapons incidents. The countries have an agreement for exchanging information on any incident which has potential for misinterpretation. India has been providing prior information about its missile tests to a set of countries, including Pakistan.

Another stream[4] of writings, basically sponsored by the Pakistani establishment, points out security imperative of Pakistani nuclear weapons. Within this stream, there are two sub streams: one justifies Pakistani nuclear weapon on the assumption that India has been possessing nuclear weapons even before 1998, and Pakistan's nuclear weapon would counter or deter Indian nuclear weapons; the second justifies it espousing the conventional superiority of India. It is a different matter that India has been sending assurances through signals that its acquisition of advanced military capabilities such as nuclear missiles or submarines are not meant for Pakistan. There is a common understanding that these advanced nuclear weapons capabilities are intended to offset the growing Chinese nuclear and other forces. Actually, Pakistani establishment through these writings wants to convey a benign image of nuclear Pakistan, and as discussed, play the victim card.

Another category[5] of writings on Pakistan nuclear weapons is relating to resolving or unravelling proliferation puzzle. As discussed, Pakistan's weak industrial, technological and engineering base forced Pakistan to look outside for its arsenals. Because of its aggressive nature, Pakistan faced hurdles in acquisition of even conventional weapons but somehow it managed to procure several major platforms. However, the operation of non-proliferation norms, rules, guidelines and treaties as well as agreements, purchase of nuclear weapons and their delivery capabilities became difficult. To beat non-proliferation restrictions, Pakistan helped develop a proliferation network with some state and non-state actors. The writings of this category give details of technical as well as political issues involved with the clandestine acquisition. Some of them indeed have very fascinating elements.

The fourth category[6] of writings on Pakistani nuclear weapons is devoted on assessing the danger of Pakistani nuclear weapons falling in the hands of Jihadis. Most of the writings have come in the last two decades. These works examine the relationship between Pakistan's nuclear establishment and Jihadi elements. As Pakistan's scientific establishment and army both are infiltrated by Jihadi elements, it is quite natural for the academic community to probe the relationship. Some of the works on the proliferation network have also discussed the Jihadi and non-state actors' involvement with Pakistani nuclear weapons. However, a couple of books came up to counter the idea of Jihadi nuclear Pakistan.

Notwithstanding writings on the Pakistani nuclear weapons, the current need to study dynamics of the Pakistani nuclear weapons is much more crucial than before. Pakistan believes in maintaining ambiguity and opted for an unwritten doctrine. The "First Use Doctrine" for Pakistan came as a natural option as the objectives of Pakistan's nuclear weapons has been war prevention and deterring India of any potential military aggression in response to Pakistan's act of terror. The proclaimed first use policy projected somehow as 'use or lose policy' and created serious security complications. The much-cherished achievement of the full spectrum deterrence of Pakistan is unstructured and amorphous. Pakistani military officials and even politicians use the phrase to allude to anything relating to its nuclear weapons and the delivery systems. It is not only because of its pronouncement on battlefield strategy but also because of the Pakistani nuclear mindset—a set of bigoted policies framed against India. Isn't the Jihadi mindset guiding nuclear weapons a bigger danger to India and the world? Moreover, in recent years, Pakistan's endeavour to provide a nuclear shield to its terror attacks or sponsorship to such attacks have become manifest and obvious. The dominant powers of the world seem to have reconciled to the Pakistani nuclear blackmail.

The Pakistani understanding views NASR as the ultimate tool in an event of a Preventive War. It is developed to threaten India from acting against terror attacks, by lowering the nuclear threshold. It is seen as a game changer in the current scenario of Ballistic Missile Defence programme being pursued by India. However, one way of looking at it can be that Pakistan attempts to draw international attention to the military asymmetry between India and Pakistan so as to protect itself from Indian aggression. What must also be noted is the danger of sub delegation of NASR missile to Brigadier level ranked Pakistani military officers.

This emerging nuclear trend is extremely dangerous for the countries which are its adversary or adversaries. The development of NASR may also alter the existing battlefield scenario. India may use the second-strike option as a response to a NASR by massively striking on Pakistani force in any part of the world. NASR provides for a lowering of nuclear threshold, but leaves the battlefield open to massive retaliatory sub-nuclear or nuclear exchange on Pakistani leadership or value targets, while incurring minimal value loss to the Indian side (if NASR is employed). It is important to note that the recent deployment of INS Arihant adds as a credible second-strike option.

In recent years what has also been significant that Pakistan has used the threat of nuclear war rather too often. Prime Minister Imran Khan after the revocation of Article 370 in 2019 has tried to flag the nuclear threat multiple times projecting Pakistan's desperation and anxiety to deal with the Indian decision on the status of Kashmir.

The aim of the book is to have a deeper understanding of Pakistan's complex security dynamics from a wide range of experts belonging to varied fields. The book is divided into three parts. The first section of the book discusses various security dimensions of the Pakistani state.

Leading experts have tried to unfold critical challenges for Pakistan including—Pakistan's economy and the unending crisis, complexities of the China-Pakistan Economic Corridor (CPEC), regional extremism and terrorism, the question of Baloch marginalisation, Indus Water Treaty and Pakistan's unending Afghanistan dilemma. The second section of the book focuses on the armed forces of Pakistan—Army, Navy and Air Force and evaluates the nuclear aspect. The third section of the book elaborates and assesses the nuclear dimensions. Pakistan's grand strategy, the full spectrum deterrence, missile build-up, nuclear proliferation and the TNW debate.

Experts have tried to unfold critical challenges for Pakistan. The second chapter by Lt Gen Ata Hasnain converses Zia's doctrine in great details. The chapter analyses three basics of Pakistan's strategy against India—nuclear balance with India, employment of irregular warfare as a subset of proxy, hybrid conflict and religious radicalism. The chapter examines why Pakistan is likely to pursue its policy of intimidation against India treating Jammu and Kashmir as a battleground.

The third chapter by Jayadeva Ranade discusses in detail the contours of the China-Pakistan Economic Corridor (CPEC). The CPEC is seen by China as an extension of its global reach and influence and Pakistan views the corridor as a solution to its economic woes. The chapter brings out the disadvantages of the CPEC for Pakistan and also discusses the challenges of CPEC in Pakistan.

The fourth chapter by Tilak Devasher reviews the socio-economic marginalisation of Balochistan during the last seven decades. The chapter elaborates that despite its strategic importance Baluchistan today is a mosaic of conflicts and fault lines that have intensified, and the region experiences varying degree of violence. Baloch struggle with the exploitation of their natural resources and inadequate allocation of funds for development.

Pakistan's economic crisis has been a constant struggle for the policy makers. The economic mismanagement and lack of investment in development expenditure has multiplied Pakistan's insecurities and led the country in a vicious cycle of external borrowing. The fifth chapter by Riya Sinha examines the causes of Pakistan's economic crisis. The chapters analyses the deficits in Pakistan's annual budget planning, and highlights the missed opportunities for economic reform by the state.

There have been frequent and strong debates in India regarding the abrogation of the Indus Water Treaty in response to Pakistan's continued cross-border terrorism and using the provisions of the Indus water Treaty with a better Treaty or using the provisions of the Treaty to inflict punishment on Pakistan. India-Pakistan strained relationship is marked by increasing mistrust, but the treaty has stood the test of time and remains uninterrupted till date. The sixth chapter by Uttam Sinha provides details of the Indus Water Treaty, critical Indian projects which have been questioned by Pakistan to delay implementation of the storage facilities on the western rivers and what are the potential options with India.

The seventh chapter by Shakti Sinha elaborates on Pakistan's Afghanistan dilemma. The chapter is very special as this was author's last writing which he sent to us before he said his final goodbye on 4 October 2021. Shakti Sinha was undoubtedly one of the leading scholars on Afghanistan and his personal experience on ground gave him a deep understanding of the Afghan issues. The chapter argues that Afghanistan is a product of the internal dynamics of Pakistan, specifically the Pakistan military's ambition to "become and remain the sole arbiter of power within the country." Pakistan's Afghanistan strategy has aimed to"prevent an alleged fear of being encircled by an India-Afghanistan alliance."

The chapter eight by Lt Gen Hooda describes the ambitions, dominant beliefs, organisational culture and values of the Pakistan Army. The Pakistan army theoretically supports the democratic set up but in practice believes in controlling the state of affairs. The chapter discusses the interests of the army and its belief in sub-conventional warfare. The author provides an insight into in army's conventional war fighting doctrine and what the future looks like.

The ninth chapter by AVM Amit Aneja provides a detailed history of the Pakistan Air Force (PAF) and force structure. The study explores the key vulnerability and tactical compulsion of the PAF. The author offers an insight in Pakistan strategic Air Force Command which is one of the major commands of the PAF and addresses the critical question of use of air power under the nuclear overhang.

Pakistan's ambition to acquire sea based nuclear deterrent has been talked about by the policymakers in Islamabad repeatedly. The development is critical in the context of regional nuclear dynamics. The tenth chapter by Vijay Sakhuja stipulates a comprehensive understanding of Pakistan's naval strategic thinking, desire to develop nuclear strike capability from the sea and policy formulations for the developments of sea based deterrent.

The eleventh chapter by Rajiv Nayan provides a comprehensive analysis of Pakistan's nuclear grand strategy. Pakistan's acquisition of nuclear weapons is not without any objective and it has a strategy to mobilise resources or means for its acquisition. Keeping the focus on India may help it in the mobilisation of resources and providing the legitimacy to its nuclear bomb in the country and to an extent outside, but the grand strategy of Pakistan's nuclear weapons seems to be establishing it as a custodian of the Islamic civilisation, which may facilitate its hegemony over a broad region comprising South, Central and West Asia. The chapter elaborates on Pakistan's nuclear objectives, its proliferation network, alliances and the grand strategy post Balakot strikes.

For decades policymakers in Pakistan have been relying on using terror as a foreign policy tool against India with the threat of the use of nuclear weapons. India's stance on the probability of a conventional war under the nuclear overhang did challenge Pakistan's conviction about New Delhi's restraint in responding to the Pakistan-sponsored acts of terror. To be able to deny India any space for conventional retaliation Pakistan has claimed to develop a Full Spectrum Deterrence. The twelfth chapter by Shalini Chawla is an elaborate assessment of the evolution of the Pakistan's unwritten nuclear doctrine which relies on a projection of uncertainty. The chapter traces the genesis of the nuclear doctrine and assesses what Pakistan implies by achieving a *Full Spectrum Deterrence*.

Pakistan has a variety of ballistic and cruise missiles with diverse range capabilities—air, ground and sea. The thirteenth chapter by Rajaram Nagappa is an exhaustive study of Pakistan's ballistic and cruise missiles. The chapter specifies Pakistan's missiles programme and assesses that "Pakistan appears to be some distance away from achieving credible second-strike capability".

Pakistan has been quite pleased with the idea of the tactical nuclear weapons and sees its short range missile NASR as a part of "strategy of assured deterrence" as Adil Sultan puts it. In fourteenth chapter Manpreet Sethi argues the logic and rationale of the TNWs from Pakistan's perspective and discusses India's position which treats all nuclear weapons at the same level. She argues convincingly that Islamabad's use of TNWs would not earn any concessions on India's doctrine of massive retaliation.

Pakistan's nuclear programme relied on external assistance extensively and the Pakistan's proliferation network did raise many questions. The fifteenth chapter by Arjun Anand and Arushi provides an insight into the past and future trends of Pakistan's nuclear proliferation network.

The sixteenth chapter is a concluding chapter by Shalini Chawla and Rajiv Nayan. The chapter assesses overall Pakistan's nuclear thinking and positioning and evaluates what would be its future nuclear posturing. The chapter analyses the internal and external dynamics of Pakistan and the fault lines which have added to the insecurities of the *nuclear Pakistan.*

We would like to thank all the authors for contributing comprehensive chapters and providing frank analyses. We thank the Department of Atomic Energy for the financial support. The staff of Pugwash India was extremely cooperative which facilitated the completion of the project. We wish to thank KW Publishers, Ms Kalpana Shukla and her team for smoothly executing the project.

Notes

1. Riedel, Bruce O., *Deadly Embrace: Pakistan, America, and the Future of the Global Jihad*, The Brookings Institution Press: Washington, D.C., 2011, pp. x-xi.
2. "Remarks by the President on a New Strategy for Afghanistan and Pakistan," White House, Office of the Press Secretary, 27 March 2009.
3. Some examples, Mario Esteban Carranza, *South Asian Security and International Nuclear Order: Creating a Robust Indo-Pakistani Nuclear Arms Control Regime*, Routledge, 2009; Hooman Peimani, *Nuclear Proliferation in the Indian Subcontinent: The Self-Exhausting Superpowers and Emerging Alliances*, Praeger, 2000; Naeem Salik, *The Genesis of South Asian Nuclear Deterrence: Pakistan's Perspective*, Oxford University Press, 2010; Z. Davis, *The India-Pakistan Military Standoff: Crisis and Escalation in South Asia,* Palgrave Macmillan; 2011; Rizwana Abbasi and Zafar Khan, *Nuclear Deterrence in South Asia: New Technologies and Challenges to Sustainable Peace*, Routledge, 2019; Devin T. Hagerty, *The Consequences of Nuclear Proliferation: Lessons from South Asia*, The MIT Press, 1998.
4. A few examples, Mansoor Ahmed, *Pakistan's Pathway to the Bomb: Ambitions, Politics, and Rivalries,* Georgetown University Press, 2022; Usama Butt and N. Elahi, *Security, Strategy, and the Future of the Islamic-nuclear Nation*, Continuum, 2010; Haider Nizamani, *The Roots of Rhetoric: Politics of Nuclear Weapons in India and Pakistan*, Praeger, 2000; Christoph Bluth and Uzma Mumtaz, *India-Pakistan Strategic Relations: The Nuclear Dilemma*, Ibidem Press, 2020; Feroz Khan, *Eating Grass: The Making of the Pakistani Bomb*, Stanford Security Studies, 2012; Naeem Salik, *Nuclear Pakistan Seeking Security and Stability*, CISS Press, 1921; Mark Fitzpatrick, *Overcoming Pakistan's Nuclear Dangers,* Routledge, 2014.
5. Prominent works are: Masood Ahmed Khan, *Pakistan and Nuclear Weapon Proliferation: A Historical Analysis of the Pakistani Nuclear Program 1947-1990*, BiblioScholar, 2012; Adrian Levy and Catherine

Scott-Clark, *Deception: Pakistan, the United States and the Global Nuclear Weapons Conspiracy*, Penguin Books Ltd, 2007; Gordon Corera, *Shopping for Bombs: Nuclear Proliferation, Global Insecurity, and the Rise and Fall of the A.Q. Khan Network*, Oxford University Press, 2006; Ayesha Siddiqa-Agha, *Pakistan's Arms Procurement and Military Buildup, 1979-99: In Search of a Policy*, Palgrave Macmillan, 2001; Jennette Hermann, *Pakistan China Nuclear Deal and International Concerns*, Alpha Edition, 2018; Henrik Stålhane Hiim, *China and International Nuclear Weapons Proliferation: Strategic Assistance,* Routledge, 2018; David Albright, *Peddling Peril: How the Secret Nuclear Trade Arms America's Enemies*, Free Press, 2010; International Institute for Strategic Studies, Nuclear Black Markets: Pakistan, A.Q. Khan and the Rise of Proliferation Networks, 2007.

6. For example, Douglas Frantz and Catherine Collins, *The Nuclear Jihadist: The True Story of the Man Who Sold the World's Most Dangerous Secrets ... And How We Could Have Stopped Him*, Twelve Books, 2007; Muhammad Jawad Hashmi, *Nuclear Terrorism in Pakistan: Myth or Reality*?, LAP LAMBERT Academic Publishing, 2012; J. Ryne Danielson, *A Nuclear Jihad: The Effect of Nuclear Weapons on Non-State Violence in the India-Pakistan Conflict,* Appalachian State University, 2012; David Armstrong and Joseph Trento, *America and the Islamic Bomb: the Deadly Compromise*, Steerforth Press, 2007.

SECTION 1
Pakistan's Security Dynamics

2. Pakistan's Lethal Combine: Nuclear Weapons, Military Adventurism and Religious Extremism

Syed Ata Hasnain

Many in India and around the world wonder why Pakistan remains committed to existential *hara-kiri* by following awkward policies involving the continued strengthening of its nuclear arsenal, the nurturing of religiously extremist 'friendly' terrorist groups and an avowed intent of retribution against India for the humiliation of 1971. Where did this deadly combination come from? How does it impact regionally and internationally and what will it take to force Pakistan to abjure and stop relying on these policies for its national security? That basically forms the theme of this chapter. To take it forward there is a need to delve into many of the historical aspects over the last 75 years.

Prior to 1971, Pakistan lived on a flawed perception of superiority over India, in almost every field. Much of this came from a perception of its religious orientation; the belief that Islam was the most modern faith and superior to all others. Being unsuccessful in giving itself a solid foundation in terms of leadership, polity, governance or economy, it lived under the mistaken belief of its civilisational superiority. This manifested most in its security outlook and led it to suicidal military standoffs with India. Its military leadership had the distinct advantage of having served as part of the undivided British-Indian Army, with soldiers of different faiths. Despite this, a mistaken delusional belief came to form part of its mindset that it could militarily defeat India and force the resolution of legacy territorial disputes in its favour, purely due to a superior fighting prowess of its soldiers based upon divinity. Military prowess, it believed, would also give it the right to sit at the high table within the comity of Islamic nations, particularly the Arab nations. While every pointer towards larger good gave it a direction towards an amicable co-existence with its larger neighbour (India) as part of the South Asian subcontinent, it veered towards a policy of acrimony.

Much of it also came from the deliberate choice it made of aligning with the West which made it the recipient of some US largesse both in economic and military terms. It attempted to follow the Turkish model of Kemal Ataturk, who had consciously steered Turkey away from the Arab and Persian world to give it a European character. Pakistan perceived that its future would be hamstrung by its linkage with India in the Indian subcontinent, especially with the kind of socialist policies contemplated and later pursued by Indian Prime Minister Jawaharlal Nehru. It wanted to dilute its South Asian identity and acquire a part Arab identity. Culturally and ethnically, it was never possible but ideologically, the linkage could work and give Pakistan a greater Islamic identity; something it has nurtured.

The military defeat suffered by India at the hands of China in a brief border war reinforced the perception of India's comprehensive weakness, leading Pakistan to trigger the conflict of 1965 in the hope of a short, swift military victory, resolution of territorial disputes in its favour and projection of the perceived civilisational superiority to attain a dominant position in the subcontinent. That the war was indecisive was not helpful for India. Pakistan to the day, celebrates Victory Day on 6 September each year, an anniversary of events of 1965 that Pakistan continues to project as examples of its superiority. Six years later, the India-Pakistan War of 1971 proved decisive in favour of India, leading to the division of Pakistan and the creation of Bangladesh. It should have changed mindsets, but did not; in fact a new obsession began . First came a perception sold to the Pakistani nation that the military setback in 1971 happened due to the disloyalty of the Bengali Muslims to their faith. It was reinforced by the idea that in the western military theatre of war, Pakistan held its own because India did not have the advantage of the east, where the Bengali Muslims had cooperated with it.

Delusional perceptions of superiority may be good for nations to retain self-pride and pass on the mantle of a high moral belief to subsequent generations. Pakistan did exactly that. However, to cater to the idea of self-pride, it placed itself on a path of near permanent confrontation with India on a couple of counts: The first was the issue of national ego linked to faith. It manifested in a desire for retribution without clear aims. The second was a competitive desire arising out of a wrong strategic perception. When India conducted its first nuclear test at Pokhran in 1974, it was clearly aimed as a response to the test conducted by China in 1964. Pakistan perceived the military differential between India and itself becoming even wider. Located next to an adversary against whom it had just been vanquished in a military confrontation, it had no intention of allowing such a differential to become a persistent issue of insecurity for Pakistan. Zulfiqar Ali Bhutto famously declared his intent to go nuclear "even if we have to eat grass ...". From thence on there was a passion behind Pakistan's search for nuclear technology in league with clandestine networks. Through the 1980s, the doctrine of ambivalence was played out, projecting last-wire capability with bouts of denial of any progress at all. It was designed to confuse the response from India. Simultaneously, it was dubbed the Islamic Bomb to line up the Islamic world behind Pakistan.

In 1977, Zulfiqar Ali Bhutto was overthrown in a coup by General Muhammad Zia-ul-Haq. Although Bhutto was vehemently anti-India, the Pakistan Army could not resist getting back to power to plan retribution against India for the loss of East Pakistan (Bangladesh). The Zia Doctrine was progressively conceived and has been the basis of Pakistan's strategy against India since the 1980s, modified from time to time. It comprised three basics—nuclear balance with India, employment of irregular warfare as a subset of proxy, hybrid conflict and religious radicalism. Military adventurism was a part of this doctrine. However, this needs further explanation. The Zia Doctrine was designed for retribution, securing entire Jammu and Kashmir (J&K), weakening India and prevent it achieving its aspirations. Its ingredients were as follows:

- A basic assumption existed that India could not be defeated on the conventional battlefield and its economy could not be matched to consider a long-drawn conventional military confrontation.
- The conventional asymmetry could, however, be overcome through nuclear parity which would limit India's options and throw up perceptions of nuclear redlines which by themselves would act as part deterrence. A redline is considered an act the execution of which, causes apprehension in the minds of the defender, of a situation of potential military defeat or strategic status that could become the highest existential threat.
- The doctrine assumed that, below the threshold of redlines, it would be possible to target India, exploiting its fault lines of faith, caste, regionalism, ethnicity and linguistics. To that, it could apply irregular warfare, nuclear blackmail and occasional military adventurism.
- International support was essential for such a strategy along with a strong strain of information warfare and denial strategy. Going beyond that, it perceived the need for religious affinity for the support it would obtain. The idea of confrontation using irregular warfare and information warfare—both with an Islamic colour—emerged progressively, even as success against the Soviet invasion of Afghanistan was gained.

The doctrine was not a one-time conception. The geopolitical environment of South Asia and the Middle East helped it evolve and J&K was to be the testing ground. How did this happen?

- 1979 proved to be one of the most significant years. Three issues concerning the geopolitics of the Middle East, South Asia and Political Islam came into prominence, almost together. The first was the revolution in Iran which brought Shia Islam to the fore, with fears that it would take the lead in the further march of Islam. The second was the siege of the Mecca Mosque by a renegade group of the Ikhwan in Saudi Arabia, forcing the

French Special Forces to enter the Mosque. It put the Saudi Royal Family under tremendous pressure from the powerful clergy to do more for the promotion of the Saudi brand of Islam which is decidedly more obscurantist. The third was the Soviet invasion of Afghanistan for various geostrategic reasons which are not being focused upon here.

- All three events occurred in close proximity of each other; in fact within eight weeks. Three nations were most affected by the run of events—the US, Saudi Arabia and Pakistan. The Saudi concern for an Iranian surge brought home the necessity of ensuring that Iran's eastern flank remained Sunni with the Saudi brand, that included Pakistan and Afghanistan.
- The US did not wish to see Iranian domination under its Islamic strain, nor Soviet presence so close to Pakistan and the Indian Ocean. Together with Saudi Arabia and Pakistan, the US launched a war by proxy to defeat the Soviets. Pakistan gained the status of a front line state, with transnational Islamic mercenaries, bankrolled by Saudi Arabia and armed by the US.
- The war continued for nine years and met the needs of all three allies. It set the stage for Pakistan's future strategies in all the spheres it desired. First, it gained prominence with Saudi Arabia and the US and came to be treated as the core partner on Afghanistan. Second, it promoted the Saudi brand of Sunni Islam through the acceptance of its funding and the presence of its clergy in the seminaries set up to cultivate the three million Afghan refugees who poured across its western frontier with Afghanistan. The Afghan Taliban was created in these camps and rose to take control of Afghanistan in 1996.

The lessons from the proxy war in Afghanistan encouraged Pakistan to launch its own proxy war in J&K. It had all the ingredients necessary for the adventurism it embarked upon. Bankrolling the resistance there, it provided a steady stream of experienced mercenary fighters freed from Afghanistan after the exit of the Soviet Union. It also prepared sufficient strength of Pakistani mercenaries to keep the pipeline active.

With adequate human resources to keep the resistance in J&K alive, its nuclear ambivalence was projected for deterrence. In addition, it concentrated on creating financial conduits and deep networks in J&K which helped spread the Saudi form of Sunni Islam to steadily replace the Sufi nature of J&K's Islamic faith. The latter was considered too close to the Indian concept of Islam which harped on tolerance, acceptance, plurality and balance. The path of proxy war against India has been steady since 1989. In 1998, India and Pakistan went overtly nuclear. Pakistan appeared to get more confident with this, judging that India was sufficiently deterred to launch conventional operations against it in response to large-scale acts of terror which appeared to cross the threshold of acceptance. Military adventurism was a follow-up when the campaign, in Pakistani perception, was going as per design. Kargil 1999 may have been General Musharraf's show but its antecedents were all laid by the military arrogance of the Pakistan Army. Failure at Kargil did not deter Pakistan or give it any perceptions of the impossibility of its long-term vision of retribution against India.

Emergence of Pakistan's 'Ecosystem' and its Threat Potential

The Zia doctrine placed Pakistan in a situation of permanent low-intensity conflict with India. At the same time, Pakistan's perception of Afghanistan being its strategic depth also led it to focus on a system by which it could retain sufficient influence over its affairs to prevent an Indian footprint expanding in its backyard. For the last many years this linkage has been primarily with the Afghan Taliban. On its borders to the east and west, Pakistan has chosen to be in confrontation, which needs an awkward ecosystem within Pakistan to progress—finances of a dubious nature from drug cartels, gun-running, religious institutions which churn out jihadi elements, sufficient other human resources to keep the jihad factory alive, intelligence networks, and clergy to keep the ideological fervour in place. Most of this finds no favour in the upper strata of society, but has managed to permeate the lower middle class, creating a larger radical footprint. Since the military, police and intelligence gives this ecosystem a virtual official flavour, there is reverse osmosis too into these institutions. The assassination of the Governor of Punjab Salman Tasir and the eulogising of his assassin Mumtaz Qadir, are clear indicators of how deep-rooted extremism in Pakistan has come to be.

The ecosystem which has emerged was perceived by the deep state within Pakistan as something beneficial to its security. It promotes the dominant position of the stakeholders such as the army, intelligence services, police and clergy, none of whom wish to be divested of the opportunities to be in positions of power. However, after the Lal Masjid incident in 2007 in Islamabad, where the army was employed against jihadi elements, none of these stakeholders were capable of curbing the rapid rise of self-empowered jihadis in the form of the Tehrik-e-Taliban Pakistan (TTP). They almost grudgingly realised the genie that had been created and continued to treat this nebulously until the TTP's strike at the Army Public School, Peshawar in December 2014, which triggered a wake-up call. The TTP fought the Pakistan Army and paramilitary forces virtually to a standstill. Its rise gave impetus to other long-existing radical elements in Pakistan to up the ante. The Sipaha-e-Sahiba and Lashkar-e-Jhangvi , two anti-Shia and anti-minority jihadi groups, have been in existence for long, until recently vanquished under *Operation Zarb-e-Azb* in 2014. Pakistan continued to treat the issue of jihadi threats casually, as these mostly manifested externally—in India and Afghanistan. However, these good times could not last forever. Those who ran the ecosystem internally also had larger ambitions beyond it just remaining under the control of the deep state.

After 2001 when the US launched its operations in the Af-Pak region, it was obvious that the Taliban and Al-Qaida had deep links inside Pakistan, persistently denied by the Pakistan leadership. The radical leadership itself was safely ensconced in Pakistani cities of Quetta, Karachi and Peshawar. The anti-Shia groups were being financed by external agencies from the Middle East. In Karachi, the Muttahida Qaumi Movement (MQM) of Altaf Hussain held strong mobilising capability and could tie Pakistan's largest city into knots, a capability it continues to hold even today, although at a slightly marginalised level. Quite obviously, the ecosystem which should have been under control of the deep state was never really so, and Pakistan's internal security issues came to the fore after 2007, forcing a commitment of almost one-third of the Pakistan Army's field deployable strength towards internal security.

A prudent way of viewing Pakistan's security compulsions is that it has three areas of focus. First, there are the internal security threats brought on by the wayward jihadi groups of different hues. There are groups within control of the deep state and some well outside, manifesting as friendly and unfriendly groups. Many of these groups have a capability to acting outside Pakistan's boundaries and are therefore useful to the deep state and form a part of the ecosystem. The second area of focus is Afghanistan, where Pakistan retains its influence through the use of proxies to neutralize Indian and Iranian influence. The third is J&K, where the 30-year proxy war has seen ups and downs, but friendly groups such as Lashkar-e-Taiba (LeT) and Jaish-e-Muhammad (JeM) remain the main proxies. They too, form part of the ecosystem as Pakistan's friendlies. At any time, Pakistan juggles with the three areas of focus and places priorities as per the currency of opportunities or threats.

Pakistan claims and projects to the world that it is one of the nations most affected by terrorism and radical extremism, without admitting that it has suffered purely from the blowback of its own policies of nurturing an ecosystem which has promoted such radical extremism. However, in June 2014, Pakistan, then clearly in the throes of a major internal disorder, launched *Operation Zarb-e-Azb,* which was conducted professionally and received further impetus after the attack on 16 December 2014 at the Army Public School, Peshawar. The National Action Plan (NAP) was then launched, which included setting up of military courts for the trial of alleged terrorists. Yet, despite the launch of this operation, the friendlies who act as proxies in Afghanistan and India (J&K), were spared. The LeT or Jamat-ud-Dawa (JuD)—as it is known after the US passed strictures against it—and the JeM have a deep hold in Punjab. Targeting them under any circumstances would mean internal security and anti-terror operations in Pakistan's heartland, from where most of the elements of the deep state hail; the Pakistan Army and intelligence services in particular. This is not acceptable for various other reasons, including political influence in the most populous province.

The ecosystem set up by the deep state with nebulous control over various entities, is an ever-persistent threat internationally, because the core centre of Islamic radicalism lies within Pakistan. While *Operation Zarb-e-Azb* may have militarily neutralised a large number of terrorists, the networks in the form of the ecosystem remain reasonably functional and always have the potential for resurgence. Why is this worrisome in terms of global terror threats? It needs to be remembered that both Al-Qaida and the Islamic State (IS) are in a state of suspense. Al-Qaida is in a better position due to its proximity to the Taliban, but the IS has little moorings and is scouting locations for its next big campaign. With the US withdrawal from Afghanistan expansion of violent extremism into Central Asia too has serious potential. With the continued existence of the ecosystem of violent extremism within Pakistan, there is every possibility of resurgence of transnational regional networks. The nations of the region do not have sufficient cooperation mechanisms to neutralise this potential. India too is seriously vulnerable. The IS has not found favour in Pakistan or Afghanistan, but it has the capacity to overcome most resistance and use scientific methods of modern terror to expand its cause.

The Failing Pakistan Economy and US Bailout

With the prevailing internal security situation over the last five years and the political instability arising out of the Pakistan Army's insistence of having an army-friendly political dispensation in power, created further turbulence, putting governance on a virtual hold. This led to a failing economy which had to be bolstered by loans from China, Saudi Arabia and the UAE. It also came under Financial Assistance Task Force (FATF) surveillance. Pakistan's economic woes, which have reduced its foreign exchange reserves to just US$ 7 billion, have left it vulnerable and there is insufficient energy and commitment to overcome these. Luck has however, favoured Pakistan in this position of virtual doom. The US under the Biden Administration has made a final withdrawal in August 2021 without full conflict termination arrangements which would have seen an exit without relative stability. Pakistan has once again been catapulted to prominence and a strategic space has opened for competition. A divided Taliban far from being a monolith is struggling to control the situation and run the country with Pakistan as yet the main stakeholder. There are also Russia, China and Iran which have retained their embassies in Kabul. International recognition seems yet far. For Pakistan it is a considerable turn around towards an advantageous situation with the Taliban 2.0 now in control. While Pakistan yet remains dependent upon US largesse for financing of any IMF loans the US control over Pakistan appears to have diluted. The US will yet be dependent on Pakistan to ensure stability of Afghanistan and hence its attitude towards Pakistan's Afghanistan policy will largely be coloured by Pakistani need.

The strategic significance gained this time may be short-lived, as the Taliban does not appear to be in any mood for compromise with the full realisation that it is in a position of advantage. Pakistan is unlikely to be in a position to deliver, although it has the convergence of Chinese, Russian and the US interests in the support that it is receiving. With the US now out of Afghanistan there is expectation that Pakistan with support of the Taliban 2.0 will once again trigger unrest and instability in J&K. In reality the situation is quite different to what it was in 1989 when the Soviet troops withdrew and Pakistan with the assistance of transnational mercenary Islamic terrorists could take us by surprise across a loosely secured LoC. Thirty years since then India has far too much experience and resources to prevent a repetition. Besides anything else India's efforts in the last few years since 5 August 2019, after the amendment of Article 370, have focused on a lot of right things. These include the dismantling of different networks which form the ecosystem of J&K and help Pakistan, the terrorists and the separatists fight their battles against India in different domains.

Pakistan will be even less compliant on delivering any form of stability in the region that the big powers are hoping for. The coming years, therefore, remain crucial for the region and it is not a particularly apt time for the Indian establishment to conduct any experiments in J&K which can upset the apple cart of relative stability gained over three years.

Pakistan and the Future Approach to J&K

Post-Pulwama and Balakot, Pakistan's strategic thinking appears skewed by the idea that for all provocation by it, every Indian military response which is below the threshold of an all-out conventional war, is manageable. It further believes that in case of an all-out conventional war, its nuclear deterrence is well in place. What Pakistan does not appreciate is that India is a matching nuclear state with a far larger and stronger set of armed forces. Redlines need not be crossed to attain strategic and military objectives. In any case, mutually-assured destruction is not something Pakistan can hope to survive with, as part of any nuclear doctrine.

None of the above is likely to appeal to Pakistan's way of thinking. It is therefore likely to continue pursuing its policy of intimidation against India, treating J&K as the battleground after the temporary back-step it has taken due to FATF pressure. Without big power pressure and actually acting to the interest of the big powers on Afghanistan, Pakistan will remain dangerously inclined towards India. This is a time when India should be examining the larger picture in the subcontinent and not be in any hurry to give triggers within J&K which could up the ante and draw Pakistan's support in a bigger way. It should work towards dismantling the ecosystem of the separatists in J&K and the tentacles of the Pakistan deep state which exist in J&K and are capable of an upsurge faster than can be realised by many in the Indian establishment. The current handling of J&K under Governor's rule has succeeded to some extent in taking apart the networks on which resurgence is usually based. Yet, it will be a fallacy to believe that enough has been done in this field. These systems are far too extensive to be taken apart in a season. Patience will be a virtue here.

Safety and Security of Pakistan Nuclear Assets

Pakistan's nuclear weapon assets can be viewed differently. On the one hand, the Pakistan Army as the custodian of national security is a responsible organisation for the national cause. It has a professional system of structuring the command and control of the nuclear assets which have been physically secured. Yet, any set of armed forces can be vulnerable and Pakistan's history of *coup de tats* and major internal security turbulence situations can have spin-offs which can be unpredictable. Pakistan has made itself vulnerable and highly suspect by the international community due to the awkward ecosystem it has created, comprising 'friendly' terrorists and various transnational underworld elements including crime syndicates. It is a well-known fact that the US and the West consider the possibility of a nuclear weapon falling into the hands of transnational terrorists as one of the most serious threats to international security. A miniature 'nuke' is not possessed by Pakistan and even a tactical nuke would require a delivery system. Yet, we cannot discount the genius of improvisation the terrorists are capable of. After all, 9/11 was not something any of us could imagine. Given Pakistan's geostrategic location and the role it plays in big power interests, an implosion within is unlikely; more so, this will also be ensured by big powers. Adding to the argument is the fact that the Pakistan Armed Forces, even with their rogue reputation, remain professional and can withstand the effects of what the ecosystem can bring to bear in terms of social and religious turbulence.

What the international community needs to be geared up for are the continuing threats to international order that can emanate should the ecosystem throw up greater non-state ambitions of expanding this to transnational proportions. Finance forms the core of this as does the spectre of religious radicalism, both of which can remain under the radar despite official efforts. Playing geopolitical games with FATF control and not offsetting the radical efforts which emanate from the Middle East, will hurt international interests. This is where India's role comes into focus. As the nation most affected by the Pakistan shenanigans, it is up to it to ensure constant sensitisation of the international community, a task much more difficult than imagined. India's information-based diplomacy needs to be strengthened manifold with long-term aims in mind.

Conclusion

Nothing is likely to change in a hurry in Pakistan's internal security-related landscape and neither will any of its overall security focus dilute anytime in the future. The international community will undoubtedly monitor the very important geostrategic space that Pakistan occupies, but the following areas which could spin out of control to the detriment of international interests, must remain under its focus:

- Its internal ecosystem must not be allowed to strengthen to give it any more capability to act with impunity against the interests of stability and order in Afghanistan and India.
- The international community must work in conjunction with powerful Islamic nations to limit Pakistan's religious extremism.
- It must continue to monitor Pakistan's nuclear assets and help to build controls under international monitoring. This will a major challenge as Pakistan has resisted all controls in the past.
- Pakistan's full cooperation must be sought on preventing any resurgence of the IS or Al-Qaida on its soil under cover of the 'friendly' radical elements.
- Pakistan's economic crisis must be used to force it to retract from support to, and nurturing of, 'friendly' terrorist organisations such as the JuD and JeM, even as diluting of the ecosystem is in progress.
- Importantly, to reduce chances of an India-Pakistan armed standoff, Pakistan must be pressurised to pull back from the dangerous game of proxy war and retribution in J&K. If Pakistan desires to enter into talks with India, as it keeps insisting, the international community can play a positive role in getting it to realise the futility of the efforts given the differential that exists between the two countries, notwithstanding nuclear parity.

3. CPEC and Challenges for Pakistan

Jayadeva Ranade

China's 'One Belt, One Road' (OBOR), which was first proposed in September 2013 and combines the twin initiatives of the Silk Road Economic Belt and 21st Century Maritime Silk Road, is a grand concept that envisions China girdling the globe. Potentially covering 55 per cent of the world GNP, 70 per cent of the global population, and 75 per cent of known energy reserves, it is essentially a plan for a China-built land and sea transportation artery to link China's production centres with markets and natural resource centres around the world. At the same time, it will harness much of China's hitherto idle economy, manpower and infrastructure-technology reserves to get much-needed returns. The initiative blends geopolitical and diplomatic objectives and has a strong domestic agenda.

The 'Belt Corridors' run along the major Eurasian Land Bridges, through China-Mongolia-Russia, China-Central and West Asia, China-Indochina Peninsula, China-Pakistan, Bangladesh-China-India-Myanmar. The Maritime Silk Route or "Road" is the maritime equivalent of the 'Belt Corridors' and comprises a network of planned ports and other coastal infrastructure projects that dot the map from South and Southeast Asia to East Africa and the northern Mediterranean Sea.

While Chinese officials and academics emphasise the economic aspects and commercial advantages of OBOR, it includes geopolitical and diplomatic objectives. Implementation of OBOR will augment China's economic influence in the participating countries. The strategy of disbursing them large sums as loans and aid will enhance the financial power that China already exercises through its trading relationships.

Huang Yiping, a Professor of Economics at Peking University's National School of Development, assessed in February 2015, that OBOR represents a sea change in China's international profile. According to him, OBOR has ended the phase of low-profile diplomacy based on Deng Xiaoping's advice to "hide your capabilities and bide your time" and transformed China into "a new great power" which "is trying to supplement the international economic order". Huang Yiping sought to justify China's more active role as an attempt to redress the limited role given to developing countries in international institutions and in line with former US President Barack Obama's demand that China take on more responsibility for providing international public goods. A Renmin University report similarly asserted the need to "supplement, not challenge" the existing order because of the "zero-sum thinking" which ensured that OBOR projects were greeted with scepticism including in China's immediate neighbourhood. Taking note of the challenges ahead, Huang Yiping conceded that: "One Belt, One Road is a good international economic strategy, but for now it is certainly not an easy one".

The most publicised bilateral commitment to OBOR was the investment pledged for the China-Pakistan Economic Corridor (CPEC) by Xi Jinping during his two-day visit to Pakistan in April 2015. The CPEC is the first leg of OBOR to be operationalised and is China's flagship venture. It traverses a distance of approximately 2,000 km from Kashgar in China's Xinjiang region till the port of Gwadar in Balochistan. When launched it was a $45 billion economic and development package that could grow to around $60 billion. Of the $45 billion, energy sector projects were around $34 billion whereas the infrastructure sector accounted for approximately $10 billion.

CPEC will include the construction of industrial parks, agricultural farms, railways, airports, roads, a fibre-optic network, energy-generating projects including one of the world's largest solar farms, and a high-speed train between Karachi and Peshawar that will travel over 160 km per hour. All these projects will be built according to Chinese plans with Chinese labour and connected to Chinese businesses. The project will also build a new telecommunications network linking Pakistan with China and through China, to Europe.

CPEC includes a number of initiatives in Pakistan that are not only economic in nature, but have cultural and civic implications. The Safe Cities initiative, for instance, is primarily designed to safeguard Chinese workers from Pakistani terrorists, but will also transform many of Pakistan's cities. The Safe Cities project includes building new, safer buildings in urban centres, training local police and military in anti-terrorist and bomb detection techniques, and the use of lighting and cameras to create safe zones in all Pakistani cities. It is also preparing to protect the CPEC inside Pakistan. A secure fibre-optic link has been laid connecting Kashgar, the headquarters of China's People's Liberation Army (PLA)'s South Xinjiang Military District with the Pakistan Army GHQ at Rawalpindi, highlighting the close military coordination between Pakistan and China. The PLA's Western Theatre Command established in 2016 is also tasked to safeguard Chinese workers, investments and projects in the CPEC in addition to protecting China's land frontiers. China at the same time informed Islamabad that it is creating a Division-strength "private army" for deployment in the areas covered by the CPEC. Chinese security organisations have begun functioning in Pakistan. China has already put in place a domestic legal basis for the deployment of Chinese troops and security personnel to protect Chinese investments and workers abroad. The operational tasks assigned to the PLA's Western Theatre Command represent the first of such arrangements.

While this project will no doubt create safer cities, many are concerned that much of the traditional areas of some of these historic cities will be destroyed to build newer, albeit safer, neighbourhoods.[1]

Disadvantages to Pakistan

Assessments of the CPEC's benefits to Pakistan vary considerably, but a study by Deloitte[2] is interesting. Pointing out that the volume of trade between Pakistan and China had increased to US$ 16 billion by

2014-15, the study alluded to impending benefits. It estimated that if all planned projects were implemented, their value would exceed all foreign direct investment in Pakistan since 1970 and would be equivalent to 17 per cent of Pakistan's gross domestic product (GDP) in 2015. It further estimated that the CPEC will create some 700,000 direct jobs during 2015-2030 adding up to 2.5 percentage points to the country's growth. Importantly, it noted that the Karakoram Highway between Rawalpindi and the Chinese border will be completely reconstructed and overhauled and Pakistan's railway network will be extended to eventually connect to China's Southern Xinjiang Railway in Kashgar. Almost 80 per cent of China's oil is currently transported over 16,000 km from the Strait of Malacca to Shanghai, but once Gwadar becomes operational this distance would reduce to less than 5,000 km. The CPEC will simultaneously open immense economic opportunities for Pakistan and physically connect China to its markets in Asia, Europe and beyond. According to *China Daily*, the energy projects would provide up to 16,400 MW of energy altogether with over 10,400 MW of energy generating capacity developed between 2018 and 2020 as part of the corridor's fast-tracked "Early Harvest" project.

The assessment of the Deloitte study is not mirrored in the numerous comments and articles by Pakistani politicians, journalists and academics. While they are appreciative that the CPEC has brought a massive influx of much-needed infrastructure aid and investment to Pakistan, they are very apprehensive that Pakistan risks losing sovereignty to China. The study fails to take into account the high energy production cost of these power plants. With fuel mandated to be imported from China's Xinjiang Autonomous Region, the cost per unit of electricity generated by the new power plants would be double the present, imposing a very high burden on the consumers. Early indicators suggest the time and production estimates are exaggerated. Politicians in Pakistan's provinces have complained for the past year that locals are not getting employment in CPEC projects and are not even being allowed access as the sites are 'protected' by 10-foot high perimeter walls. Pakistan media reports claim around 9,800 locals were hired for the construction of the 392 km highway from Multan in Punjab to Sukkur in Sindh. Similarly, the Suki-Kinari hydropower project in Khyber Pakhtunkhwa is expected to create more than 4,000 jobs. In terms of jobs actually created, it is reported that the China Machinery Engineering Corporation (CMEC)'s Thar lignite mining and coal-fired power plant in Sindh has created over 1,000 jobs so far, while the Sahiwal power plant, southwest of Lahore in Punjab province 'hired 3,000 locals'. The actual figures of employment are at great variance with the predicted figure of 700,000.

On the other hand, there has been a huge influx of Chinese labour. Chinese restaurants, grocery stores, guest houses and language centres have opened across Pakistan, aimed mainly at the country's growing population of Chinese citizens. The supermarket shelves are lined with products manufactured in China:[3] everything from noodles to hardhat construction helmets, sea kelp to stationery, spice mixes to industrial meat grinders. Consequently, there has been no benefit to Pakistan's economy as no money is coming in through the service sectors as well.

Politicians, academicians and journalists have voiced serious concerns about Pakistan's mounting debt to China and the anticipated high cost of electricity from the new energy projects. Expressing concern about the viability of the CPEC, Ali Malik, a researcher with the South Asia Program at the Hudson Institute in Washington DC, pointed out on 4 January 2017, that "most of Pakistan's urban centres are located in the east, not the west and that inter-provincial resentment and differences have flared, with the western provinces accusing the centre of being partial to the country's eastern portion, where majority of Pakistan's economic bases are located."

There are other questions about the economic viability of the CPEC, for which the bulk of financing has come in the form of loan-based financing, and not unconditional grants from the Chinese Government. Though the loans are given to individual construction companies involved with the projects, there are significant risks to the Government. Many of the power projects are under sovereign guarantees, thus making the Pakistani Government responsible if these companies fail to meet their debt obligations. Pakistan's current liabilities (debt), both private and public, have reached a staggering 75 per cent of GDP (Rs 22.5 trillion).

According to a *Financial Times (FT)* report, Pakistani officials feel that lending money to Pakistan also favours China, as it does not wish to disclose details of the loans that are part of the CPEC project.[4] "The Chinese are not keen on Western institutions learning the minute details of [financing of] CPEC projects," an unnamed official in Islamabad was quoted as saying. "An IMF programme will require Pakistan to disclose the financial terms to its officials." According to the *FT* report, prior to the April 2018 loan of $1 billion, Pakistan had borrowed almost $1.2 billion from Chinese banks since April 2017. Pakistan's Prime Minister Imran Khan and China's Premier Li Keqiang met in November 2018 after which China agreed to provide aid for Pakistan's deteriorating economic situation. On the other hand, some people have alleged that China's generosity may worsen Pakistan's financial difficulties.

Additional worries are that the CPEC's success depends entirely on Pakistan's ability to export goods and services and show a strong rise in exports. Pakistani analysts warned that these sectors of the economy would have to compete with the influx of cheaper Chinese imports that have the potential to strangle the domestic market. Chinese imports have, incidentally, already grown from 4 per cent in 2010 to 9 per cent in 2015. Economists say that if this downward trend of exports and increase in imports continues, Pakistan will face a serious balance of payments crisis. Others suggest that Pakistan is already on the verge of experiencing a crisis, as the Pakistan government expected in June 2021 that debt servicing will rise to 35 per cent of the total budget outlay of Rs 8.4 trillion for the next fiscal year. It has set aside Rs 3.1 trillion for interest payments and repayments on domestic and foreign loans.

There is a general view that in order to safeguard its economic future Pakistan must be cautious in how it implements and administers completion of the CPEC. More importantly, they assert that the central government must be honest about the nature of Chinese investment, as Pakistan risks losing its sovereignty and being beholden to China and exploited by it for its natural resources and geostrategic location.

For China, however, the centre-pieces of the CPEC are the Gwadar Port and the area of the Karakoram in the north. It has eyed Gwadar for years and agreed to fund its development only after Pakistan agreed to grant it "sovereign guarantees to the port facilities" in 2007. Gwadar is important for China's maritime ambitions. As China enlarges its Navy and retains a permanent presence in the Indian Ocean, its aircraft carriers, other surface warships and submarines will require a base. The importance of Gwadar for China is emphasised by the inclusion of Gwadar International Airport and other major development works of Gwadar Port in the CPEC's first phase,with completion originally targeted for 2017. By 2021, however, project completion targets appear to have got extended for various reasons. A total of nine projects valued at approximately US$ 1 billion, each intended to augment China's commercial and military capacity, are planned in and around Gwadar. China is reported to have established electronic eavesdropping posts at Gwadar.

The CPEC's first phase also includes expansion of the Karakoram Highway, connecting Pakistan's railway network to China's Southern Xinjiang Railway to Kashgar, and placing of a secure fibreoptic line between Kashgar and Rawalpindi, all projects of military significance. What is really interesting is that when tensions rose early last year because of Pakistani complaints about the rising costs and the slow pace of work, China sought to assuage Pakistan and said many of the projects around Gwadar would take the form of grants! The security of Gwadar is a source of continued concern for the Chinese and has imposed a heavy financial burden on Pakistan. In January 2016, the Pakistan Navy decided to deploy two additional Marine Battalions to provide round-the-clock security at Gwadar. On 21 September 2016, in the wake of the deterioration in India-Pakistan relations over Kashmir, Chinese Premier Li Keqiang publicly expressed reservations and told Pakistan's former Prime Minister Nawaz Sharif that he "hoped" Pakistan could continue to provide protection to the CPEC and Chinese personnel in Pakistan.

The official Chinese newspaper *Global Times* similarly warned that "the increasing cost of security is becoming a big problem in efficiently pushing forward the project." In November 2016, during the inaugural Kashgar-Gwadar cargo run and subsequent transfer of the containers to waiting vessels at Gwadar Port, Pakistani officials went to great lengths to allay Chinese concerns and the Pakistan Navy deployed ships and aircraft to provide security cover to ensure safe and secure transit.

Since Gwadar became operational, the role of Pakistan's maritime forces has increased and the Pakistan Navy has been assigned special responsibility to protect the Gwadar seaport project and more than 500 Chinese nationals working there, from offshore threats. Pakistan has set up a Special Security Division (SSD) under a Major General, solely for protecting CPEC construction sites. With China refusing to provide any financial assistance towards security expenses of the CPEC, the Pakistan Government on 24 September 2016, decided to meet such expenses by adding 1 per cent more to the cost of all central energy projects and recovering it from consumers through the National Electric Power Regulatory Authority. This cess is to help the Pakistan Army meet expenses incurred on the SSD. The Senate Standing Committee on Planning Development and Reform has protested over Pakistani citizens being billed for providing security to Chinese nationals in Pakistan.

Pakistani politicians are already complaining about the annual US$ 12 million expenditure on the SSD, which is now expected to double. The success of the CPEC and Gwadar Port depends on having a safe and secure maritime environment in the Arabian Sea and Indian Ocean region in general. Envisaging attacks by militant groups or insurgents on seaports and vessels, and use of the container vessels to smuggle weapons, drugs, etc., Pakistan has strengthened maritime security capabilities. This includes: intensifying security patrols and coastal exercises; creation of Coastal Watch Stations; establishing a Joint Maritime Information Coordination Centre (JMICC); establishment of the Force Protection Battalion of the Pakistan Marines; and more robust maritime security activities jointly by Pakistan and China. Collaboration in building naval craft has been stepped up. China and Pakistan have agreed to jointly construct the F-22P Frigate in addition to the Azmat and Jalalat-class fast-attack craft and corvettes for the Pakistan Maritime Security Agency.

In June 2015, Pakistan's Ministry of Defence Production signed a contract with M/s China Ship Trading Company for construction of seven Maritime Patrol Ships, four of which are being built in China and the others at the Karachi Shipyard and Engineering Works. The China Shipbuilding Industry Corporation (CSIC) will also provide Pakistan's Navy with eight attack submarines. Pakistan has to pay for these vessels. Other serious issues threatening the development of Gwadar have surfaced, with Pakistani analysts implying that China has undue interest in Gwadar Port. Gwadar is described as an "island isolated in an arid landscape with roads and railways linking it to the rest of the nation." The city's water supply dam has dried up following three years of drought. The existing desalination plant does not work and there is no more water. Unless Gwadar gets its full road and rail connectivity, the port cannot flourish. Gwadar additionally symbolises the sense of alienation felt by many in Balochistan, who suspect that most of the benefits of the CPEC are going to outsiders.

However, the non-flexible and strict terms and conditions imposed by Beijing have led to unsuccessful negotiations on some projects between Islamabad and the Chinese Government. In November 2017, Pakistan backed away from the Diamer-Basha Dam project due to its "unrealistic" terms and conditions, and China taking ownership of the entire project was stated to be unacceptable by former Prime Minister Shahid Khaqan Abbasi. The Diamer-Basha Dam is excluded from the list of CPEC Projects and the Pakistan Government is now funding the project on its own after some changes in the project's design. The new Pakistani Government has also rejected China's proposal to build a US$ 60 billion coal-fired power plant under the "China-Pakistan Economic Corridor". The Pakistani daily *Dawn* reported that Prime Minister Imran Khan, who took office in August 2018, officially informed

Beijing that the country is not interested in building the Rahim Yar Khan power plant.

Besides this, Chinese influx is creating fissures in the feudal Pakistani society. A recent scandal in Pakistan was unearthed where Chinese men, with the help of collaborators in Pakistan, married young Pakistani women after making cash payments to their families and brought them to China. The human trafficking issue gained widespread attention in April, 2019 when Pakistani television broadcaster ARY News raided a compound in Lahore, where several Chinese men were discovered with six Pakistani wives, two of whom are 13 years old. ARY News reported the men paid Rs 400,000 ($2,820) to each of the women's families, who were also promised Rs 40,000 in monthly payments and a Chinese visa to a male relative of the bride. Some of the women entered into forced marriages, and one contacted the broadcaster, which led to the expose. The Chinese Embassy in Pakistan issued a statement on 13 April 2019 conceding that while some unlawful matchmaking centres earned illegal profits from brokering cross-national marriages by victimising Pakistani and Chinese youth, the reports of organ sales were "misleading and groundless."

Challenges for CPEC in Pakistan

The major problems that the CPEC faces in Pakistan include regional and ethnic differences and conflicts. Created in 1947 as a country for the Muslims of the Indian sub-continent, Pakistan is in fact composed of several, not always friendly, ethnic enclaves. Pakistan's four provinces and two autonomous areas generally, but not perfectly, represent these groups. These ethnic groups include the Punjabis, who make up almost 45 per cent of the national population and dominate the national government; the Pashtun, a conservative tribal group who live in the Khyber-Pakhtunkhwa Province and make up about 17 per cent of Pakistan's population; the Sindhis who live in large feudal estates in Sindh Province including the city of Karachi, and constitute about 14 per cent of the country's population; the Baluch who live in the relatively poor area of Baluchistan and make up less than 4 per cent of Pakistan's population; and the Muhajirs, who are the descendants of the refugees who fled India in 1947 and do not have a province of their own, but reside in Karachi and areas around that city and make up about 8 per cent of the country's population. Other groups include the Kashmiris, the Brahuis and the Saraikis from Multan.

Regional and ethnic rivalries and feuds have played a major role in Pakistan's short history. For instance, although the official language of Pakistan is Urdu (and English), it is only spoken as a native language by about 8 per cent of the population. Urdu, in fact, was the language spoken by the Muslims in the Indian Subcontinent, but not by the people who lived in the area that is now Pakistan.

These ethnic and regional rivalries do not just represent differences in culture or language, but also represent bitter rivalries for national political and economic dominance. This clash of cultures is particularly exhibited in the tension between the military, dominated by the Pashtun, and the Punjabis who control the apparatus of the national government. The military has stepped in several times since 1947, declaring martial law and replacing incompetent and corrupt national governments.

Balochistan, which has a potentially pivotal role in the CPEC, is another province in ethnic turmoil. It is the largest province and has many natural resources. However, the Baloch have the lowest standard of living of any ethnic group in Pakistan and feel alienated from the Pakistani power structure. Due to this, in part, a number of militant Baloch separatist groups have emerged and have been causing trouble.

The fear among many Pakistanis is that CPEC will only enrich the Punjabis (some have suggested that the "P" in CPEC stands for Punjab), since the Punjabis control the national government, while leaving the rest of Pakistan relatively poor.[5] This is especially a concern of the Baloch and the Pashtun, who have already seen many of the CPEC programmes directed away from their provinces and towards the Punjab or Sindh provinces. The obvious case is of the new highway being built as part of the initiative between Kashgar and Gwadar. One of the routes in the original plan, referred to as the Western Route, was to go through the Khyber-Pakhtunkhwa Province. However, the route was changed by Islamabad to avoid that province. The route is now planned to run largely through the Punjab and Sindh provinces. True, a large section of the route will be through Balochistan, but largely in the remote areas of the southern section of the province, and will therefore not benefit Balochistan much. Both the provincial governments of the Khyber-Pakhtunkhwa and Balochistan have voted against the CPEC and have petitioned the national government in Islamabad to include more projects in provinces other than the Punjab.[5]

The fate of the project in Balochistan is key to the ultimate success of CPEC, since the use of the port of Gwadar is one of the project's key elements. Increasing calls in Balochistan for the creation of a separate state and ensuing armed conflict pose an enormous challenge to the corridor. Baloch nationalists oppose the project as the demographic balance could ultimately turn against them, making them a minority in their own province as other ethnic groups move into the province. Even presently, the Baloch people only make up about 55 per cent of the population of Balochistan. This anger towards the CPEC has increased to the point that Chinese citizens have been kidnapped and killed by Baloch militant groups.

On 13 May 2017, gunmen killed ten Chinese labourers working on the CPEC project in Gwadar. The attack was carried out by the Baloch Liberation Army (BLA), a group reportedly fighting for an independent homeland for the Baloch. A spokesperson for the BLA said:[6] "This conspiratorial plan, CPEC, is not acceptable to the Baloch people under any circumstances."

In addition, the CPEC, and with it, China's cultural and economic incursion into Pakistan, is reminiscent to many of when the British ruled the Indian Subcontinent from 1858 to 1947. China's influence in Pakistan is not of the same nature—China does not officially claim to govern the country—but there are similarities which many in Pakistan have noticed and this could trigger considerable ethnic and regional pushback against the projects.

Militant Islam

Pakistan was created in 1947 as an avowedly Muslim country. As a result Islamic doctrines, laws, and institutions have been a part of Pakistan since the beginning. However, though Islamic political parties have always been active, in the last couple of decades a new kind of Islamic militancy has emerged. These orthodox militant parties include home-grown groups such as the Tehrik-e-Taliban and the Lashkar-e-Jhangvi, which are local or regional organisations with specific agendas internal to Pakistan. One target of these groups are the religious minorities in Pakistan, including the small Christian minority and the Shia Muslims whom they consider heretics and idol worshipers. These groups strongly oppose foreign intervention, including by the Chinese, and will constitute a challenge to the CPEC.

Other militant Islamic groups are connected to, or supported by, trans-national Islamic movements. These include the Lashkar-e-Taiba (LeT) and the Harkat-ul Mujahideen. Also, increasingly active in Pakistan are elements of the Islamic State, al-Qaeda, and the Afghan Taliban. These groups have been responsible for a number of terrorist attacks in Pakistan. Militant Islamic movements have deep roots and can be traced back to the beginning of Pakistan. They received a fillip in the 1980s when the United States and Saudi Arabia, among others, poured considerable amount of money into creating Madrasas on the Afghan-Pakistan border to recruit and train Afghan Mujahideen to fight the Soviets. The Pakistani military and powerful Inter-Services Intelligence participated in this effort and continue to retain their links and nurture them. These Islamic militant groups are useful to the Pakistani military establishment in many ways and especially for the low-intensity conflict against India in Kashmir. But these militant Islamic groups also harbour a profound and deep hatred against the West, especially the United States, and favour orthodox Islam.

These militant Islamic groups would, therefore, potentially be particularly dangerous for the Chinese projects in Pakistan. China does not have a good image in the Islamic world and its treatment especially of the Uyghurs in Xinjiang province has generated resentment. An indication of this was visible when Hafiz Saeed of the LeT warned then Prime Minister Nawaz Sharif against Pakistan's "new best friend" and asked him to inquire about their treatment of Muslims in Xinjiang during Ramzan. This resentment will fester. The presence of thousands of Chinese workers and their habits and customs will offend the orthodox Muslims residing in rural Pakistan where the CPEC projects are sited. Attacks on Chinese citizens in Pakistan have already taken place and will continue. Although the Chinese will create safe places for their workers, there will be a continual threat of violence against its citizens in Pakistan.

In conclusion, it is clear that the CPEC will confront many problems in Pakistan. These include the threat to Chinese workers and personnel from the largely conservative rural Muslim population of Pakistan and the Balochis who apprehend being marginalised in their home province. Other difficulties will centre on Pakistani reappraisal of the CPEC and China's financial agreements on CPEC projects. Allegations that they are heavily skewed in China's favour are gaining ground. The IMF and World Bank too, at the instance of the US, have insisted that Pakistan provide detailed accounts for CPEC projects. A Pakistan whose economy is in dire straits and which is seeking loans from them, will have fewer alternatives. The accusation that Pakistan risks losing sovereignty to China is emotive and has the potential to spread. It could get aggravated with the presence of Chinese security personnel in Pakistan, which has already triggered local tensions and fights. China will, however, not want to jeopardise its huge strategic investment in Pakistan and will want to keep the relationship in good repair. It additionally has important military ambitions of acquiring Gwadar Port and securing a large chunk of Pakistan-occupied-Kashmir and adjacent areas.

A difficult proposition for China and Pakistan in the longer term will be to resolve their widely differing objectives. Their objectives are almost at cross-purposes—while China has a larger strategic objective and views the corridor more as an essential stepping stone towards global leadership, Pakistan sees it just as a solution for its economic difficulties.

Disclaimer: The article was written by Mr Jayadeva Ranade for the Pugwash Project in May 2020.

Notes

1. Corr, A., "China Will Suppress Terrorism, Diversity, and Democracy in Pakistan", *Forbes,* 2017, at https://www.forbes.com/sites/anderscorr/2017/05/15/china-will-suppress-terrorism-diversity-and-democracy-in-pakistan/—662cb4db5cd6. Accessed on 20 April 2019.
2. "How will CPEC boost Pakistan economy?", at https://www2.deloitte.com/pk/en.html. Accessed on 19 April 2016.
3. Asad Hashim, "Pakistan: A slice of China in Islamabad", Al-Jazeera, at https://www.aljazeera.com/indepth/features/2017/08/pakistan-slice-china-islamabad-170830081303813.html. Accessed on 25 April 2019.
4. "Pakistan seeks more loans from China to avert currency crisis", *Financial Times*, at https://www.ft.com/content/1256ceaa-802c-11e8-bc55-50daf11b720d. Acessed on 24 April 2019.
5. Shah, R., "China's Trouble with Pakistan's Turbulent Democracy", *The Diplomat*, 2017, at http://thediplomat.com/2017/01/chinas-trouble-with-pakistans-turbulent-democracy/. Accessed on 20 April 2019.
6. "Gunmen kill 10 labourers in Balochistan's Gwadar", Al-Jazeera, at https://www.aljazeera.com/news/2017/05/gunmen-kill-10-labourers-balochistan-gwadar-170513111330168.html. Accessed on 21 April 2019.

References

Abdul Manan, "12 sites proposed for special economic zones in Balochistan, K-P", *The Tribune*, at https://tribune.com.pk/story/1026167/12-sites-proposed-for-special-economic-zones-in-balochistan-kp/. Accessed on 12 January 2016.

Asad Hashim, "Pakistan: A slice of China in Islamabad", Al-Jazeera, at https://www.aljazeera.com/indepth/features/2017/08/pakistan-slice-china-islamabad-170830081303813.html. Accessed on 25 April 2019.

Corr, A. (2017), "China Will Suppress Terrorism, Diversity, and Democracy in Pakistan", *Forbes*, at https://www.forbes.com/sites/anderscorr/2017/05/15/china-will suppress-terrorism-diversity-and-democracy-in-pakistan/—662cb4db5cd6. Accessed on 20 April 2019.

"CPEC Mess: Chinese company building Gwadar Port operating in Pakistan illegally", lawmakers told, 14 March 2018, Zee News, at http://zeenews.india.com/world/cpec-mess-chinese-company-building-gwadar-port-operating-in-pakistan-illegally-lawmakers-told-2089425.html. Accessed on 15 March 2018.

"Chinese to Outnumber Baloch Natives by 2048", *The Nation*, at http://nation.com.pk/national/29-Dec-2016/chinese-to-outnumber-baloch-natives-by-2048/amp. Accessed on 29 December 2016.

Falak Arreba, "Angry Balochis Oppose China Pakistan Economic Corridor", 22 October 2017, *The Sunday Guardian*, at https://www.sundayguardianlive.com/world/11369-angry-balochis-oppose-china-pakistan-economic-corridor. Accessed on 29 December 2017.

"Gunmen kill 10 labourers in Balochistan's Gwadar", Al-Jazeera, at https://www.aljazeera.com/news/2017/05/gunmen-kill-10-labourers-balochistan-gwadar-170513111330168.html. Accessed on 21 April 2019.

Kiyya Baloch, "Can China's Gwadar Port Dream Survive Local Ire?", *The Diplomat*, at http://thediplomat.com/2014/12/can-chinas-dream-of-a-pakistan-port-survive-local-ire/. Accessed on 17 December 2014.

"Pakistan seeks more Loans from China to Avert Currency Crisis", *The Financial Times*, at https://www.ft.com/content/1256ceaa-802c-11e8-bc55-50daf11b720d. Accessed on 24 April 2019.

Saibal Dasgupta, "China to Seal Border with Pakistan to Curb Terror", *The Times of India*, 11 January 2017.

Sattar Khan, "Gwadar—Pakistan's impoverished colony or an economic hub?", DW, at http://www.dw.com/en/gwadar-pakistans-impoverished-colony-or-an-economic-hub/a-19185999. Accessed on 14 April 2016.

Shah, R. (2017), "China's Trouble with Pakistan's Turbulent Democracy", *The Diplomat*, at http://thediplomat.com/2017/01/chinas-trouble-with-pakistans-turbulent-democracy/. Accessed on 20 April 2019.

Shakil FM, "Pakistan Seeks Bailout from China and Saudis Instead of IMF", 4 April 2018, *Los Angeles Times*, at http://www.atimes.com/article/pakistan-seeks-bailout-china-saudis-rather-imf/http://www.cpecinfo.com/home.

4. Balochistan's Socio-Economic Marginalisation: The Security Implications

Tilak Devasher

Balochistan is perhaps Pakistan's most strategic province for a variety of reasons. It has almost 44 per cent of the country's landmass and two-thirds of its coastline. It shares borders in the north and north-west with Afghanistan and in the west with Iran. In the east are the Pakistani provinces of Sindh, Punjab and in the north parts of Khyber-Pakhtunkhwa (KP). Its 760-km coastline has an approximately 180,000 sq. km exclusive economic zone that is largely untapped. The province is located near the Strait of Hormuz through which passes nearly 40 per cent of the world's oil supplies. Its geographical proximity to the oil and gas deposits of the Central Asian region further adds to its strategic importance.[1] It also provides access to the Arabian Sea and the Indian Ocean, to land-locked Afghanistan, the Central Asian states as well as the Xinjiang province of China.

Three of Pakistan's naval bases are located on the Baloch coast—Ormara, Pasni and Gwadar. Pakistan's nuclear testing site is located in Chagai in Balochistan while the expanse of the province provides Pakistan the flexibility to disperse its nuclear arsenal.

The proximity of the main opium producing centres in Afghanistan—the provinces of Helmand, Kandahar and Zabul—to Balochistan and the Chaman border crossing makes it crucial in smuggling narcotics out of the country.

Balochistan's location, adjoining Afghanistan, made it important to the US in the 'War on Terror' for carrying out operations against the Taliban after 9/11. Logistic support to the US forces was provided through airfields in Pasni and Dalbadin in Balochistan. Drone attacks against the Taliban were launched from Shamsi, another air base previously leased to Arab sheikhs for hunting the Houbara bustard. After the US campaign against the Taliban that began in November 2001, Balochistan became a significant exit route for Al-Qaeda and Taliban fighters seeking safe havens in Pakistan. Balochistan was also a critical link in the US supply chain for its troops in Afghanistan from Karachi via the Chaman border crossing.

Location apart, Balochistan's treasure-trove of minerals and energy resources makes it critically important. According to a famous Baloch proverb, 'A Baloch may be born without socks on his feet, but when he grows up every step he takes is on gold.'[2] Balochistan is reputed to have vast mineral and energy resources, including natural gas, as also reserves of coal, gold, copper, silver, platinum, aluminum and uranium. Reqo Diq, Saindak, Sui[3] and Chamalang produce a wealth of resources like copper, gold, natural gas, coal and other minerals.

Decades ago, noted American author Selig Harrison had written, 'If it were not for the strategic location of Balochistan and the rich potential of oil, uranium, and other resources, it would be difficult to imagine anyone fighting over this bleak, desolate and forbidding land.'[4] Since he wrote, Balochistan has become the key to the energy security of Pakistan. The rising requirement for energy resources has resulted in increasing the economic and strategic salience of the province. It is this assured access to natural gas resources that is the prism through which Pakistan looks at Balochistan. As Robert G. Wirsing puts it, energy security is now a foremost national priority. Resultantly, Balochistan's economic and strategic importance has been enhanced exponentially making it crucial for Pakistan to deal with the growing separatism in the country.[5]

Despite its strategic importance or perhaps because of it, Balochistan today is a montage of conflicts and faultlines that have escalated into varying degrees of violence. These range from those between the Baloch nationalists and the state; inter-and intra-tribal feuds and clashes; ethnic faultlines, sectarian conflicts and terror strikes. Not surprisingly, Balochistan, even seventy years after Pakistan's creation, has been described as 'an edgy place';[6] 'a boiling cauldron of ethnic, sectarian, secessionist and militant violence, threatening to boil over at any time';[7] 'an active volcano that may erupt anytime with dire consequences.'[8]

The figures speak for themselves (Table 4.1).

Table 4.1: Fatalities, Suicide Attacks and Explosions

A FATALITIES						
Period	Incidents	Civilian	SFS	Extremists	Unknown	Total
2014-2018	692	1110	477	917	151	2647
B SUICIDE ATTACKS						
Period	Incidents	Civilian	SFS	Extremists	Unknown	Total
2014-2018	39	352	124	54	05	530
C EXPLOSIONS						
Period	Incidents	Civilian	SFS	Extremists	Unknown	Total
2014-2018	253	566	201	64	61	892

Source: http://www.satp.org/datasheet-terrorist-attack/fatalities/pakistan-balochistan. Accessed on 2 February 2019.

Why is Balochistan such an enduring security problem for Pakistan? One reason is that the most persistent and bitter conflict between the Baloch nationalists and the state has been continuing in some form or the other since Pakistan's forcible accession of the princely state of Kalat (as the bulk of Balochistan was then known) in 1948. The conflict has intensified due to the federal government treating the province as a colony, exploiting its resources without giving much back to improve the lives of the people. While memories of the forcible accession linger, it is the socio-economic marginalisation of the province during the last seven decades that has been responsible for the present security situation. In fact, contrary to the state's narrative of the so-called 'foreign hand' being responsible for the unrest and fomenting violence, it is chronic underdevelopment and socio-economic backwardness of the region that has alienated the population and compelled many to take up arms against the state.

A new element of the alienation is the perception that the Baloch identity is being systematically erased. This feeling of insecurity has been accentuated due to developments like the persisting military operations in the province with its off-shoots of enforced disappearances and 'kill and dump' policies; the exclusion of the Baloch in decisions pertaining to mega projects like the China-Pakistan Economic Corridor (CPEC) and development of the Gwadar Port; the fear of being turned into a minority in their own province due to the large influx of Chinese and Punjabis to run these projects, etc.

Not surprisingly, the Baloch frequently ask what has being a part of Pakistan given them? What Prince Abdul Karim wrote from exile in Afghanistan, to his brother the Khan of Kalat Mir Ahmad Yar Khan in 1948 seems as if it could have been written in 2019:

> "... the Pakistan people are not only more aggressive than the British, but they are also in the habit of biting off their own friends... From whatever angle we look at the present government of Pakistan, we will see nothing but Punjabi fascism. The people have no say in it. It is the Army and arms that rule... There is no place for any other community in this government, be it the Baluch, the Sindhis, the Afghans or the Bengalis ... total Punjabi Fascism rules supreme everywhere".[9]

It is this feeling of not being an equal partner in the Federation borne out of the reality of socio-economic marginalisation during the past seven decades that has created a serious security situation for Pakistan. For the Baloch the socio-economic marginalisation has made the conflict in essence over identity—to preserve their resources, culture, language and ultimately all that it meant to be a Baloch.[10] A Human Rights Commission of Pakistan (HRCP) team in 2003 'noticed discontent almost everywhere in Balochistan because of the widely shared perception of the people's exclusion from public affairs. They felt deprived and ignored.'[11] In 2009, the HRCP reported that a section of the Baloch had concluded that they were being viewed as enemies of the state; 'they feel abandoned by the people as well as political forces in the rest of the country. There is a sense of isolation, rejection and dejection.' It cautioned that the 'sense of deprivation and suppression is deep rooted in Baloch nationalist identity; the establishment's failure to negotiate and compensate further isolates a population that has long put up with armed and aggressive tactics to curb the struggle for their rights.'[12]

Such a feeling has persisted over decades. *Jabal*, the official organ of the Baloch People's Liberation Front had stated in July 1977:

> "In Islamabad's calculations Balochistan is a vast estate for plunder, an arid desert floating on oil and minerals. A large part of their political strategy is dictated by the desire to extract this treasure for the benefit of the Pakistani bureaucratic bourgeoisie and foreign imperialist interests.... The Pakistani oligarchy needs Balochistan's oil and minerals to overcome the severe economic crisis gripping the whole country."[13]

The Federal government has often tried to co-opt the Baloch with developmental projects, but none of them have achieved any measure of success. As Baloch journalist Malik Siraj Akbar puts it, 'development' itself has different meanings for the Baloch and the federal government. For the Baloch, development is linked with the creation of employment opportunities and consequent improvement in their standard of living. For Pakistan, development means obtaining Balochistan's mineral wealth and to expedite the development of the Gwadar Port and the CPEC.[14] The Baloch would, however, want that these resources be first used for the uplift of Balochistan itself, rather than for the rest of Pakistan. A conflict is thus inherent in the situation.

Economic Exploitation

Exploitation of the natural resources of Balochistan and inadequate allocation of funds for development is a major component in the alienation and resentment in Balochistan.

Overview of Balochistan's Economy

According to a study by noted economist Kaiser Bengali titled 'A Cry for Justice: Empirical Insights from Balochistan,' in 2011 the approximate GDP growth rate of all three provinces was 4.9 per cent, while for Balochistan, it was 2.8 per cent, which showed that the province was lagging behind. He warned that if policies and attitudes remained unchanged, it would fall even lower.[15]

Bengali also noted that the 25-year development expenditure analysis showed that from 1990 to 2001, the average share of Balochistan was 3.9 per cent of the total development expenditure in the country, which translated into 0.18 per cent of GDP.[16] This, according to the Balochistan Government's Budget White Paper 2016-17 'underpins the fact that historically Balochistan's economy has largely under-performed compared to its potential. The underlying facts behind this weak economic performance of the province include volatile political and security environment, and structural bottlenecks.'[17]

Whenever someone asks the federal government about how they plan to improve the economic condition in Balochistan, the standard reply these days is 'China-Pakistan Economic Corridor (CPEC).' The federal government proudly claims that the Corridor will prove to be a game-changer and change the fate of the people of Balochistan. Unfortunately, these are nothing more than hollow claims. The proposed Economic Corridor will only pass through a portion of the province and cannot change the lives of all the people of the province.[18] Second, there is no guarantee that the people of Balochistan will get jobs after the establishment of this Corridor. In the past, the Baloch have been ignored in mega projects such as the Saindak copper-gold project, the Reko Diq project and the Gwadar Port project.[19] CPEC is unlikely to be the solution to the employment problems, let alone the economic problems of Balochistan.[20]

Issue of Natural Gas

At the centre of economic exploitation is the issue of natural gas. Balochistan's natural gas production has been critical to the development of the Pakistan economy. Cheap gas from Balochistan ushered a new chapter in the history of industry and economy of Pakistan. According to the Balochistan Government's Budget White Paper 2015-16, if gas from Sui was not available, the country would have to import oil as a substitute, spending at least US$ 3 billion per annum.[21] However, while Sui gas was instrumental in setting up of industries all over the country, the benefits of their gas deposits have eluded the Baloch. In fact, the way in which the gas from Balochistan has been exploited, violates the constitutional provisions for the supply of gas. As per Article 158 of Pakistan's Constitution: "The Province in which a well head of natural gas is situated shall have precedence over other parts of Pakistan in meeting the requirements from that well head".

Natural gas was struck in Sui located in the Bugti tribal area of Balochistan in the early 1950s. Once operationalised, it produced approximately 45 per cent of the country's total gas. However, the town of Dera Bugti was supplied with gas in the mid-1990s, almost forty years after gas was discovered in the district. Likewise, while most of Punjab has access to gas, Balochistan's provincial capital Quetta was supplied with natural gas only as late as 1980.[22] In May 2014, the Ministry of Petroleum and Natural Resources informed the Senate that out of the 32 district headquarters of Balochistan, only 13 had natural gas facility and 59 per cent of the urban population in the province was deprived of it.[23] In comparative terms, almost 97 per cent of Punjab's urban population has access to gas.[24]

In 1995, Balochistan contributed nearly 56 per cent to Pakistan's total output of natural gas, but by 2007 its share had dropped to 22.7 per cent. That year it consumed only 5.81 per cent of the country's total output.[25] According to Frederic Grare, provincial consumption was only 17 per cent of its own production, with 83 per cent of its natural gas being provided to the rest of the country for industrial and household use.[26]

Apart from low consumption of its own gas, the second issue is of royalty and specifically the quantum of royalty. Balochistan receives a 12.5 per cent royalty from its natural gas revenues. However, this royalty and gas development surcharge was made admissible only after 1991, 39 years after discovery of natural gas in Balochistan. Thus, for decades, Balochistan had lost out on royalty.[27] Moreover, the royalty is based on a well-head price that was far lower than that of other provinces. Balochistan's average gas field well-head price in rupees per MMBTU was Rs 66.34; for Sindh, it was Rs 142.57 and for Punjab it was Rs 162.93. The differentiated well-head price was due to it being based on per capita provincial income in 1953, resulting in a well-head price in Balochistan that was far lower than in Sindh and Punjab. Consequently, Balochistan received far less royalties than the other provinces.[28] The well-head price of gas was enhanced to Rs 163.13 MMBTU only in 2009-10.[29]

Not surprisingly, the Baloch 'interpret the disparity between the value of gas produced in Balochistan and the poverty of the province as a consequence of their exploitation by outsiders.'[30] The militants have responded to this situation by forcibly preventing further exploration and extraction in regions that are resource-rich, such as the Bugti and Marri homelands.[31] In addition, the Baloch are determined to increase the cost of the conflict for Islamabad by launching periodic attacks on pipelines and installations, disrupting gas supplies.[32]

Economic exploitation of Balochistan has been summed up by Kaiser Bengali who notes that empirical evidence shows that Balochistan has suffered and continues to suffer systematic economic exploitation, discrimination and neglect. He laments: 'We have taken much from Balochistan and given very little to it.... How can a province be so rich in resources and yet suffer from abject poverty. This is a saga of massive resources transfer, colonial-style political and economical management.'[33]

Socio-Economic Deprivation

The impact of the economic marginalisation is clearly reflected in the socio-economic deprivation in the province that has been highlighted in several credible reports.

In a report in 2008 the World Bank[34] held that Balochistan had the weakest *long-term growth, the worst quality of employment and the weakest social development* (emphasis added) performance of all provinces. From 1972-73 to 2004-05, the economy expanded 2.7 times in Balochistan, 3.6 times in NWFP and Sindh, and 4.0 times in Punjab. As a result, the growth divergence has widened historic income differences and Balochistan's per capita income level of $400 in 2004 was only two-thirds of Pakistan's level. Balochistan's rate of structural change and urbanisation was also lower than elsewhere. According to the report, Balochistan scored lowest among the provinces on key indicators such as education, literacy, health, water and sanitation for 2006/07.

Other reports and surveys confirm this grim picture of Balochistan.

Poverty

The Sustainable Development Policy Institute's (SDPI) report estimated poverty levels using 27 indicators pertaining to four dimensions of well-being, i.e., education, health, living conditions, and assets ownership.[35] The report not only highlighted the districts where poverty was high but also tracked the changes in poverty levels in individual districts over a five-year period, 2008 to 2013. In 2012-13, the multi-dimensional poverty headcount was 62.6 per cent of the population of Balochistan, 39.3 per cent of KP, 37.5 per cent of Sindh, and 24.3 per cent of Punjab. Of this, 46.2 per cent of the population of Balochistan was living in extreme poverty compared to 26.6 per cent in KP, 24.6 per cent in Sindh and 15.4 per cent in Punjab. At the national level, 18.6 per cent of the population was living in extreme poverty.

Based on poverty headcount ratios, districts were classified into five zones or quintiles. The geographic concentration of poverty was evident from the fact that out of 56 districts in the bottom two quintiles (poverty figures ranging from 72.6 per cent to 96.4 per cent in the bottom quintile and from 50 per cent to 72 per cent in the fourth quintile), 23 or half were from Balochistan, 11 from Sindh, 8 from KP, and two from Punjab. Districts that were largely rural and had low population were the ones with the highest headcount ratio.[36]

According to a 2017 report prepared by the United Nations Development Programme (UNDP) and the Oxford Poverty and Human Development Initiative (OPHI), titled "Multidimensional Poverty in Pakistan", Balochistan was rapidly sliding back on all human development indicators. According to it, 71.2 per cent of the population in Balochistan was victim of multi-dimensional poverty. Rural areas were even worse where 84.6 population lived under stifling multi-dimensional poverty. This explained the pathetic state of human development indicators in the province.[37]

The report cautioned that while the China-Pakistan Economic Corridor (CPEC) could potentially boost economic activities it also had the potential to further entrench existing inequalities by concentrating these opportunities in the already developed and least poor districts.[38]

Moreover, the Benazir Income Support Programme (BISP) that has been giving over a billion dollars a year across the country to poor families,[39] 'is systematically biased against what is by far the poorest province in the country.' Based on the 2017 Census, and BISP's latest data, 16 per cent of Pakistani households received unconditional transfers from BISP. The percentage of Balochistan's population covered by BISP should have been the highest given its poverty levels, but it is not. Only around 13 per cent of the households in Balochistan were beneficiaries, though residents of Balochistan were more than twice as likely to be poverty-stricken as a resident of Punjab. Twenty-five per cent of Khyber-Pakhtunkhwa (KP)'s households, and 22 per cent of the far richer Sindh, received BISP transfers. To achieve KP's level of coverage, it is estimated that an additional 235,759 women in Balochistan should be getting a stipend. In other words, nearly a quarter million of Balochistan's families were being deprived of what should rightfully be theirs.

According to Dr Kaiser Bengali, the first national coordinator of the BISP, the reason for this was that a larger portion of Balochistan's population wasn't surveyed in the nationwide poverty census concluded in 2011 due to their living in isolated, inaccessible settlements across the vastness of Balochistan.[40]

Unemployment

It has been estimated that the number of unemployed persons in Balochistan (0.06 million) constitutes about 20 per cent of the total number of unemployed persons (3.05 million) in Pakistan. This indicates a disproportionate high number compared to

Balochistan's 6 per cent of the total population of Pakistan.[41] Worse, unemployment is increasing; a 2007 study on demographic transition, education and youth employment found that young people in Balochistan were twice as likely to be without a job as their Punjab counterparts.[42]

Excluding Quetta, the other districts in Balochistan provided little or no employment opportunities for the people. Agriculture that was the primary source of employment in Balochistan has been badly affected by shortages of water and electricity.

Human Development Index (HDI)

Based on the Pakistan Social And Living Standards Measurement (PSLM) survey for the year 2014-15, a study carried out by the Social Policy and Development Centre (SPDC), Karachi, developed regional HDIs.[43] On this basis, the estimated HDI for Pakistan and the provinces for 2014-15 was: Pakistan-0.524; Punjab-0.550; Sindh-0.506; KP-0.476; Balochistan-0.407. Of the bottom 15 districts according to the estimated values of HDI, two were in KP (Tor Ghar and Kohistan) and two in Sindh (Kashmore and Tando Mohd Khan). The remaining 11 districts were in Balochistan. No district of Punjab was placed in this cluster of bottom 15 districts.[44]

The top 15 districts of Pakistan in terms of HDI contain 12 districts in Punjab, one in Sindh (Karachi) and two in KP (Abbottabad, Haripur). These districts lie in the category of medium level of development. Barring Karachi, all districts of Sindh and Balochistan belong to the low level of human development.[45]

Comparatively speaking, the lowest category district in Punjab is Rajanpur with an HDI of 0.425. This is higher than 24 districts of Balochistan. There are only four districts in Balochistan that have a higher HDI than Rajanpur, the district with the lowest HDI in Punjab. In fact, the HDI of the lowest district in Balochistan, Dera Bugti, is 0.297 as compared with the 0.425 of the lowest district in Punjab.[46]

The magnitude of HDI shows the extent of disparities in the level of human development.

Food Security and Malnutrition

According to a report, 13 most underfed districts in Pakistan were from Balochistan (minimum intake of food measured by calories). The entire generation in Dera Bugti in Balochistan is reported to be malnourished. A recent report on malnutrition and food poverty has disclosed that two out of three households in Balochistan cannot afford a proper meal and 83.4 per cent of the children in the province are facing severe malnourishment. Eighty-three per cent of the children of Balochistan have no access to health, education and opportunities.[47]

The situation had deteriorated so much that the then Provincial Health Minister Mir Rehmat Baloch felt the need in May 2017 to call for the imposition of a nutrition emergency in Balochistan, as the nutritional situation of the mother and the child was alarming in the province. He added that according to a survey, 52 per cent of the children suffered from stunting and 40 per cent were underweight.[48] This reveals the grim picture of the living conditions of the population especially mothers and children. Nutrition is clearly the victim of serious neglect in Pakistan and especially in Balochistan. Over the decades, successive governments have paid little attention to the issue, resulting in the current alarming statistics. Poor spending on healthcare, weak institutions, erratic funding by donors and a culture of negligence are cited as the main reasons for the existing situation. As the *Daily Times* put it, 'Unfortunately the ordinary citizens of Pakistan have been left at the mercy of a dysfunctional health system, negligible health facilities and often vacuous and unskilled practices of the health staff.'[49]

Millenium Development Goals (MDGs)

Despite tall claims, fancy promises and international commitments, Pakistan has not made much headway in fulfilling its MDG commitment. As per a UNDP report, Balochistan in 2015 was the worst performing province in most if not all areas of the MDGs. The report showed that at the current rate of progress, no MDG could be achieved in its entirety in the province. Its performance while completely off track and below the national average for almost all indicators was especially of grave concern in health and education related indicators. Forty-three per cent of the children were underweight against a target of 20 per cent, reflecting a severe lag in performance. Similarly, in MDG 2, in all three indicators—net primary enrolment ratio, completion/survival rate and literacy rate, performance was lower than the national average and considerably behind the targets. Balochistan was also under-performing in five indicators of child mortality with a staggeringly high infant mortality rate by national standards. In MDG 5, progress was especially lagging for all indicators—at 785 deaths per 100,000 live births, the maternal mortality ratio deserved immediate attention.[50]

Education

According to the Adviser to the Balochistan Chief Minister on education, over 1.6 million children of school-going age were not in schools. However, according to a report released by the Academy for Educational Planning and Management (AEPAM), a federal government institution, more than 1.8 million children were out of school in Balochistan. Education Statistics for 2014-2015 launched in February 2016 by the Ministry of Federal Education's Academy of Educational Planning and Management, estimated that 24.02 million children between the ages of 5-16 were out of school in Pakistan. Balochistan had the highest percentage of out-of-school children at 70 per cent, followed by Sindh at 56 per cent and Punjab at 44 per cent, and Khyber- Pashtunkhwa with the lowest percentage of out-of-school children at 36 per cent.[51]

By the Government's own admission, of the 22,000 plus settlements in the province, the Government had Government-run schools (primary, secondary and high schools) in only about 12,500 of them.[52]

The situation regarding girls' education is far worse. Girls continue to suffer severe disadvantage and exclusion in Balochistan. A staggering 75 per cent of girls aged between 5 and 16 are out of school compared to 65 per cent boys within the same age group in Balochistan, according to the NGO Alif Ailan. There is one girls' high school every 77 km^2. Owing to scarcity of high schools for them, girls in the respective area have little option but to give up their education after completion of middle school.[53]

School drop-outs is another major issue. Every year 130,000 students enrol in schools but only 61,000 appear in matriculation examinations out which only 30,000 are able to pass while the number of university pass-outs is 3,000.[54]

At an all-Pakistan level, 11 out of the 16 districts in Pakistan with the worst Net Enrolment Rate (NER) record were in Balochistan; none of the districts in the province lay in the highest quality of district education rankings. Of the 32 districts in Balochistan, 23 districts had an education score of less than 50 per cent.[55]

The Economic Survey of Pakistan 2011-2012 provides a comparative survey of literacy rates (10 years+) in Pakistan and the provinces (Table 4.2).

Table 4.2: Literacy Rate in Pakistan

	2008-09			2010-11		
	M*	F#	T@	M*	F#	T@
Pakistan	69	45	57	69	46	58
Punjab	69	50	59	70	51	60
Sindh	71	45	59	71	46	59
KPK	69	31	50	68	33	50
Balochistan	62	23	45	60	19	41

Source: The Economic Survey of Pakistan 2011-2012
Notes: *Male; # Female; @ Total

Social Indicators

Balochistan has the poorest social indicators in the country.

The maternal mortality rate (MMR) in Pakistan is 276 (per 100,000 live births), whereas according to 2006-07 data, Balochistan had the highest MMR—785 per 100,000 live births, almost three times the national average, while the MMR for Punjab stood at 227 per 100,000 live births. The current MMR and female reproductive health demographics of Balochistan can only compete with war-torn

Somalia—with an MMR of 1000 and Liberia, with an MMR of 770 per 100,000 live births.

Only 43 per cent of children are fully immunised in the province against a national average of 78 per cent. According to the Extended Programme on Immunisation (EPI) coverage survey 2001, only 35 per cent of the children in the age group of 12-23 months were fully immunised at that time, showing marked deterioration.[56] Balochistan accounted for 7 out of the 9 districts in Pakistan with the lowest full immunisation rate, including the four districts with the worst record. Balochistan's performance would look even worse without the exclusion of Dera Bugti and Kohlu in the Pakistan Social and Living Standards Measurement (PSLM) sample due to security reasons. Additionally, UNICEF reported that there was no vaccination centre in 39 per cent of the union councils in the province. In 2011, the province recorded the highest incidence for polio cases in the world: a total of 62 out of a worldwide 169.[57]

The province also remains deprived of basic health facilities. High infant mortality rates (IMR) prevailed with 158 out of a 1,000 children dying before five years of age. Even the Democratic Republic of Congo's average of 126 is lower while Pakistan's national average of 70 is less than half. According to another report, the IMR in Balochistan is high with wide urban-rural and male-female variation. In rural areas, mortality rates for children under the age of five (U5MR) are at 164 per 1,000 live births, much higher than that of urban children (130 per 1,000 live births).[58]

While Pakistan as a whole lags behind in the social sector, Balochistan lags far behind other provinces in all indicators. The poor social fabric has been largely due to the lack of economic growth that has stunted attempts to improve the lot of the people. It is understandable that with such a weak social sector—with low-level literary rate and poor and inadequate healthcare services, for instance—for Balochistan to embark on economic development is an uphill task.

One argument advanced for the deplorable conditions in Balochistan is that the population is low and area is vast. Thus, far more expenditure would have to be expended to achieve the same economic benefits as in the other provinces. This is a self-serving justification since any government would try and bring all the provinces to one level rather than focusing only on the already developed ones, even if they have much larger populations. Allowing Balochistan to lag behind in the name of smaller population is indicative of treating the population of the province as second-class citizens. As a federation, the federal fiscal system is expected to bring about equalisation among federating units, provision of public services and socio-economic development indicators.[59] This is something that Pakistan has clearly failed to do.

To conclude, for the Baloch, discriminations by the Pakistani (Punjabi) state began with the creation of Pakistan itself when their independence was snatched and when their national identity began to be smothered. Over the decades, the continued exploitation of the province's natural gas and other resources for the benefit of Punjab; the resultant appalling socio-economic indices of the province; the construction of mega projects like Gwadar deep-sea port and the CPEC that do not factor-in Baloch aspirations and could turn them into a minority in their own province; the brutal tactics of enforced disappearance and especially the wanton 'kill and dump' policy adopted by the Army have congealed the alienation of the Baloch.

Facing continued subjugation, a growing section of the Baloch have resorted to arms. They seem to have chosen to fight to survive rather then submit and be marginalised in their own homeland. As Declan Walsh put it, "Balochistan's dirty little war ... highlights a very fundamental danger—the ability of Pakistanis to live together in a country that, under its Islamic cloak, is a patchwork of ethnicities and cultures." He quotes Haris Gazdar, a Karachi-based researcher saying, "Balochistan is a warning of the real battle for Pakistan, which is about power and resources, and if we don't get it right, we're headed for a major conflict."[60]

For Pakistan, the security implications of a disturbed Balochistan are dire. Given the economic and strategic importance of Balochistan, it cannot afford to fail. However, its policies that are responsible for the socio-economic marginalisation of the province are actually ensuring just the opposite.

The moot question is whether the security situation in Balochistan could improve with real economic development, improvement in social indicators, more investments in education and health and allowing the Baloch to use their resources for their benefit first?

The short answer is perhaps, yes. However, as things stand, such measures are unlikely to be taken simultaneously. For one thing, the military is averse to provincial rights and autonomy. Under the government of Imran Khan, feelers were put out about tinkering with the 18th Constitutional Amendment that had devolved powers to the provinces. For another, Pakistan has gone too far down the road in terms of commitments to the Chinese on Gwadar and the CPEC, to tweak the projects to give the Baloch a stake. For most of the Baloch themselves, it no longer about economics alone. They have come to see so-called development projects as further examples of the exploitation of the resources of Balochistan for the sake of the Punjabi state. For most Baloch, it is now about preserving their national resources, their honour, about their survival with dignity in their own lands, about protecting their national identity, culture and language, in a word, about independence. Pushed to the wall, facing marginalisation and subjugation, an increasing number of Baloch have picked up the gun for the sake of preserving their rights. This is the direct consequence of Balochistan's socio-economic marginalisation.

Disclaimer: The chapter has been extracted from the author's book "Pakistan: The Balochistan Conundrum" published by HarperCollins India in 2019. The article was written and submitted by Mr Tilak Devasher for the Pugwash project in May 2020.

Notes

1. Government of Balochistan, 'Budget White Paper 2015-16' , at www.kcci.com.pk/Rnd/wp-content/uploads/2017/07/White-Paper-2015-16-2.pdf. Accessed on 27 February 2018.
2. A Baloch proverb, cited in Farhan Hanif Siddiqi, *The Political Economy of The Ethnonationalist Uprising In Pakistani Balochistan, 1999-2013*, Quaid-i-Azam University, Islamabad, January 2015, at https://www.researchgate.net/publication/272183981_Political_Economy_of_the_Ethno-nationalist_Uprising_in_Pakistani_Balochistan_1999-2013. Accessed on 3 March 2018.

3. Gas from Sui is in a league by itself as discussed later in the chapter.
4. Selig S. Harrison, *In the Shadow of Afghanistan: Baluch Nationalism and Soviet Temptations*, Carnegie Endowment for International Peace, Washington, DC 1981, p. 7.
5. Ibid.
6. Declan Walsh, 'Pakistan's secret dirty war', *The Guardian*, 29 March 2011, at https://www.theguardian.com/world/2011/mar/29/balochistan-pakistans-secret-dirty-war. Accessed on 27 February 2018.
7. Naveed Hussain, 'Fiddling While Balochistan Burns,' *The Express Tribune*, 15 August 2012, at https://tribune.com.pk/story/422060/fiddling-while-balochistan-burns/. Accessed on 27 February 2018.
8. Human Rights Commission of Pakistan (HRCP), 'Pushed to the Wall, Report of the HRCP Fact-Finding Mission to Balochistan' October 2009, at http://hrcp-web.org/hrcpweb/wp-content/pdf/ff/14.pdf. Accessed on 3 March 2018.
9. Inayatullah Baloch, *The Problem of Greater Baluchistan: A Study Of Baluch Nationalism*, Steiner Verlag Wiesbaden Gmbh, Stuttgart, 1987, pp. 191-92.
10. Muhammad Ijaz Laif and Muhammad Amir Hamza, 'Ethnic Nationalism in Pakistan: A Case Study of Baloch Nationalism during Musharraf Regime', *Pakistan Vision,* Vol. 10, No. 1, 2010.
11. Human Rights Commission of Pakistan (HRCP), 'Human Rights in Balochistan and Balochistan's Rights: Report of a Fact-Finding Mission, October 2003', at http://hrcp-web.org/hrcpweb/wp-content/pdf/ff/20.pdf p-59. Accessed on 3 March 2018.
12. HRCP 2009, n. 8.
13. 'Imperialism, Oil and the Balochistan Revolution', *Jabal,* July 1977, p. 6, cited in Selig Harrison, n. 4, p. 171.
14. Malik Siraj Akbar, 'Why Pakistan Is Embarrassed to Talk About Balochistan', *Huffington Post*, 13 March 2014, at http://www.huffingtonpost.com/malik-siraj-akbar/why-pakistan-is-embarrass_b_4937159.html. Accessed on 3 March 2018.
15. Zoya Anwer, 'Balochistan has no say in national policy making', *The News*, 12 February 2018, at https://www.thenews.com.pk/print/279759-balochistan-has-no-say-in-national-policy-making. Accessed on 27 February 2018.
16. Ibid.
17. Government of Balochistan: 'Budget White Paper 2017-18, p. 8, at http://www.balochistan.gov.pk/index.php?option=com_docman&gid=1474&Itemid=677. Accessed on 3 March 2018.
18. Adnan Aamir, 'Unemployment in Balochistan', *The News*, 27 April 2015, at http://www.adnan-aamir.com/2015/04/unemployment-in-balochistan.html. Accessed on 27 February 2018.
19. Frédéric Grare, 'Pakistan: The Resurgence of Baluch nationalism', South Asia Project No. 65, January 2006, Carnegie Endowment for International

Peace, at http://carnegieendowment.org/files/CP65.Grare.FINAL.pdf. Accessed on 27 February 2018.

20. Adnan Aamir, n. 18.
21. Budget White Paper 2015-16, n. 1.
22. International Crisis Group, 'Pakistan: The Worsening Conflict In Balochistan', *Asia Report* No. 119, 14 September 2006, at https://d2071andvip0wj.cloudfront.net/119-pakistan-the-worsening-conflict-in-balochistan.pdf. Accessed on 3 March 2018.
23. Budget White Paper 2015-16, n. 1.
24. Iftikhar Firdous, 'Deprived Province: 59% of Balochistan Without Natural Gas', *The Express Tribune*, 26 May 2014, at https://tribune.com.pk/story/713135/deprived-province-59-of-balochistan-without-natural-gas/. Accessed on 2 March 2018.
25. Ibid.
26. Frédéric Grare, n. 19.
27. Government of Balochistan: 'Budget White Paper 2016-17, n. 17, p. 19.
28. Ibid.
29. Ibid.
30. Paul Titus, 'Introduction' in Sylvia Matheson, *The Tigers of Baluchistan,* Oxford University Press, Karachi, 1998, p. xx.
31. Explaining why the Marris opposed oil exploration in their lands, Nawab Khair Bakhsh Marri said: 'We saw what happened in the Bugti area, where they have "developed" the Sui gas, 80 per cent of which goes out of Balochistan to make others rich'. Selig Harrison, n. 4, p. 47.
32. International Crisis Group, n. 22.
33. Cited in Zoya Anwer, n. 15.
34. World Bank, 'Pakistan: Balochistan Economic Report—From Periphery to Core', No. 40345-PK May 2008.
35. Arif Naveed, Geof Wood and Muhammad Usman Ghaus, 'Geography of Poverty in Pakistan—2008-09 to 2012-13: Distribution, Trends and Explanations', p. iii, Joint Report By Pakistan Poverty Alleviation Fund & Sustainable Development Policy Institute (SDPI), Islamabad, 2016.
36. Ibid.
37. Naseer Memon, 'The Balochistan conundrum', *The News*, 16 April 2017, at http://tns.thenews.com.pk/balochistan-conundrum/#.Wr-gY62B06g. Accessed on 2 March 2018.
38. Arif Naveed, Geof Wood and Muhammad Usman Ghaus, n. 35.
39. Deserving families are selected via a nation-wide poverty census (last completed in 2011) and receive Rs 4,700 a quarter, paid to the woman of the house.
40. Assad Ahmad, 'Balochistan's missing Poor', *Dawn*, 24 March 2018, at https://www.dawn.com/news/1397227/balochistans-missing-poor. Accessed on 31 March 2018.
41. Pakistan Institute Of Legislative Development And Transparency (PILDAT), *Balochistan: Civil-Military Relations*, Islamabad, March

2012, p. 35, at http://www.pildat.org/publications/publication/cmr/issuepaperbalochistanconflictcmr.pdf. Accessed on 3 March 2018.

42. Sher Baz Khan, "Unemployment on rise, says ADB; *Dawn*, 22 May 2007, at https://www.dawn.com/news/248191. Accessed on 27 February 2018.
43. Haroon Jamal, 'Quantifying Sub-National Human Development Indices from Household Survey Data', Social Policy and Development Centre (SPDC), Karachi, May 2016, at http://www.spdc.org.pk/Data/Publication/PDF/RR-96.pdf. Accessed on 3 March 2018.
44. Ibid., pp. 5-6.
45. Ibid., p. 7.
46. Ibid., p. 8.
47. Sadia Ali, 'The Poor Daughter of Balochistan', *The News*, 17 August 2016, at https://www.thenews.com.pk/print/142987-The-poor-daughter-of-Balochistan. Accessed on 3 March 2018.
48. Saleem Shahid, 'Call For Nutrition Emergency In Balochistan', *Dawn*, 1 May 2017, at https://Www.Dawn.Com/News/1330316/Call-For-Nutrition-Emergency-In-Balochistan. Accessed on 2 March 2018.
49. 'Malnutrition in Balochistan', Editorial, *Daily Times*, 2 May 2017, at www.dailytimes.com.pk. Accessed on 2 March 2018.
50. 'Millennium Development Goals', UNDP in Pakistan, 2015, at http://www.pk.undp.org/content/pakistan/en/home/post-2015/mdgoverview.html. Accessed on 3 March 2018.
51. Monis Ali, 'The education crisis in Balochistan', *Daily Times*, 27 October 2016, at http://dailytimes.com.pk/opinion/27-Oct-16/the-education-crisis-in-balochistan. Accessed on 27 February 2018.
52. Syed Fazl-E-Haider, 'Education in Balochistan Fails to keep pace', *Pakistan and Gulf Economist*, 31 July 2017, at http://www.pakistaneconomist.com/2017/07/31/education-in-balochistan-fails-to-keep-pace/. Accessed on 27 February 2018.
53. Mohammad Zafar, '75% Girls Out Of School In Balochistan', *The Express Tribune*, 4 July 2016, at https://tribune.com.pk/story/1135714/provincial-govt-challenge-75-per-cent-girls-school-balochistan/. Accessed on 27 February 2018.
54. Ibid.
55. Alif Ailaan, 'The State of Education in Balochistan', at https://d3n8a8pro7vhmx.cloudfront.net/alifailaan/pages/496/attachments/original/1473163108. Accessed on 3 March 2018.
56. Abdul Wahab, 'A Province in Peril', *Newsline*, June 2009, at http://newslinemagazine.com/magazine/the-final-showdown/. Accessed on 2 March 2018.
57. Government of Balochistan, 'Balochistan Education Sector Plan 2013-2017', at http://aserpakistan.org/document/learning_resources/2014/

Sector_Plans/Balochistan%20Sector%20Plan%202013-2017.pdf, p. 8. Accessed on 3 March 2018.

58. Abdul Wahab, n. 56.
59. Ibid.
60. Declan Walsh, n. 6.

5. Pakistan's Economic Crisis: Lessons Unlearned

Riya Sinha

Introduction

Since its formation, Pakistan has seen cyclical economic crises marked by years of high inflation and low growth in the Gross Domestic Product (GDP). In the last few years, Pakistan's GDP growth has witnessed a huge slump—from 5.8 per cent in 2017, to 1 per cent and 0.5 per cent respectively in 2019 and 2020. GDP growth showed an improvement in 2021 and stood at 5.6 per cent before the economic crisis started to further intensify. The current economic crisis is not a new phenomenon; it has roots in the various short-term and unsustainable measures adopted by successive governments since the 1960s and the reversal of policies for political reasons thereafter. This is particularly exemplified by the fact that the 18 IMF supported programmes since 1958[1] have not been able to strengthen Pakistan's economy.[2]

The political cycle of Pakistan's economic crisis has been analysed by Mohammad Yaqoob, Former Governor, State Bank of Pakistan:[3]

> "A casual review of the speeches and statements of successive government representatives in Pakistan during the last two decades will lead an objective observer to conclude that there has been a consistent pattern of each government criticizing the economic management of preceding governments, praising their own policies and programs and complimenting themselves for doing a better job, but in reality adhering to similar short-term, and short-sighted, approach to economic management with similar results."

Some scholars call Pakistan the 'sick man of South Asia.'[4] Apart from the dwindling GDP growth, the country also ranks low in the global corruption index published by Transparency International (117 out of 180 in 2018).[5] In the World Bank's Ease of Doing Business Report 2020, Pakistan has made improvements and is ranked among the top 10 improvers; however, the relative ranking continues to be low (108 out of 190).[6] Furthermore, rising debt servicing obligations coupled with low exports and heavy reliance on imports, mean that both domestic revenue and foreign exchange reserves are shrinking, leaving little for the country to fund its recuperation back to an annual economic growth of at least 6 per cent.[7]

The case of Pakistan's economic crisis has remained a curious one for many scholars, observers and analysts. For decades, the country's economy has shown signs of mismanagement, stemming from poor decision-making coupled with rampant corruption in policy implementation. Yet, Pakistan has managed to leverage the narrative of a 'weak' state and topped it with threats to its nuclear capability as well as its geographic location to attract resources from external donors—a move that has sustained the economy thus far. The geostrategic importance of Pakistan is more now than ever before, especially after it became the biggest beneficiary of China's Belt and Road Initiative (BRI) through the development of the China-Pakistan Economic Corridor (CPEC).[8]

This chapter aims to address the key question that has irked many observers—why does Pakistan's economy face an economic crisis every few years? A closer analysis of Pakistan's budget documents reveals the main structural imbalances that continue to plague the economy. The first part of this chapter highlights the key challenges that have been recurrent in Pakistan's economic crisis over the years. Despite years of reform policies, the challenges remain unaddressed mainly due to gaps in implementation. However, Pakistan's economy has not always been vulnerable. The second part of the chapter focuses on three key missed opportunities in Pakistan's economic history that could have changed the economic fate of the country. Finally, highlighting the current IMF programme, the chapter argues that it may be another failure if Pakistan does not address the underlying causes of economic imbalance, and this can have lasting security repercussions for the region.

Problems in the Economy

The *Pakistan Economic Survey 2018-19* identified a four-fold problem with the economy: (a) high fiscal deficit, (b) current account deficit (CAD) highest in the history of the country, (c) debt liabilities are so big that debt servicing takes a large portion of the budget and (d) depletion of foreign exchange reserves.[9] Low revenue growth, and large-scale increase in public spending led to widening of Pakistan's fiscal deficit in FY2019 to 6.5 per cent of the GDP (2.5 per cent higher than budgeted). The public debt widened to approximately 75 per cent of the GDP and due to an increase in the trade deficit fuelled by rise in imports (as a result of the high domestic demand), the CAD too rose to 6.3 per cent of the GDP from 4.1 per cent in the previous year.[10] The sectoral outlook is also very dismal; industrial manufacturing decreased by 3 per cent between July and January FY2019 and major agricultural crops such as cotton, wheat and rice witnessed a decline in production due to water shortage.[11] As a result, the exports did not pick up despite a depreciating exchange rate, further widening the CAD. In May 2019, the inflation rate in Pakistan increased to 9.1 per cent from 4.2 per cent in the preceding year.[12]

In addition to the above, an overvalued exchange rate, an accommodative monetary policy, and weak institutions, contributed to deterioration of the international reserves, which by January 2019 had fallen to just US$ 6.6 billion.[13] It was only after seeking short-term financing from Saudi Arabia, United Arab Emirates and China that the reserves increased to US$ 10.5 billion in May 2019. However, this figure was enough to sustain only two months of imports.[14] Furthermore, as per the State Bank of Pakistan, the total public debt accumulated by Pakistan as in June 2019 stood at Pakistani Rupees (PKR) 31.786 trillion, a staggering 81.8 per cent of the GDP. In April 2021, Pakistan's external debt was approximately US$ 90 billion, out of which US$ 24.7 billion is owed to China. In June 2022, Pakistan's total debt and liabilities stood at 89.2 per cent of GDP. Total external debt and liabilities stood at approximately 37 per cent of the GDP.

This deteriorating economic condition built the case for Pakistan to seek credit from the IMF. While the short-term loans from bilateral and multilateral creditors has provided for a short-term relief, they fail to address the underlying structural problems of the economy. Therefore, the debt obligations of Pakistan are likely to increase. While the Federal Budget for FY2020 and FY2021 did set an ambitious target for bringing the economy back on track, the following points identify the key structural impediments that the policy-makers will have to address:

1. *Errors in Estimation of Revenue Collection:* Revenue forecasting has been one of the weakest strands of Pakistan's economy, wherein the estimation gap between the budgeted and actual revenue collection has always been high. Studies show that is because the forecasts are not based on macro-economic models, but rather on policy changes such as tax measures, improving tax collection efficiency.[15] Several issues in Pakistan's economy are based on the Government's inability to predict actual revenue collection figures (Table 5.1). This leads of reallocation of expenditure. The high debt servicing obligations of Pakistan, increasing share of the defence budget, and high subsidies to

Table 5.1: Pakistan's Budgetted and Actual Revenue Estimates

Fiscal Year	Budgeted Gross Revenue Receipt# (PKR million)	Actual Gross Revenue Receipt (PKR million)	Difference (Percentage)	Change in Defence Expenditure	Change in Development Expenditure*
2014-15	3,945,504	3,952,472	0.18	2.8%	-10.0%
2015-16	3,419,997	3,597,142	5.18	-0.7%	-5.5%
2016-17	4,915,575	4,737,354	-3.63	-2.2%	-10.9%
2017-18	5,310,317	4,992,486	-5.99	8.6%	-20.7%
2018-19	5,660,505	5,031,628	-11.11	3.4%	-28.0%
2019-20	6,716,624	5,504,000	-22.03	10.6%	-22.8%
2020-21	6,573,000	n/a	n/a	n/a	n/a

Source: Issues of Federal Budget in Brief from 2014-2021.
Notes: #Gross Revenue receipt consists of both tax and non-tax revenue.
*Includes Federal PSDP, development expenditure outside PSDP and the development loans and grants to provinces.

state-owned enterprises mean that the budget cuts are usually made in the development sector. In the last five years, the development expenditure has been slashed majorly irrespective of the increase or decrease in gross revenue receipts (Table 5.1). As a result, the effects of these are seen notably in major developmental areas such as health, education, and water (explained further below).

2. *High Fiscal Deficit Due to Low Tax-to-GDP Ratio*: The Federal Board of Revenue (FBR) is the main tax revenue collecting body in Pakistan for both direct and indirect taxes. In the Budget for FY2020, the Government of Pakistan set an ambitious FBR revenue collection target of PKR 5.5 trillion, increasing it over 35 per cent from FY2019.[16] This target was tailored to meet the IMF loan conditionalities. To achieve this, the Government adopted measures such as reduction of the income tax slab from PKR 12 lakh per annum to 6 lakh per annum, increasing sales tax, etc., and reduced the current expenditure. The revenue collection target is difficult to achieve because Pakistan has one of the lowest tax-to-GDP ratios in South Asia and the world.[17] This is also one of the major contributors to the high fiscal deficit in the country.

Figure 5.1: Tax-to-GDP Ratio (Percentage)

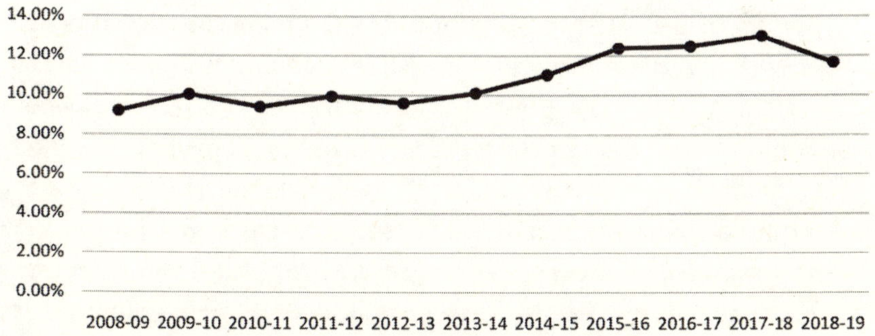

Source: Ministry of Finance, Government of Pakistan.

Figure 5.2: Pakistan's Fiscal Deficit (2009-2019)

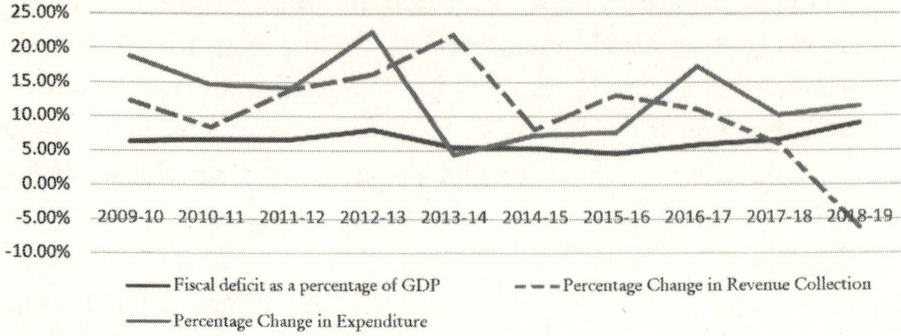

Source: Ministry of Finance, Government of Pakistan.

In FY2019, the fiscal deficit was 8.9 per cent of the GDP, increasing from 6.6 per cent in the previous year and the highest in 28 years.[18] Data shows that even when the economy was performing well, the fiscal deficit was lower due to reduction in expenditure rather than increase in the revenue (Figures 5.1 and 5.2). In FY2019, the tax-to-GDP ratio stood at 11.6 per cent, a decline from 13 per cent in FY18 (Figure 5.1). The Government of Pakistan requested the IMF to reduce the FBR target by PKR 300 billion, to PKR 5.2 trillion.[19] Given the decline in trade and short-fall in the July-October revenue collection target (PKR 1.28 trillion instead of PKR 1.48 trillion[20]), it became important to revise the revenue collection target. Furthermore, the increasing debt servicing obligations, as explained in the next point, only paint a dismal picture for containing the increasing fiscal deficit.

3. *High Foreign and Domestic Debt:* It is common knowledge that high debt will slow down the economy. In FY2019, Pakistan's total external debt stood at US$ 104 billion. This figure is likely to increase to US$ 133 billion by FY2024,[21] if Pakistan gets the required loans from bilateral partners as envisaged by the IMF programme.[22] The year-on-year growth in Pakistan's total debt was 32.8 per cent in FY2019.[23] As a result, debt servicing requirement is also high; in FY2019, Pakistan's total debt servicing was PKR 3,445 million, out of which 68.26 per cent was interest payment on the government's external and internal debt.[24] During the same period, the domestic debt was 88 per cent of the total government debt, the main source of which was borrowing from the banks.[25]

This reflects the accommodative monetary policy of the State Bank of Pakistan. The State Bank of Pakistan predicted,[26] the increase of both internal and external debt in FY2020, comprising 10.3 per cent of the GDP.[27]

4. *Inability to Curb Current Account Deficit (CAD):* In the budget speech FY2020, the Finance Minister of Pakistan highlighted that the goal was to halve the CAD from US$ 13 billion in FY2019 to US$ 6.5 billion in the fiscal year.[28] For this, the government has vowed to take steps such as improving mechanism for tax refund, supporting duty structure on raw materials, and providing electricity and gas at a competitive (or subsidised) cost. In order to boost exports, the government has provided subsidised gas and electricity, loans at low interest rate. Pakistan managed to reverse the current account deficit from US$ 284 million in September 2019 to a surplus of US$ 99 million in October 2019.[29] Pakistan reported a surplus after four years. However, this reduction in deficit is largely attributed to reduction in imports rather than increase in exports.[30] This massive reduction in imports will affect the revenue collection through taxation, cause inflation to rise and indicates slowing economic activity in the country.
5. *Cyclical Crisis in the Energy Sector:* In Pakistan, the Water and Power Development Authority (WAPDA) distributes electricity, whereas the tariff is determined by the government. As a result, energy tariffs (gas and power) have been used by successive governments as political tools. For instance, when fuel oil prices increased in 2007, the government did not pass the price hike to consumers because of it being an election year. This decision widened the fiscal deficit.[31] Furthermore, the demand-supply gap in Pakistan's power sector has been widening. This is attributed to the challenges in power generation as well as lack of capacity to transmit energy across the country.[32] However, the power sector is riddled with corruption, heavy financial losses, and bureaucratic delays. Poor and inequitable management of the power sector in different provinces has also led to excessive shortages and in turn, has affected the growth of industries in

the state. Circular debt is one of the major problems affecting the power sector.[33] It arises from the inability of the power generating and distributing companies to clear their dues as a result of 'non-recovery of bills and losses in transmission and distribution.'[34] In FY2019 and 2020, the Government of Pakistan took several measures to reduce circular debt, including revision of power and gas tariff, campaign against defaulters and power thieves and removing transmission bottlenecks.[35] In October 2019, Pakistan's circular debt rose to PKR 860 billion.[36]

High Defence Expenditure vis-à-vis Development Expenditure as a Cause of the Economic Crisis

Globally, Pakistan has one of the highest defence expenditures as a share of the total Government expenditure. In 2019, 18.4 per cent of Pakistan's total federal expenditure was for military purposes. By comparison, India and China spent 8.8 per cent and 5.4 per cent, respectively, on defence expenditure in the same year (Figure 5.3).

Figure 5.3: Defence Expenditure as a percentage of Total Government Expenditure

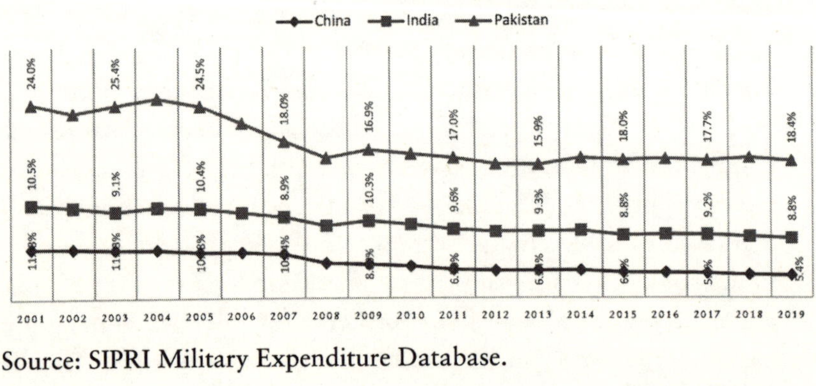

Source: SIPRI Military Expenditure Database.

Despite years of economic crisis, Pakistan's defence expenditure continues to form a significant portion of the total Government expenditure, whereas development expenditure has been declining. It is also reported that Pakistan's defence budget is much higher than projected in the budget document, as it includes important components such as military pensions.[37] The reported components

Table 5.2: Pakistan's Current Expenditure on Defence and Development

Fiscal Year	2016-17			2017-18			2018-19			2019-20		
	Budgeted (PKR billion)	Revised (PKR billion)	% of GDP	Budgeted (PKR billion)	Revised (PKR billion)	% of GDP	Budgeted (PKR billion)	Revised (PKR billion)	% of GDP	Budgeted (PKR billion)	Revised (PKR billion)	% of GDP*
(a) Defence Affairs and Services	860	841	2.8	920	999	3.0	1,100	1,137	2.9	1,152	-	2.6
(b) Development Expenditure (Overall)	1,050	936	5.3	1,340	1,062	4.7	1,152	829	1.8	949	-	2.1
(b.i) Water Resource Division	31	31	0.1	36	35	0.1	79	38	0.1	85	-	0.2
(b.ii) Education Affairs and Services	84	84	2.2	90.5	90.8	2.4	97.4	97.1	0.25	77	-	0.2
(b.iii) Health Affairs and Services	12	13	0.9	12.8	12.9	1.0	13.9	13.9	0.5	11	-	0.02

Source: Issues of Federal Budget in Brief from 2014-2019.

Note: * Based on IMF projection of Pakistan's GDP to be Rs 44,446 Billion in FY2020.

of the defence budget include defence services (civil works, assets, employee-related expenses, etc.) and defence administration. Additionally, the Defence Production Division is listed under the PSDP. Furthermore, Pakistan's military expenditure exceeds the budgeted expenditure every year. This is a result of its arms race with India, as well as its geostrategic position with respect to Afghanistan and its internal terrorism threats.[38] It is also estimated that Pakistan spends approximately 10 per cent of its defence budget on nuclear expenditure.[39] Studies indicate that increasing the defence budget does not have any adverse impact on the economy on its own; however, this must be supported with a corresponding increase in the development budget to manage the economy.[40]

Post-1977, Pakistan has tried to establish itself as a security state by increasing defence expenditure and reducing the development expenditure (Table 5.1). This single-minded approach to security—encompassing only defence—has led the other developmental sectors such as health, education and water to suffer. This has had far-reaching consequences on the economic development of Pakistan. In education, Pakistan ranks 113 out of 120 in UNESCO's Education-for-All Development Index (EDI).[41] Illiteracy is widespread and almost 23 million children aged 5-16 years are not in school.[42] Despite this, Pakistan spends just 2 per cent of its GDP on education.[43] The situation is made worse by the fact that 65 per cent of male and 79.8 per cent of the female population is in the age-group of 15-24 years and is unskilled.[44] Public spending on health, nutrition and education is only 3 per cent of the GDP.[45] In the health sector, expenditure as a percentage of the GDP has been increasing only marginally (0.97 per cent in 2017-18; 0.91 per cent in 2016-17 and; 0.77 per cent in 2015-16).[46] This, despite the fact that Pakistan has the lowest life expectancy in South Asia (66.6 years in 2017, compared to 68.8 in India and 75.5 in Sri Lanka), high infant mortality rate, second highest maternal mortality rate and the highest under-5 mortality rate. The urgency of increasing spending in the health sector is indicated in the *Economic Survey of Pakistan 2018-19*: "Health sector of the country faces tough challenges and there is a dire need to enhance the budget allocation for health aggressively by federal and all provincial governments, especially development expenditure so that increased and better quality health facilities may be available across the country". In a similar vein, depletion of water reserves is one of the biggest threats to Pakistan's economy. The per capita availability of water has decreased from 5,260 cubic metre in 1951 to 935 cubic metre in 2019.[47] For a country that uses 93 per cent of its freshwater resources in agriculture,[48] the decline in water resources is alarming because the total water availability for both kharif and rabi crops is decreasing every year (–18.1 per cent in 2018-19).[49] This is affecting the production of major crops such as cotton, sugarcane, rice and wheat, that also form a major part of Pakistan's export basket.

Figure 5.4: GDP Growth 1960-1980 (percentage)

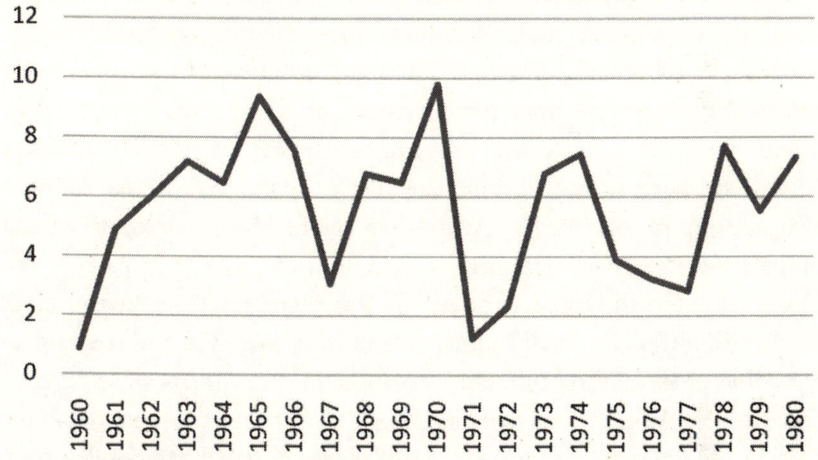

Source: Pakistan Bureau of Statistics.

Despite claims of a defence budget cut in FY2020 Federal Budget, the actual figures do not show any significant change. However, in comparison, there has been a consistent decline in the actual spending on development expenditure over the years. As a result of this, Pakistan today faces a bigger threat from the non-traditional security areas than the traditional security areas.

Periods of High Growth and Missed Opportunities

While Pakistan's current economic situation may be alarming, the country's economy has witnessed periods of high growth in the 1960s,

1980s and early 2000s when the average GDP growth was between 6 and 7 per cent.[50] Interestingly, during all the three periods, Pakistan was under military rule and the high growth was largely the result of high inflow of foreign aid. This, coupled with some economic reforms, enabled high GDP growth in the country. However, the failure of the Government to bank on the high growth rates has resulted in an economy that is inherently weak, as detailed in the earlier section. This section elaborates on the periods of high economic growth in Pakistan's history and identifies three key missed opportunities that could have prevented the recurring economic crisis.

The first period of relatively high economic growth was the 1960s. This period was marked by recovery in the agricultural sector due to the Green Revolution that resulted in an increase in agricultural productivity, particularly of wheat and rice.[51] The modernisation of the agricultural sector also paved the way for development of new markets in small towns, and new value-chain industries in bigger cities.[52] This growth could have been sustained had it not been for the 1965 India-Pakistan War, the opposition faced by Ayub Khan against the backdrop of signing of the 1966 Tashkent Agreement with India, and the 1971 India-Pakistan War, that led to the creation of Bangladesh (Figure 5.3). Failing to bank on the growing economy by slowly liberalising subsidies and creating an equitable profit among different provinces in order to increase revenue collection and build trust between the civilians and the army, was the *first missed opportunity* towards the economic re-structuring of Pakistan.

Figure 5.5: GDP Growth 1980-2000 (percentage)

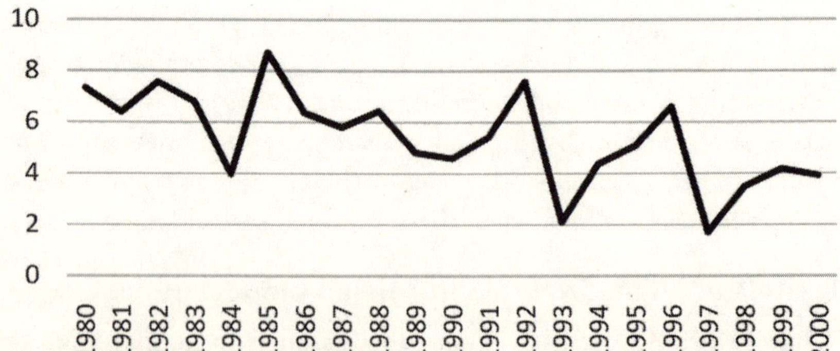

Source: Pakistan Bureau of Statistics.

Zulfikar Ali Bhutto of the Pakistan's Peoples Party (PPP) came to power in December 1971. In light of the heavy losses incurred during the 1971 war with India and the separation of East Pakistan, coupled with PPP's socialist outlook,[53] he nationalised industrial, commercial and financial assets in the period between 1972-74 in order to ensure that the private sector benefitted the poor and there was an equitable income distribution. Even educational institutions were nationalised during this time. This nationalisation of key sectors was the first step by the government in controlling the economy and reshuffling the developmental priorities. This period also marks the beginning of a decline in the tax-to-GDP ratio, that is, the number of people paying taxes declined, signalling a rise of the informal economy.[54]

1977 onwards, under General Zia-ul-Haq, Pakistan made a move to re-establish itself as a security state. This was the beginning of the increase in the defence budget. The rationale for this was rooted in two developments during this period—(a) Pakistan's defeat in the 1971 war, and (b) pumping of money from the IMF and the US that made re-allocation of resources possible in the budget.

The banking crisis, with its roots in Bhutto's nationalisation policy, heightened during the military rule of Zia-ul-Haq. In his effort to make Pakistan an Islamic Republic, he introduced Islamisation of the banks wherein the commercial and investment banks were no longer permitted to charge interest on loans or pay interest on deposits kept by them. The Government also introduced *Zakat*, which was managed by *Zakat* committees. Zia also supported the United States in training the Mujahideen after the Soviet occupation of Afghanistan in 1979. In return, the US supported Pakistan with aid throughout the 1980s that led to filling up of the foreign exchange reserves and hid the deficiencies of nationalistic and Islamic economic policies on Pakistan's economy. Writings suggest that this huge inflow of foreign aid has been one of the causes of the low tax-to-GDP ratio, or tax evasion in Pakistan.[55] In 1986, Pakistan signed the Structural Adjustment Loan with the World Bank, and in 1988, signed an Extended Fund Facility (EFF) with the IMF of US$ 516 million, the highest amount disbursed by the IMF to any country till then.[56] In spite of attracting 'location rent' from the US, becoming the largest beneficiary of the IMF, and facing a relative period of political stability, Pakistan failed to mobilise the economic resources to bring macro-economic stability and focus on development. This marks the *second missed opportunity* in Pakistan's economic history to revive the economy. Pakistan initiated the Economic Reform Order[57] in 1991, however, it took two years to show results due to the political turmoil that started after the death of Zia-ul-Haq and lasted till 1993.

Since 2001, Pakistan has been the beneficiary of the US Coalition Support Fund (CSF), a fund that reimburses allies for cost incurred by the war on terror wherein the US military makes use of local transport infrastructure. Pakistan has received more than US$ 33 billion in US assistance since 2002 and approximately US$ 14 billion in CSF.[58] While the foreign exchange reserves spiked between 2001-2008, Pakistan failed to leverage this economic condition to bring about slow but gradual changes in the economy that could have reduced the impact (if not averted) of the 2008 global crisis on Pakistan's economy and the 2013 balance of payment crisis. This period reflects the *third missed opportunity* in Pakistan's economic re-structuring.

Figure 5.6: GDP Growth 2001-2019 (percentage)

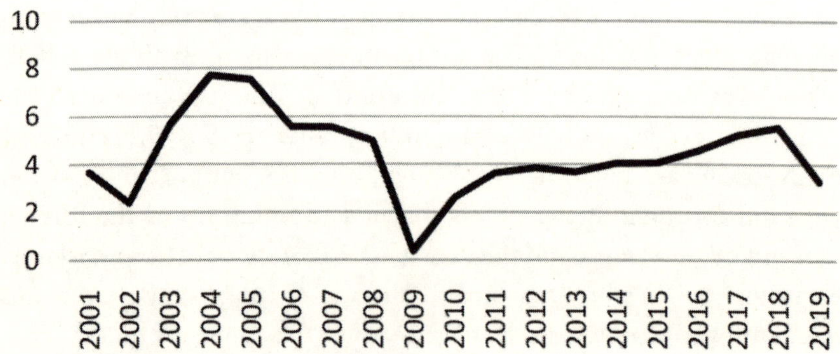

Source: Pakistan Bureau of Statistics.

The current economic crisis and the IMF bailout conditionalities have once again established the norms under which restructuring of

Pakistan's economy must take place. Given the geopolitics developing in the region, Pakistan will need to tread carefully and ensure that the current fiscal crisis does not translate into another missed opportunity. To achieve this, the IMF programme is important.

Pakistan and the IMF

In July 2019, the IMF Executive Board's approval for a US$ 6 billion credit line for Pakistan came as a sign of relief to the country's dwindling economy. The 39-month long Extended Fund Facility (EFF) Arrangement was expected to put Pakistan's economy 'on a path of sustainable and balanced growth and increase in per capita income.'[59] This credit was extended to Pakistan in the backdrop of a growing fiscal deficit, overvalued exchange rate, depleted international reserves and loss-making state-owned enterprises. According to the State Bank of Pakistan, in FY 2019, Pakistan's debt from the IMF stood at approximately US$ 6.1 billion. By the end of FY 2021, this increased to about US$ 6.5 billion.

Overall, Pakistan has had 22 arrangements with the IMF under different heads. However, 18 out these have not been completed.[60] The current arrangement (22nd) is under the General Resource Account (GRA) wherein the IMF lends to the 'not-so-poor' countries undergoing economic crisis. With the GRA, the loan has been provided under the Extended Fund Facility (EFF). This is Pakistan's sixth EFF Arrangement since 1980 and is only slightly less than the previous EFF package obtained in 2013 (see Figure 5.7), from US$ 6.4 billion in 2013 to US$ 6 billion in 2019.

Figure 5.7: Pakistan's EEF Arrangements with the IMF (US$ billion)

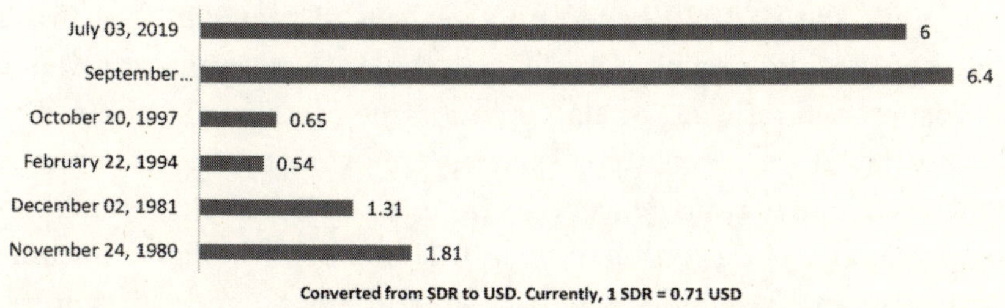

Source: International Monetary Fund.

The largest credit taken by Pakistan was in a stand-by arrangement in 2008 of SDR 5169 million (approximately US$ 7.2 billion) when the CAD increased to 8.50 per cent of the GDP. Pakistan's quota at the IMF is SDR 2031 million. According to IMF's stand-by and existing arrangements, a member can borrow up to 145 per cent of its quota annually and 435 per cent of its quota cumulatively in an arrangement. In the latest EFF, Pakistan has borrowed 210 per cent of its quota.

To address Pakistan's current economic upheaval, a comprehensive support programme was developed to stabilise the economy. The key elements of the programme include fiscal consolidation, market-driven exchange rate, energy sector reforms, structural reforms in governance and expansion of social spending.

It is also expected that the fund-supported programme will potentially gather broader support from Pakistan's multilateral and bilateral creditors to the tune of US$ 38 billion. This financial assistance is expected to further support the current EFF.

An analysis of the previous years' IMF statement on Pakistan (EFF documents) and macro-economic scenario, reveals Pakistan's trend of completing the programme without addressing the underlying structural problems. So far, Pakistan's track record on programme implementation has been weak, leading to incomplete reforms or policy reversals post completion of the programmes. Likewise, there exist similarities between the recommendations of various IMF statements on Pakistan. The need for fiscal consolidation by raising the tax-to-GDP ratio, improvement of monetary policy, and structural and governance reforms were a part of the statement on the 2013[61] and 1997[62] credit to Pakistan, which it failed to complete.

While the FY2020 Federal Budget was in tune with the IMF's reforms, it did set some unrealistic ambitions[63] in terms of revenue collection and reforms, as elaborated in the preceding sections. The authorities have taken steps such as removal of GST exemptions and preferential rates (except in food and medicine), elimination of personal income tax credits and deductions for higher income brackets, and strengthening tax on real estate and agriculture, among others.

The review team expressed satisfaction at the economic reform process, though much needs to be achieved to meet the key elements of the programme. However, while focussing on the achievements of the government such as increasing reserves, stable exchange rate, reducing fiscal deficit and contained domestic credit,[64] the impact of underlying factors such as decreasing exports and imports and rising inflation, are not being assessed. The structural deficiencies of Pakistan's economy will not be resolved unless a holistic review of Pakistan's economic conditions is conducted.

Conclusion

With economic growth declining since 2018, the ascent to power was not been easy for former Prime Minister Imran Khan. He inherited a structurally weak economy from his predecessors and spent his time in office reaching out to donors seeking bailouts, aids, and loans to stabilise the economy. Pakistan's economic condition can improve if it can find a way to leverage its geostrategic location and this time, couple it with strong internal economic policies to bring sustainable change to its economy.

This chapter has made an attempt to review Pakistan's economy and its defence budget since 2001. Despite periods of economic crisis, Pakistan's defence budget has been increasing, whereas the share of development expenditure in the federal budget has been decreasing. Pakistan spends 18.4 per cent (2019) of the total Government expenditure on defence. This is guided by the political nature of Pakistan's budget as well as threats faced both externally and internally. While the FY2020 and 2021 budgets were prepared under the looming shadow of IMF's conditionalities, the dismal share of PSDP expenditure reflects the economic priorities set by Pakistan. An increase in the defence budget may not, by itself, be a causal factor of economic crisis, however, the decreasing share of development expenditure deepens the crisis. Pakistan spends only 2 per cent of its GDP on education, and 0.97 per cent in health. Within this, there are significant variations between various provinces. This poses a high non-traditional security threat to the state.

After winning the general elections in July 2018, Prime Minister Imran Khan vowed to make Pakistan an "Islamic welfare state" on the lines of Medina, where "... widows and the poor are taken care of."[65] However, in months after the election, the steps taken by his government to bring stability back to the economy by cutting the development expenditure by 21 per cent while leaving the defence budget unaffected in absolute terms, were reminiscent of similar steps taken by his predecessors. Furthermore, the tax-to-GDP ratio, an important indicator of a welfare state, is struggling to increase. The tax officers have been reluctant in implementing tax reforms and with increasing inflation and fall in trade, the trading community has become apprehensive about paying taxes.[66] Instead of relying on austerity measures, the government needs to undertake structural re-thinking to bring Pakistan's economy back on track. This particularly involves re-analysing the country's defence and development expenditure.

Notes

1. This refers to the General Resource Account (GRA) Arrangements of the IMF and excludes the four programmes sought by Pakistan under the Poverty Reduction Growth Trust (PGRT) Arrangement. 'List of IMF Arrangements with Pakistan', at https://www.imf.org/external/np/fin/tad/extarr2.aspx?memberKey1=760&date1key=2019-04-30. Accessed on 22 September 2019.
2. Masood Ahmed. 2018. 'Why does Pakistan Have Repeated Macroeconomic Crisis?" Centre for Global Development', p. 7, at https://www.cgdev.org/sites/default/files/why-does-pakistan-have-repeated-macroeconomic-crises.pdf. Accessed on 27 July 2019.
3. Mohammad Yaqoob, 2011. 'The Causes of Economic Crisis in Pakistan and Its Remedial Measures.' State Bank of Pakistan Research Bulletin, 7(1), 2011, at http://www.sbp.org.pk/research/bulletin/2011/Vol-7-1/1Yaqoob.pdf. Accessed on 28 July 2019.
4. Shahid Javed Burki , and Adnan Naseerullah, 2016. 'Pakistan's Economy: Domestic Dissent and Foreign Reliance,' in Christophe Jaffrelot (ed.), *Pakistan at The Crossroads: Domestic Dynamics and External Pressures,* 2016. Columbia University Press, New York, p. 165.
5. Transparency International, *Corruption Perceptions Index 2018,* Berlin, 2019.
6. World Bank's Ease of Doing Business Report 2020, Pakistan improved 28 points to rank 108.

7. When Pakistan's economy was performing well in the 1960s and early 2000s, the average GDP growth rate was registered at 6 per cent. The years 1954 and 1965 have recorded highest and second highest GDP growth rate in Pakistan's history at 10.22 per cent and 9.38 per cent, respectively (see Figures 3, 4 and 5).
8. Zamir Ahmed Awan, 'Pakistan support for BRI stays strong ahead of forum', *China Daily*, 2019, p. 8, at http://www.chinadaily.com.cn/a/201904/09/WS5cac063aa3104842260b5252.html. Accessed on 27 July 2019.
9. *Pakistan Economic survey 2018-19*, Economic Adviser's Wing, Finance Division, Government of Pakistan.
10. State Bank of Pakistan Economic Data.
11. 'IMF Statement on Pakistan', at https://www.imf.org/en/Publications/CR/Issues/2019/07/08/Pakistan-Request-for-an-Extended-Arrangement-Under-the-Extended-Fund-Facility-Press-Release-47092. Accessed on 27 July 2019.
12. State Bank of Pakistan Economic data, n. 10.
13. Ibid.
14. Panos Mourdoukoutas, 'IMF Will Either Make or Break Khan's Pakistan', *Forbes*. 25 July 2019, p. 3, at https://www.forbes.com/sites/panosmourdoukoutas/2019/07/25/imf-will-either-make-or-break-kahns-pakistan/#78690da13703. Accessed on 3 August 2019.
15. Muhammad Ali Qasim and Mahmood Khalid, 'Accuracy of Revenue Forecast: Analysis of Pakistan's Federal Revenue Receipts', *Forman Journal of Economic Studies,* 12, January-December 2016, at https://www.fccollege.edu.pk/wp-content/uploads/2017/03/Paper-3-Accuracy-of-Revenue-Forecast-Analysis-of-Pakistan's-Federal-Revenue-Receipts-by-Muhammad-Ali-Qasim-and-Mahmood-Khalid.pdf. Accessed on 30 July 2019.
16. In the previous budget (FY2019), Pakistan had set an annual target of revenue collection at PKR 4.4 trillion, however, the actual Federal Board of Revenue (FBR) collection amounted to PKR 3.82 trillion. See Budget in Brief 2019-20. Ministry of Finance, Government of Pakistan, p. 7, at http://www.finance.gov.pk/budget/Budget_in_Brief_2019_20.pdf. Accessed on 30 August 2019.
17. In Pakistan, the tax-to-GDP ratio was 11.6 per cent in FY2019, whereas in Bhutan, the ratio is 12 per cent and in Nepal the ratio is 21 per cent. Source: Ministry of Finance Government of Pakistan and World Bank Statistics at https://data.worldbank.org/indicator/GC.TAX.TOTL.GD.ZS. Accessed on 30 July 2019.
18. Faseeh Mangi, "Pakistan's Fiscal Deficit Rises to Highest in 28 Years." *Bloomberg,* 27 August 2019, at https://www.bloomberg.com/news/articles/2019-08-27/pakistan-s-fiscal-deficit-rises-to-highest-level-in-28-years Accessed on 30 July 2019.

19. Shahbaz Rana, 'Pakistan requests IMF to cut tax target by Rs 300b', *The Express Tribune,* 1 November 2019, at https://tribune.com.pk/story/2091063/2-pakistan-requests-imf-cut-tax-target-rs300b/. Accessed on 27 July 2019.
20. Ibid.
21. "IMF statement on Pakistan", n. 11.
22. 38 billion.
23. Pakistan Debt and Liabilities Summary, State Bank of Pakistan.
24. "State Bank of Pakistan Economic Data", at http://www.sbp.org.pk/ecodata/index2.asp. Accessed on 3 August 2019.
25. Pakistan: Summary of Consolidated Federal and Provincial Budgetary Operations, 2018-19, Ministry of Finance, Government of Pakistan.
26. State Bank of Pakistan, 'The State of Pakistan's Economy', *Third Quarterly Report for the Year 2018-19,* 2019, at http://www.sbp.org.pk/reports/quarterly/fy19/Third/Complete.pdf. Accessed on 3 August 2019.
27. "IMF statement on Pakistan", n. 11, p. 30.
28. Budget Speech FY2020.
29. 'Pakistan Posts Current Account Surplus in October,'*Newsweek Pakistan,* 19 November 2019, at https://www.newsweekpakistan.com/pakistan-posts-current-account-surplus-in-october/. Accessed on 27 July 2019.
30. Ibid.
31. Idrees Khawaja, Tahir Mahmood and Usman Qadir, 'Social Impact of Global Recession in Pakistan', *Pakistan Economic and Social Review,* 48 (2), Winter 2010, pp. 261-278.
32. Maha Rehman, 'Pakistan's electricity generation has increased over time. So why do we still not have uninterrupted supply?', *Dawn.* 10 June 2019 at https://www.dawn.com/news/1430728. Accessed on 12 August 2019.
33. Afia Malik, 2016. 'Tackling the Energy Crisis', in Rashid Amjad and Shahid JavedBurki (eds.), *Pakistan: Moving the Economy Forward,* Cambridge University Press, Cambridge, UK, p. 108.
34. Ministry of Finance. 'Budget Speech 2019-20', p. 15, at http://www.finance.gov.pk/budget/budget_speech_english_2019_20.pdf. Accessed on 19 August 2021.
35. Ibid.
36. 'Active circular debt of Pakistan's power sector hits Rs860b', *The Express Tribune,* 8 October 2019, at https://tribune.com.pk/story/2075176/2-power-sectors-active-circular-debt-hits-rs860b/. Accessed on 20 August 2021.
37. Shane Mason, 'Military Budgets in India and Pakistan: Trajectories, Priorities, and Risks, at https://www.stimson.org/wp-content/files/file-attachments/Military-Budgets-India-Pakistan-Trajectories-Priorities-Risks-Oct2016.pdf.pdf. Stimson Center (Washington DC), 2016, p. 23.
38. Muhammad Azfar Anwar, Zain Rafique and Salman Azam Joiya, 'Defense Spending-Economic Growth Nexus: A Case Study of Pakistan', *Pakistan Economic and Social Review*, 50 (2), Winter 2012, pp. 163-182.

39. Shane Mason, n. 37, p. 33.
40. Muhammad Azfar Anwar, et al., n. 38, p. 178.
41. The Education-for-All Development Index (EDI), *Global Education Monitoring Report 2016,* UNESCO, at https://en.unesco.org/gem-report/sites/gem-report/files/GEM_Report_2016_2nd_edition_Statistical_Tables.pdf. Accessed on 3 August 2019.
42. Tilak Devasher, "Education: An Emergency," in *Pakistan: Courting the Abyss*, HarperCollins, New Delhi, 2016.
43. Ministry of Finance, Government of Pakistan, 'Education', *Pakistan Economic Survey 2018-19,* at http://www.finance.gov.pk/survey/chapters_19/10-Education.pdf. Accessed on 10 August 2019.
44. Ibid.
45. Ministry of Finance, Government of Pakistan, 'Health and Nutrition', *Pakistan Economic Survey 2018-19,* at http://www.finance.gov.pk/survey/chapters_19/11-Health%20and%20Nutrition.pdf. Accessed on 9 August 2019.
46. Ibid.
47. 'Per capita water availability may fall to 860 cubic metres', *The Express Tribune*, 28 June 2019, p. 1, at https://tribune.com.pk/story/2002420/1-per-capita-water-availability-may-fall-860-cubic-metres/. Accessed on 12 August 2019.
48. Ibid., p. 11.
49. Ministry of Finance, Government of Pakistan. 'Agriculture, *Pakistan Economic Survey 2018-19,* at http://www.finance.gov.pk/survey/chapters_19/2-Agriculture.pdf. Accessed on 12 August 2019.
50. 'National Accounts', Pakistan Bureau of Statistics, at http://www.pbs.gov.pk/national-accounts-tables. Accessed on 12 August 2019.
51. Faiz Mohammad and Mian M. Aslam, 'Wealth Effects of the Green Revolution in Pakistan,' *The Pakistan Development Review,* 25 (4), 1986, Papers and Proceedings of the Third Annual General Meeting of the Pakistan Society of Development Economists (August 10-12), pp. 489-513.
52. Shahid Javed Burki, 'Introduction', *Historical Dictionary of Pakistan.* The Scarecrow Press Inc., Oxford, United Kingdom), 2006, p. 17.
53. In its interim constitution, the PPP set its motto as 'Islam is our faith; Democracy is our polity; Socialism is our economy; All power to the people'. See Rafi Raza, 1997. 'Origin and Growth of the PPP', in *Zulfiqar Ali Bhutto and Pakistan 1967-77*, p. 4, reproduced by H. Panhwar Sani.
54. Shahid Javed Burki, n. 52, p. 19.
55. Kamal Assad, 'Tax Evasion in Pakistan: Determinants and Requisite Policy Interventions', *European Online Journal of Natural and Social Sciences* 8(1), 2019, Special Issue on Advancement of Business and Management Science, p. 187.
56. Jamil Nasir, 2012. 'IMF Programs in Pakistan (1988-2008)—An Analysis,' at https://criterion-quarterly.com/imf-programs-in-pakistan-1988-2008-an-analysis/. Accessed on 3 August 2019.

57. It included liberalising of foreign exchange regime, lifting of controls on investment, privatisation of public sector enterprises and provision of incentives to domestic and foreign investors.
58. Phil Stewart and Idrees Ali, 'Exclusive: Pentagon cancels aid to Pakistan over record on militants,' Reuters, 2 September 2018, at https://www.reuters.com/article/us-usa-pakistan-military-exclusive/exclusive-pentagon-cancels-aid-to-pakistan-over-record-on-militants-idUSKCN1LH3TA. Accessed on 20 August 2019.
59. 'IMF Country Report: Pakistan', July 2019, at https://www.imf.org/en/Publications/CR/Issues/2019/07/08/Pakistan-Request-for-an-Extended-Arrangement-Under-the-Extended-Fund-Facility-Press-Release-47092. Accessed on 5 August 2019.
60. Daniel F. Runde, 'An Economic Crisis in Pakistan Again: What's Different This Time?', 31 October 2018, at https://www.csis.org/analysis/economic-crisis-pakistan-again-whats-different-time. Accessed on 27 July 2019.
61. Press Release, 'IMF Statement on Pakistan', September 2003, at https://www.imf.org/en/News/Articles/2015/09/14/01/49/pr13322 Accessed on 3 August 2019.
62. Press Release, 'IMF Statement on Pakistan', October 1997, at https://www.imf.org/en/News/Articles/2015/09/14/01/49/pr9748. Accessed on 3 August 2019.
63. Riya Sinha and Prateek Joshi, 'Pakistan's Budget FY2020: Unrealistic Ambitions', Vivekananda International Foundation, New Delhi, 2019.
64. Masood Waqar Khan, 'Lurking Dangers', *The News,* 26 November 2019, at https://www.thenews.com.pk/print/574317-lurking-dangers. Accessed on 20 August 2021.
65. 'Imran Khan Vows to Make Pakistan an Islamic Welfare State on Lines of Medina', News18, 26 July 2019, at https://www.news18.com/news/world/imran-khan-vows-to-make-pakistan-an-islamic-welfare-state-on-lines-of-medina-1824913.html. Accessed on 20 August 2021.
66. Mubarak Zeb Khan, 'Tax Regime to be Reformed with Stakeholder's Consent: PM', *Dawn,* 14 November 2019, at https://www.dawn.com/news/1516576/tax-regime-to-be-reformed-with-stakeholders-consent-pm. Accessed on 2 August 2021.

6. Indus Waters Treaty: Assessing Dimensions

Uttam Kumar Sinha

Introduction

The Indus Waters Treaty (IWT), signed in 1960 between India and Pakistan, despite having functioned for the last six decades is, in the current political context, troubled. Well-wishers of the Treaty—like those who champion for a India-Pakistan dialogue—often dub it as "uninterrupted and uninterruptible". The World Bank, as a third party—pivotal in facilitating the IWT—continues to cautiously observe the implementation of the Treaty. The role of India, as a responsible upper riparian state abiding by the provisions of the Treaty, is remarkable, but it is under pressure to rethink the extent to which it can commit itself as its overall political relations with Pakistan becomes intractable. It is also important to underline that the reason the Treaty has remained 'uninterrupted', is because India allows it to work. This also goes to suggest that the Treaty can become *Quidquid voverat atque promiserat*[1] if India decides to. However, for this to be achieved, a number of politico-security and hydrological factors need to be determined as also a political consensus to abrogate the IWT in which India has invested politically and financially.

Every now and then there is a clamour for abrogating the Treaty as a response to Pakistan's support to cross-border terrorism and its intransigence. Inevitably, the discourse shifts away from the rationality of sharing the waters with Pakistan to using the shared rivers as an instrument of coercion and a tool of punishment. What emerges in the water debates with Pakistan is an interesting interplay between India's justifiable anger over Pakistan's support to cross-border terror and correcting the history of generosity. Importantly, it reopens the past and with it, the re-examination of the IWT—both the context in which it was framed and the text that was negotiated.

The basis for any river water treaty is to continuously find an equitable approach for meeting vital human needs. Water treaties, particularly in regions where scarcity and political uncertainty is high, are also a barometer to gauge state behaviour. This raises a few interesting observations: to what level does changing political climate effect existing treaties? Does signing of river water treaties lead to more cooperative ventures between the riparians concerned and thereby enhance the overall peace environment in the region? Is the negotiation process preceding the signing of a treaty a final solution or only a provision that temporarily conceals the claims and counter-claims and the real and perceived fears of the riparians (particularly the lower riparian)? Do 'the real and perceived fears' lead to non-compliance of the treaty with an overriding 'militarised' approach in which the 'possession' of water is determined unilaterally? And finally, what are the linkages associated with transboundary waters? All these questions are now beginning to haunt the IWT.

Indus Waters Treaty

It is remarkable that the IWT[2] has survived the tumultuous relationship between India and Pakistan. That the Treaty has lived is because India respects its signatory and values trans boundary rivers as an important connector in the region both in terms of diplomacy and economic prosperity.[3] There have been several occasions—the Indian Parliament attack in 2001, the Mumbai terror attack in 2008, the terrorist attacks in Uri in 2016 and the 2019 Pulwama attack—which could have prompted India, within certain conditions of the Vienna Convention on the Law of Treaties,[4] to contemplate withdrawing from the IWT. However, on each occasion, based on its cost-benefit assessments, India chose not to. The IWT is now 62, which by all means is an important milestone. But landmarks are also often accompanied by reality checks. The much-vaunted 'robustness' of the Treaty has come under serious political strain, threatening to undercut both its 'letter and spirit' and create a future that will be substantially different from its past history. It also needs to be asked whether water rationality that led to the IWT will continue to hold in the future.

Back in time, partitioning the Indus river system,[5] compromising the six rivers, was inevitable after the partition of India in 1947. The sharing formula, devised after prolonged negotiations and the World Bank's good offices, divided the Indus system into two halves. The three western rivers (Indus, Jhelum and Chenab) went to Pakistan and the three eastern rivers (Sutlej, Ravi and Beas) were portioned to India. Equitable it may have seemed, but the fact remained that India conceded 80.52 per cent of the aggregate water flows in the Indus system to Pakistan. Probably it is the only Treaty in the world that was not only volumetric (water-sharing) but also partitioning. India also gave £62 million to Pakistan to help build replacement canals from the western rivers.[6] Such generosity is unusual of an upper riparian. Pakistan should remind itself that the water-sharing having been signed for all purposes, stands settled and therefore, there can be no question of Pakistan's water rights.

Did India Compromise its Position?

It is often asked as to whether India compromised its upper riparian position more than actually required. This is a query raised in retrospect. Water was critical for India's development plans, irrigation facilities and power. It was crucial, therefore, to get the waters of the eastern rivers for the proposed Rajasthan canal and the Bhakra Dam. Without these waters both East Punjab and Rajasthan would be left dry, severely hampering India's food production. India's Prime Minister Jawaharlal Nehru, while inaugurating the Bhakra canals described it as "a gigantic achievement and a symbol of the nation's energy and enterprise". In Pakistan, however, it was an occasion of expression of strong resentment. Nehru was always conscious that the Bhakra canals should not be at the cost of reduced water supplies to Pakistan. However, he was also very clear that India's interest on the eastern rivers should be protected. Nehru at a public meeting in Bangalore stated: "So far as Pakistan and India are concerned, I have been convinced that the only policy we should pursue is one of friendship with Pakistan. So we have consistently pursued that policy. Naturally, that does not mean that we should abandon our vital interests. That is not the way to seek friendship." On the Indus waters, Nehru in the same speech goes on to say, "The Indus water dispute is one of the differences still to be settled between India and Pakistan. On all these issues India pursues a policy of candour and regard for human needs on both sides of the border and is always willing to negotiate in a friendly spirit to the end that she and Pakistan should someday come to live on their subcontinent as amicably and cordially as the United States and Canada live in North America."[7]

It is interesting to note that India's negotiating approach was in clear contrast to the position on the Farakka barrage on the Ganga in East Pakistan (which later became independent Bangladesh). Pakistan, in 1951, had objected to India's plans, fearing that such a barrage would reduce the availability of water for projects in East Pakistan. Several notes were exchanged and in 1957 Pakistan even suggested taking the matter to the UN. But India did not budge an inch. Soon after the signing of the IWT, Nehru and Ayub Khan discussed the Farakka barrage in London in 1961 but nothing concrete was decided. A number of expert-level meetings were held between 1960 and 1969 but the issue remained unresolved until 1996 when India and Bangladesh signed the Ganges Water Treaty.

Clearly, due to its strategic location and importance, the Indus basin attracted far more serious attention than the Farakka issue. The Indus tributaries passed through Jammu and Kashmir (J&K) which had received, by then, considerable international attention. In fact, David Lilienthal, the US public administrator who headed the Tennessee Valley Authority and later the Atomic Energy Commission, after visiting India and Pakistan, wrote in August 1951 in the US magazine *Collier's* that the two countries were on the edge of a war over Kashmir and the US might be drawn into it. Lilienthal had feared that "another Korea is in the making."[8] In contrast, no such pressure was manifest in the case of the Farakka barrage. Although the World Bank did show some interest in mediating the issue, India resisted the pressure quite successfully.[9]

While in India the IWT is perceived to be highly generous towards Pakistan, the view in Pakistan has been radically different. The main impression in Pakistan has been that the loss of the eastern rivers was irreparable. Commentators such as Bashir Malik have challenged the Treaty's provisions, saying that it was Nehru who manipulated the Radcliffe Award to ensure that the headworks of Ferozepur remained in India.[10] Malik grieves that the signing of the Standstill Agreement and the Delhi Agreement was a colossal error, which in the end cost Pakistan its rights over the eastern rivers, and goes on to say that India's negotiation tactics were superior to those of Pakistan.[11] He also questions the World Bank's motive behind the 1954 plan, as it was well aware that the loss of the eastern rivers would be "a rude shock to bear with [for] Pakistan." Malik writes: "It would seem as a tactical strategy to assure her, though falsely, of availability of enough flow of waters of Western Rivers."[12] He adds that the Bank's proposal "incorporated the core elements of the Indian plan. In fact she gained much more than she could ever imagine ... She got away with the total flow of 33 Million Acre-Feet (MAF) virtually for a song."[13]

Current Situation

What is disputable today has nothing to do with water-sharing, which is settled under the Treaty, but whether the Indian projects on the western rivers, in particular Jhelum and Chenab, as Pakistan claims, conform to the technical stipulations. Storages on rivers indeed create anxiety for lower riparian states and the IWT's provisions factor the water supply concerns of Pakistan. It must be noted that there is not a single storage dam that India has built on the western rivers even though the IWT allows storage entitlement of up to 3.6 MAF (million acre feet). However, this is being corrected by the Modi government since 2016.

Each project, in accordance with the IWT, requires India to provide specified information to Pakistan at least six months before the commencement of the works. Clearly the question of India acquiring capacity to manipulate or withhold the flow of water is, under the IWT's provisions, not only untenable but can also be monitored. Pakistan's objections to the projects over several decades have been tactical and less technical. Its objective principally has been to stall any water development projects in Kashmir. A prosperous and developed Kashmir increasingly locked to mainstream India is an anathema to Pakistan's leadership as it waters its subversive designs. Not surprisingly, therefore, Pakistan uses water issues to drum up hysteria over Indian regional hegemony, and its propaganda machinery works overtime.

Pakistan has cleverly used its lower riparian position to garner international sympathy and domestic incapability. The country receives 67 per cent of international waters, making it a boxed-in-lower riparian not only with India but also with Afghanistan vis-à-vis the Kabul River. The leadership articulates its vulnerability and victimhood by raising water as a "lifeline" issue, suggesting clearly that the sharing of the waters with India still remains unfinished business. A section of Pakistan's political-military leadership, given its feudal and industrial background, believes that the water issues not only help divert attention from Pakistan's inefficient water management policies and inter-provincial water disputes between Punjab and Sindh but would also provide a "back door" for international involvement, once again, in the Jammu and Kashmir dispute.

The *raison d'etre* of the IWT was precisely to de-link the water issue from territorial disputes and settle any differences within the mechanism of the Permanent Indus Commission. By linking the waters to Kashmir, Pakistan is trying to reframe the water discourse through territoriality. India, on the other hand, has been far more open to talks and concessions on water issues than territory. In the case of the Salal Dam and Tulbul navigation project, India conceded to Pakistan's demands by making structural changes to the former and suspending work on the latter, having suffered excessive siltation thereon.

Delays Hamper India's Water Utilisation

India's leadership and water development planners in the seventies lost much ground to Pakistan on the interpretation of the Treaty when it came to various projects on the western rivers. Resultantly it conceded to the technical objections raised by Pakistan. In its wisdom, India felt that the spirit of the Treaty was far more important to the overall peace and security in the region. In retrospect, India paid a huge price not only in terms of project delays and increasing cost but also gave Pakistan a context to question and challenge many of the projects that India plans to build today. It has been recorded that 27 Indian projects have been questioned by Pakistan, principally to stall progress and delay implementation of storage facilities on the western rivers.

The following section examines some of these projects starting with the Salal Hydroelectric Project (on river Chenab in the Udhampur district of Jammu and Kashmir). Interestingly, this project was conceived in 1920 but took almost four decades before the Jammu and Kashmir government started an inception study in 1961 and the construction of the project started in 1970. The design conceived of a two-stage powerhouse with a total installed capacity of 690 MW (345 MW each). The site of the powerhouse was to be 72-km upstream of Marala headworks of the Triple Canal Project, which irrigates vast areas of land in Pakistan and is fed by the Chenab and Jhelum rivers. This immediately raised concerns for Pakistan and it pitched its diplomacy to ensure that the project gets crippled. While India, in accordance with the Treaty, provided information of the project in 1974, Pakistan in 1976 raised objections and both the countries entered into a series of talks. Pakistan clearly feared that storage capacity of the Salal project could flood parts of Punjab in Pakistan or stop water from reaching the Punjab plains. India tried to convince Pakistan, as it has always done and even so today, that it would be impossible to cause flooding in Pakistan without causing damage to the territory within India's control. Eventually, India conceded and in 1978 it agreed to reduce the height of the dam.

After the Salal came the Tulbul Navigation Project, which India proposed to build in 1984 on the river Jhelum at the mouth of the Wullar Lake, India's largest fresh water lake near Sopore. The Project was aimed at facilitating proper navigation (4 ft depth) over a 20-km river stretch between Sopore and Baramulla and stabilising the water level in the Jhelum through navigation locks. The engineers argued that this would also help Uri I, Uri II and Lower Jhelum projects to generate more electricity in the lean season by providing water. Pakistan raised objection under Article I (11) of the IWT relating to "man-made obstruction" and Article III "storing any water of, or construct any storage works on, the Western Rivers". The work on the Tulbul Project was stopped in late 1987 and the discussions dragged on and in 1991, India agreed to adjust the design of the Project keeping in mind Pakistan's concern, for example to keep about 6.2 m of the Project ungated. Initially, the work at the Project was only temporarily suspended by India, for a few months, as a goodwill gesture to resolve the differences but in spite of numerous government-level meetings between the two countries, the differences remained unresolved. The Tulbul Navigational Project is now part of the Composite Dialogue Process providing Pakistan further flexibility to delay meaningful resolution of issues or possibly link it with other issues if a situation arises.

In both the cases, Salal and Tulbul, Pakistan did not refer to the Projects as 'disputed' but as 'differences'. Interestingly,just as the Salal was coming to some reasonable agreement, the Tulbul unfolded. Likewise as the Tulbul was being adjusted, the Kishanganga HEP cropped up. Each new project that India started marred the earlier efforts to reach an understanding. India's adjustment to Pakistan's demands on the Salal has resulted in huge siltation of the dam. The final commissioning of the Project took place in 1996 and by 2002 the Salal HP recorded an all-time high siltation. The 80 m reservoir depth had 25 m of siltation. The Salal Dam now has a total installed capacity of 690 MW. It is the first dam built on a rock pedestal. With six turbines each with a capacity of 115 MW, power from the Salal Dam is transmitted to the northern grid where it is distributed to the states of Jammu and Kashmir, Punjab, Haryana, Delhi, Himachal Pradesh and Rajasthan.

In the case of the Baglihar Hydroelectricity Project, Pakistan invoked the clause on Settlement of Differences and Disputes and approached the World Bank for the appointment of a Neutral Expert in 2005. This was the first time that the resolution was taken to the Neutral Expert away from the ambit of bilateral discussions. After the Neutral Expert's verdict in February 2007, which was seen as a "creative compromise", India resumed work on Stage I which was commissioned in 2008. The commissioning was earlier planned for 2005, but Pakistan's objections clearly delayed the commissioning. Stage II of the project has been worse which was earlier planned to be commissioned in the first quarter of 2008. It was finally inaugurated in November 2015, taking the installed capacity to 900 MW. The bitter dispute over the Baglihar Dam, before it was resolved through third-party arbitration, was a turning point in the history of the Treaty. But the fact that it has given rise to political debates signals that all future requirements are likely to see the technical understanding of the Treaty being overshadowed by political considerations.

The issue of the 330-MW run-of-the river Kishanganga Hydroelectricity Project on a tributary to the Jhelum is another case in point in which was delayed by Pakistan and the cost of the project escalated. This hydropower project is designed to divert water from the Kishanganga River (called Neelum in Pakistan), generate electricity, and then send the water back to the River. Construction began in 2007, but was halted in 2011 because Pakistan went to the International Court of Arbitration (ICA) claiming the Kishanganga Project would adversely affect the Neelum-Jhelum Hydropower Project it planned on the same river in 1989. In February 2013, the ICA gave an interim ruling, later confirmed in December 2013, that India could divert a minimum amount of water for power generation, and work on the Kishanganga Project was resumed. The Project was finally commissioned in 2018. Both the Tulbul and the Kishanganga are on the Jhelum. This river is critical for Pakistan as it feeds into the Triple Canal Project, the water from this project irrigates the Upper Bari Doab and is crucial during the lean season. Any storage upstream is seen as a threat to Pakistan.

Discernible Pattern

Pakistan's riparian behaviour with India has a distinct pattern. The IWT provides a multi-layer dispute resolution mechanism. A

Permanent Indus Commission, established by the Treaty, works as the first level of dispute resolution. The Commission is responsible for exchange of all information between the two countries including giving and responding to notices on either side. In case a difference arises between the two governments on 'interpretation or implementation of the Treaty' or a fact, if established, is seen as a breach of the Treaty, the Permanent Indus Commission shall first endeavour to resolve the question bilaterally. If the Commission is unsuccessful in resolving the dispute, a Neutral Expert could be appointed at the request of either Commissioner to resolve the dispute, or the two governments at other levels could also deal with the dispute. The Treaty also prescribes the constitution of an ICA to deal with certain questions with regard to implementation or interpretation of the treaty, in case the two governments agree or either of them requests.

In the first two cases, the Salal and the Tulbul, the dispute resolution was confined to the first level, i.e., the PIC and bilateral negotiations. Also, India adjusted its projects to Pakistan's demand. With Baglihar, Pakistan explored the Neutral Expert option but failed to get the desired verdict. It was also an expensive exercise. Had it remained within the bilateral format, it is very likely that India, as in the case of Salal and Tulbul, would have equally adjusted. However, the Neutral Expert's verdict was a blessing in disguise for India as it raised important technical points on dam construction,especially on sediment accumulation.

With Kishanganga, Pakistan sought the intervention of the International Court of Arbitration, as provided in Article IX. The first unit of the Kishanganga Project has been commissioned albeit with considerable delay. Here again, Pakistan failed. However, it can be argued that Pakistan's objective is clearly to delay projects in Kashmir in the hope of adding political and financial costs for New Delhi. This will remain a pattern in all the other upcoming projects on the Chenab, including the 850-MW Ratle and the 1000-MW Pakal Dul. India should be careful not to fall into the trap of legalese and dispute resolution processes.

The Project's delay and the resultant cost escalation have not been quantified specifically from the date of the Project's suspension, as a result of Pakistan objection, to the final commissioning of the projects. India needs to take the ongoing projects on the western rivers in earnest and not get trapped into Pakistan's illogical objections. It must be noted that Pakistan's lobbying power with the World Bank is well known and it uses two US-based law firms—Three Crowns and Williams & Connelly—to champion its concern. Both these law firms are well known in the US for their lobbying prowess. The World Bank, as the third party to the Treaty, has to be told in no uncertain terms that its sympathy with Pakistan is unreasonable and it should avoid playing the mediator's role; rather it should consider plans that resolve Pakistan's water wastage and inefficient usage of water.

Pakistan's Motivation

The larger question is: what are the motivations for Pakistan to raise the water issue, which by all accounts is settled under the IWT? Water issues are being politically constructed in Pakistan and its water scarcity is increasingly couched in the language of security vis-à-vis India, the upper riparian state. There is a purpose. First, water becomes an existential driver of Pakistan's perpetual enmity with India. By disregarding the much-lauded 'fairness' of the IWT, the Pakistani establishment has focused its lens on India being the upper riparian 'aggressor', 'stealing' the waters of the Indus system, and a country with 'malevolent' intentions. Pakistan wants to reframe a new set of lower-upper riparian dynamics by articulating its 'water rights' under the provisions of the Treaty by raising concerns and asking India for an explanation. It is an effort to put India on the defensive. The trajectory of the public discourse on water in Pakistan is such that water is increasingly being projected as a flash point with the political-military class benefiting from such positioning. Pakistan's leadership is noted for its heightened expressions of war over water to draw international attention.[14]

Such expressions are also for public consumption and to whip up anti-India sentiments. Water, being emotive, is a mobilising factor and unfortunately, even those who argue for cordial existence with India are unlikely to take an objective view of the water issue. For example, Hafiz Saeed, in a rally organised by the Jamaat-ud-Dawain Lahore in June 2010, called for a jihad against India, alleging that it was deliberately turning Pakistan barren. The activists in the rally were sporting posters with the message 'Water flows or blood'.[15] Second, shifting the blame to India for its water woes serves the purpose of the ruling establishment in Pakistan, which seeks to disproportionately exploit the water resources issue to its advantage. By aggressively accusing India of 'stealing' Pakistan's share of the river water, the establishment wants to absolve itself of its wrong water management policies and inter-provincial water dispute between Punjab and Sindh. Unfortunately, the debate and actions on river waters are being coloured by unnecessary jingoism. Various studies suggest that Pakistan can become water secure through efficient and sustainable resource management and better risk mitigation. The 1960 IWT settled the lifeline issue and allayed Pakistan's lower riparian fears. But the issue continues to find space in Pakistani domestic politics and its linkage to the Kashmir issue implies that any future settlement of this problem with India may reopen the case of distribution of the Indus river system. In terms of volumes of water used, the Indus basin has been over-developed. The competition today for the already overused waters in the Indus basin is many times more than what it was in the 1950s and therefore, claims to the Indus waters will only become magnified on either side. The volumetric approach in the over-utilised basin unfortunately shifts the focus from better irrigation service delivery and efficient water management.

The fundamental challenge, therefore, is to keep the differences within the framework of the Treaty and evolve a mechanism in finding solutions to the immediate and unforeseen water-related issues. While the IWT settled the issue of water-sharing, its combination of permissive and restrictive provisions relating to Indian projects on the western rivers has led to an adversarial situation in which India tries to use the permissive provisions to the highest extent possible and Pakistan applies the restrictive provisions to the utmost.[16]

It is clear that while the Treaty may have served some purpose at the time it was signed, with a new set of pressures in the changed circumstances, there is an urgent need to look at it afresh. The Treaty does not have an exit clause, so it cannot be abrogated. However, it does permit the possibility of renegotiation. Article XII of the Treaty says that it 'may from time to time be modified by a duly ratified Treaty concluded for that purpose between the two governments'. Any 'modification' that India might seek to make in order to remove some of its stringent provisions should also at a parallel level evolve a joint mechanism to study the actual flow of the water and make an assessment of the impact of climate change on the scarcity. This determination will be crucial to removing the growing misperception in Pakistan that India 'blocks' and 'steals' the Indus waters. Given Pakistan's asymmetry in terms of hydrology and economic and military resources, it will strive for a more equitable distribution of waters with India. Likewise, it will continue its proxy war hoping to force India to negotiate to its advantage on the water issue. India, on its part, is primarily concerned with state-sponsored terrorism and will only show willingness to 'talk' about 'water needs' with Pakistan and certainly not 'negotiate' on 'water rights'.

Being a lower riparian state, Pakistan's scepticism of India allows it to increasingly securitise the issue. In fact, it can justify the issue domestically and, therefore, it is not surprising that it maintains high troop levels and alertness around the canals on the eastern front, fearing that India will try to take control of the western rivers of the Indus basin. These intricate canals act as a defensive shield against a ground attack. In the case of India, the issue is more about the rationality of the Treaty, the needs and aspirations of the Kashmiris and a genuine water scarcity that has emerged because of increasing demand and the growing impact of climate change.

What should India Do?

There have been debates in India during the last two decades about: (a) the need to replace it with another improved Treaty (Indus Water Treaty-II), (b) to abrogate it and (c) to utilise the provisions of the Treaty to inflict pain on Pakistan as a counter measure.[17] Those who advocate revision argue that the Treaty is outdated in the sense that it does not take into account new realities and grounds for cooperation (proper survey of the basins for better exploitation of water resources, reconsideration of the interests of Kashmiris whose interests were overlooked, and new technologies being used for dam-making, de-siltation and ecological issues, etc.), and hence begs for revision. The advocates of abrogation argue that the Treaty has unjustly signed away more waters to Pakistan than it rightfully deserved, and has not ensured friendly behaviour from Pakistan. Moreover, it has taken undue advantage of the relevant clauses of the Treaty to stall and delay power and navigational projects in the state of Jammu and Kashmir which has hurt the interests of the people of Kashmir. Therefore, India should abrogate the Treaty unilaterally in response to irresponsible and hostile behaviour demonstrated by Pakistan ever since the Treaty was signed. There is a third perspective that centres round the optimal use of Treaty provisions. Those advocating this hold that India has been quite generous in not using the provisions of the Treaty to good effect (to store water granted by the Treaty to India) especially at a time when the problem of water scarcity has started haunting Pakistan.

In view of the third perspective, adequate attention must therefore be paid to harness maximum possible water from these rivers through multi-purpose projects. Under the Modi government (2014-2019) projects like the Ujh (storage of 0.82 MAF) and Shahpurkandi Dam (0.012 MAF) and the 2nd Ravi Vyas Link Project which can harness water flowing across border to Pakistan (about 0.58 MAF in non-monsoon period), but which were hanging fire, have become a national priority. Shahpurkandi Project on the Ravi River seeks a total production capacity of 206 MW. Jammu and Kashmir will get 20 per cent of power generated from this Project.

On the western rivers, the "permissible storage capacity" as per the Treaty provisions has not been paid serious attention in India. One of the projects identified for storage purposes is the Bursar Multipurpose Project on Marusudar River (main Tributary of Chenab) in Kishtwar district of Jammu and Kashmir. As per data provided by the government, it will store about 1 MAF, produce

1230 MW of electricity and irrigate about 100,000 hectares. The Detailed Project Report (DPR) is under preparation and no central assistance has been granted yet for the Project. The Project requires 1,665 hectares of land, including 1,077 hectares of forest land. It will affect more than 500 families in over 14 villages. The second multi-purpose project being planned is Gyspa on Bhaga River (Chenab Main)[18] in Lahul & Spiti District of Himachal Pradesh. It is supposed to store water (0.74 MAF), produce 300 MW of electricity and irrigate 50,000 hectares of land. The DPR was completed in 2017 but the work has yet to start because of resistance from local people.

These two projects need to be pursued with due sensitisation of the people about the value of such efforts, with well-planned rehabilitation and compensation measures. The state governments must be engaged effectively in this regard. For that matter, all power projects (33 under construction and 8 under planning and execution, for example Sawalkote and Ratle) should be given top priority. Out of the total capacity of 11,406 MW which is to be harnessed from the three rivers, only 3,034 MW has been tapped so far.

The Tulbul Navigation Project, which remains stalled, must now be completed despite Pakistan's objections. Pakistan, as explained earlier, termed this Navigation Project as a violation of the IWT and refuses to understand the logic of enhancing connectivity through the river which would have a rewarding effect on tourism and the economy of the state. It will be worthwhile for New Delhi to engage the local government with a view to building pressure from the people of the state for the execution of projects on the western rivers which will boost the local economy. In March 2003, the state Assembly had passed a resolution urging the Indian Government to review the IWT and revise it to accommodate the interests of the people of the state. Due attention must be given to raise popular awareness over the issue and expose Pakistani resistance to such developmental projects in the state.

In addition to reducing the leakages from eastern rivers and building storage on the western rivers within the provisions of the

Treaty, the Government must leverage Afghan interests in harnessing the development potential of the Kabul and Kunar Rivers flowing into the Indus from Afghanistan. The major tributaries of the Kabul River are the Logar, Panjshir, Kunar, Alingar, Bara and Swat Rivers. After successful completion of the Salma Dam Project on the Harirud River in Western Afghanistan and rehabilitation of Amir Ghazi and Qargha Dams by India, there is a renewed interest by the Afghan Government to construct multi-purpose water projects on the tributaries of the Kabul River with India's help.

Afghanistan does not have enough dams, reservoirs and barrages to adequately manage and control the runoff from glacial meltdown from the Hindukush during summer. As a result, it is susceptible to both severe flooding and droughts, and has little control of waterflow into neighbouring countries, especially Pakistan. There is no water-sharing agreement between Afghanistan and Pakistan till now and reports of Indian interest in Afghan rivers have made Pakistan nervous as can be seen from comments in Pakistani newspapers. Afghanistan has so far resisted Pakistani initiatives to work out some bilateral mechanism in this regard.

Conclusion

The IWT was essentially about balancing the water rights of Pakistan without compromising on the needs of India. The Treaty became possible because India agreed to make do with only 20 per cent of the total water available in the six rivers of the Indus system, giving away 80 per cent to Pakistan. India gave preference to fulfilling its immediate water needs over future needs, particularly those of the people of Jammu and Kashmir. Most international analyses ignore both these facts, i.e., the generosity on the Indian side and the genuine needs of the people of Kashmir. India needs to call Pakistan's bluff and its constant ranting on India stealing the waters of the Indus. As a first step, India needs to maximise the effectiveness of the Treaty. India allows about 5-6 per cent of the water flowing into Pakistan because of our poor water development projects, in particular creating storage capacities on the eastern rivers. It is a welcome sign that the Modi Government is paying attention to rivers in general and to fast tracking a number of projects on both the eastern and western rivers of the India Basin. Any move to abrogate the IWT without first optimising the provisions of the Treaty is a senseless option.

Notes

1. *Quidquid voverat atque promiserat* is Latin for null and void.
2. See the text of the Indus Waters Treaty, at https://mea.gov.in/bilateral-documents.htm?dtl/6439/Indus. The text in pdf is also available in the UN Treaty Collection, the World Bank and the Ministry of Water Resources, Government of India (GoI).
3. Some of the essential reads on the making of the Indus Waters Treaty are: Aloys Arthur Michel, *The Indus Rivers: A Study of the Effects of Partition*, Yale University Press, New Haven, CT, 1967; Scott Barrett, 'Conflict and Cooperation in Managing International Water Resources', Policy Research Working Paper 1303, The World Bank, May 1994; and Bashir A. Malik, *Indus Water Treaty in Retrospect,* Brite Books, Lahore, 2005. However, the most significant account of the Treaty is Niranjan D. Gulhati, *The Indus Waters Treaty: An Exercise in International Mediation,* Allied Publishers, Bombay, 1973.
4. See, https://treaties.un.org/doc/Publication/UNTS/Volume%201155/volume-1155-I-18232-English.pdf. Accessed on 9 March 2022.
5. The Indus basin is an important geophysical part of the Indian subcontinent. The Indus, together with the Chenab, Ravi, Sutlej, Jhelum, Beas and the extinct Saraswati, constitutes the basin. The Indus basin has a total area of 11,65,500 km^2 with annual available waters of 207 Billion Cubic Meters (BCM). The basin countries are Pakistan (632,954 km^2), India (374,887 km^2), China (86,432 km^2) and Afghanistan (76,542 km^2).
6. For an account of the making of the IWT read Niranjan D. Gulhati, n. 3.
7. Nehru's speech is quoted in Niranjan D. Gulhati, n. 3, pp. 160-161.
8. David E Lilienthal, 'Another Korea in the Making?', *Collier's Weekly*, 4 August 1951, pp. 22-23, at http://www.unz.com/print/Colliers-1951aug04-00022. Accessed on 9 March 2022.
9. See, Uttam K. Sinha, Arvind Gupta and Ashok Behuria, 'Will the Indus Waters Treaty Survive?', *Strategic Analysis*, 36(5), Sep-Oct 2012, p. 739.
10. Bashir A. Malik, n. 3, p. 67.
11. Ibid.
12. Ibid., p. 161.
13. Ibid., p. 169.
14. Pakistan's articulation of its lower riparian concerns tends to receive a sympathetic international audience. Water experts such as John Briscoe, who is currently Gordon McKay Professor of Environmental Engineering

at Harvard University, speak more from the lower riparian perspective (Pakistan), often but not intentionally ignoring the upper riparian accommodation (India). Briscoe's article 'War or Peace on the Indus?', published in *South Asian Idea, at* http://thesouthasianidea.wordpress.com/2010/04/03/war-or-peace-on-the-indus/ puts the onus on India, being the regional hegemon, to show restraint on the Indus basin, ignoring the fact that India has been far more generous and accommodative than any upper riparian in the world.

15. Divya Kumar Soti, 'Why Hafiz Saeed is Raking up the Indo-Pak Water Issue?', at http://intellibriefs.blogspot.com/2010/07/why-hafiz-saeed-is-raking-up-indo-pak.html. Accessed on 1 April 2022.
16. According to the IWT, India can use 3.6 MAF of storage and can irrigate up to 1.34 million acres but has not done so. Moreover, 2 MAF of water flows to Pakistan from the eastern rivers every year due to dilapidated infrastructure.
17. See the author's interview in *Firstpost,* at https://www.firstpost.com/india/indus-waters-treaty-doesnt-fit-into-current-sociopolitical-situation-of-india-pakistan-says-riverine-expert-uttam-sinha-6293351.html.
18. The Gyspa Dam project was originally conceived as a 170 MW, run-of-river hydropower project under the Himachal Pradesh State Electricity Board (HPSEB). But in August 2008, the Government declared it a 'National Water Resource' project and modified it from a mere hydro-electric project to a water storage project with capacity for hydro-electric generation.

7. Pakistan's Afghanistan Dilemma

Shakti Sinha

Introduction

Pakistan's complex relations with Afghanistan and its implications for the wider world is far more extensive than any other bilateral relation between two neighbours. Though relationships between any two countries, not just neighbours, are multifaceted, rarely are they so enmeshed as to make a bowl of spaghetti look simple. On the one hand, Pakistan's relations with, and its attitude towards, Afghanistan is a product of internal dynamics of the former, specifically its military's mission to become and remain the sole arbiter of power within that country—in order to prevent an alleged fear of being encircled by an India-Afghanistan alliance. On the other hand, these relations have also been impacted by developments outside their borders which at times have pushed the situation on to the global stage. Afghanistan has been mostly at the receiving end of this relationship, not unusual for a weaker state with a lesser weight in the global geostrategic environment. However, it is this writer's case that this blinkered view of Pakistan has prevented it from developing into the key player linking trade and economic relations between India and countries of Central Asia and West Asia. Had Pakistan played this role of a land bridge, it would have benefitted not just economically but it would have also been able to play a bigger role in regional and world affairs.

Latest Developments

At the time of writing (October 2021), Pakistan is clearly the only dominant player in Afghanistan, having successfully installed their 'boys', the Taliban in power after the US exit. Not just that, the Pakistani Army succeeded in keeping out all independent Taliban voices, including from the Doha Shura which not just negotiated the US-Taliban deal on American withdrawal but also was the face of the Taliban in dealing with the world. The expectation that the chief negotiator, Mullah Baradar, would be the Prime Minister has belied; he is one of the two Deputy Prime Ministers with Mullah Hassan Akhund pointed as Prime Minister. Similarly, Stanekzai, the head of the Doha office, is again the Deputy Foreign Minister, a job he held when the Taliban was last in power (1996-2001). The Kandahar Shura, the original group from which the Taliban was created and rose, has been largely side-lined, as being not pro-Pakistan enough. Instead, the leaders of the Haqqani network, often described as a 'veritable arm of the Pakistan Army' has been placed in important positions, with Sirajuddin Haqqani, a UN designated terrorist with a US$ 10 million bounty on his head, nominated as the Interior Minister. His uncle Khalil-ur-Rehman Haqqani is the Minister of Refugees, with two more associates, Najibullah Haqqani and Sheikh Abdul Baqi Haqqani, nominated as Minister of Communications and Higher Education, respectively. Mullah Yaqoob, the son of the founder, Mullah Omar, is the defence minister, and could be required to be a bridge between the Haqqanis and the 'old' Taliban.

This is a complete, and almost overnight, change in the Pakistan-Afghanistan relations. Since the fall of the Taliban in late 2001, and the installation of a democratic regime in Afghanistan, Pakistan shared a prickly relationship with the latter. It had then taken Pakistan a lot of time to reconcile to its perceived loss of influence; for, Taliban rule was the first, and till then the only, Afghan regime whose existence depended on Pakistani support. This was possible because the Pakistani Army officers ran the Taliban campaign, even attended their high-level meetings. Ultimately, the Taliban then ended up controlling almost 90 per cent of the territory of Afghanistan. In effect, Afghanistan was reduced to being the fifth province of Pakistan, with its administration lacking real agency. This changed completely in 2001 and has once again reversed itself.

However, since it is too early to judge how the Taliban 2.0 regime would pan out, and how much agency it would be able to exercise vis-à-vis their Pakistani mentors, this chapter would look at how Pakistan—Afghanistan relations evolved historically, stopping basically at 2020, when the Islamic Republic was very much in position.

What made post-American intervention (2001) in Afghanistan almost intolerable for the Pakistani Army is that they saw India as having re-established itself in that country. Thousands of Afghans travel to India to study, often at their own cost. Thousands more travel to India for medical treatment. In fact, the visa section at the Indian Embassy and the different consulates were besieged with visa applicants; the Indian missions at Afghanistan (and Bangladesh) issued between 150,000 and 200,000 visas each year. For the Afghans, India emerged as the development partner of choice, seen as having delivered on successful projects such as the multi-agency Northern Electricity Power System (NEPS) (that brought power to Kabul over the Hindukush), the Salma Dam (that would reduce Western Afghanistan's dependence on Iran for its electricity needs), the Zaranj Delaram Highway (that potentially offers Afghanistan access to the world by-passing Pakistan), and the building of the National Parliament. India's refusal to get involved in intra-Afghan politics meant that it did not try to have a say in the power politics of Afghanistan, unlike Pakistan or Iran, and it ensured that all sides trust India. It is no wonder that, in different surveys over the years, India showed up right at the top of countries the Afghans trust. Pakistan's inability to look at Afghanistan outside its India-prism hobbled its ability to be seen as a friend, or to play a positive role in ensuring peace, stability and development that the Afghan people desire most of all.

Historically, the United States has been the common and dominant international partner of both Pakistan and Afghanistan and during the Obama presidency realized the futility of dealing with the problems of these countries in isolation, given the torturous inter-linkages that bind the two countries together. Though it was the Obama administration that was responsible for the Af-Pak moniker, his Special Representatives were unable to begin any meaningful dialogue on ending the conflict. This position changed with Trump's assumption of office, with the US applying considerable pressure on Pakistan including name-calling and cutting back on financial support. But ultimately, the US had to reverse stand, and relied on the Pakistani Army to deliver the Taliban to the negotiating table. The US-Taliban agreement at Doha (29 February 2020), the collapse of the Islamic Republic and the de facto assumption by the Taliban in August 2021, potentially offers Pakistan a historical chance to break out of past prejudices and work to curb forces of Islamic militancy that it itself created but which threatens both countries. Whether Pakistan would be able to seize this opportunity and emerge as deliverer of peace remains an open question. In fact, there would be few takers for such an expectation.

Complicated and Multifaceted Relations

There are four historical and geographical factors that underpin Afghanistan-Pakistan relations and these, in turn, are dictated by local factors as well as their interactions with the world. Understanding these factors, along with the other more traditional ones, are key in understanding the factors that could make this relationship a non-antagonistic one.

The first of these factors arise from Afghanistan's memory of the vivisection of the Pashtun territory in 1893, following the demarcation of a border between (British) India and Afghanistan. The Afghanistan government, under Amir Abdul Rehman, was weak and financially dependent on the British and, thus unable to deny the latter's demands. The lines on the map drawn by Sir Mortimer Durand were signed into the Treaty of Gandamak and its validity was to remain for a hundred years. When the British Empire withdrew from India, leaving behind India and Pakistan as successor states, Afghanistan's government argued that the treaty stood abrogated on the grounds that one of the parties to the Treaty had exited and that it had no treaty obligations to Pakistan. Consequently, Afghanistan initially opposed the admission of Pakistan as a member of the United Nations and wanted a resolution of its claim. However, the world was still weary in the aftermath of the Second World War and the partition of India had horrendous consequences—Afghanistan simply did not matter.[1] This aspect of the Afghanistan-Pakistan relations remains important even at present and in fact, is one of the key driving factors in the unusual dynamics of this bilateral relationship.

Geography is the second feature that complicates the bilateral relations of these two neighbours. Afghanistan, a landlocked country, traditionally had two main 'ports of entry' on its Pakistan border, Torkham on the Khyber and Spin Boldak on the Quetta-Kandahar Highway. These entry points until quite recently, had near-monopolistic features, historically making Afghanistan's access to the world heavily dependent on its eastern neighbour. Now, however, an alternative is opening, as Afghanistan has had growing trade with Iran, particularly through Islam Qala, emerging as another important port of entry. The northern land ports, dormant till recently, except for the flow of Russian troops during the 1980s, are also picking up, especially through Hairatan, particularly after the extension of the Uzbek railway to Mazar-i-Sharif. The Zaranj-Delaram Road, built by India, would capable of generating significant traffic once the Chahbahar Port and associated rail-line became fully functional, though it is significantly affected by the downturn in Iran-United States relations. The dependence of Afghanistan on Pakistan has been significantly declining over the years, though with Taliban in power again, Pakistan would attempt to monopolise all trade and access of Afghanistan. Other local factors which have inhibited the use of the Highway, include insecurity in Nimroz province of Afghanistan through which it passes. However, this Highway and linkage to Chabahar alone has huge potential to develop as an alternative to Afghanistan's overwhelming reliance on the port of Karachi and on Pakistani trading and trucking interests.

A related, key long-term issue, and one that was the main reason behind the Pakistani establishment's decision to create the Taliban, has been the United States' desire to develop alternate evacuation routes for the oil and gas reserves of Central Asia, bypassing Iran and reducing the dependency on Russia. Afghanistan was central to these plans, with the proposed pipelines running to the Indian Ocean through its territory. This made it attractive for Pakistan to try and be in charge or at least in control of this strategic crossroad.[2] However, with time, this factor has diminished in importance as the Chinese have built oil and gas pipelines running eastwards from the 'Stans' to China, making the latter the biggest player in the game.

The third factor complicating relations between the two countries is the status and role of the Pakhtuns in Pakistan. Reluctant to be part of Pakistan in 1947, when they were banking on the continuance of an undivided India, the Pakhtun elites have become an integral part of the Pakistani state. This initially came from their representation in the army, a hangover of the colonial policy from the 1930s, which accelerated during the Second World War. The initiative was to change the composition of the British Indian Army to make the Punjabi Muslims and Pakhtuns as the dominant ethnicity within it.[3] This is especially so for the Pakhtuns from the settled areas of the erstwhile North-West Frontier Province (NWFP), now Khyber-Pakhtunkhwa. Ayub Khan was the first of the senior army officers, a tradition that has continued, to be part of the military-bureaucratic elite which has led Pakistan and not allowed a viable political class to develop. It is said that the Pakhtuns constitute close to a quarter of the Pakistan Army which places them distinctly above the status of the Sindhis and the Balochis, and next only to the Punjabis as the determinants of Pakistan's fate. This gives the Pakhtun elite a considerably different world view from that of their cousins across the border and even from the average Pakhtun within Pakistan.

The fourth factor which completely changed the dynamics of Afghanistan-Pakistan relations was the anti-Soviet jihad (1979-1992). It not only converted Pakistan into the gateway to Afghanistan, with money, arms and Pan-Islamic jihadis flowing in one direction, and refugees in the other, but it also ended up making Pakistan a key arbiter in Afghanistan affairs. Afghanistan-displaced persons in Pakistani camps earned their refugee status only after they enrolled in one of the seven Afghan political parties, *tanzeems*, recognised by Pakistan. All American and Saudi Arabian assistance for the jihad were routed through the Pakistan Army which determined which group would receive the assistance and how much, a role which eventually converted the Inter-Services Intelligence (ISI) into the formidable institution that it has become. Millions of Afghans came across, settled in camps and cities in Pakistan and, while a majority have returned to Afghanistan, significant numbers have stayed back. This running of jihadi camps, and other policies of the military dictator, General Zia-ul Haq, not only radicalised the Pakistani Army but also the Pakhtuns of Pakistan, which considerably dampened the spirit of Pakhtun nationalism, until then, essentially secular.

Frustrated Starts

For some time in 2007 and early 2008, it looked like relations between the two countries could take a turn for the better. Pakistan's President Pervez Musharraf's regime had become quite discredited domestically and the Pakistani Army was on the defensive. The mishandling of Chief Justice Iftekhar Chaudhry's case and the subsequent lawyers' movement, allegations of corruption in the privatisation of state-owned companies, and the economic down trend, were together taking their toll. Further, Afghanistan's President Hamid Karzai's claims of cross-border support for the Taliban had started gaining currency and the role of the Pakistani Army came under scrutiny. The Pakistani military ruler's inability to protect Ms Benazir Bhutto—she barely escaped at her Karachi homecoming and was then assassinated at Rawalpindi, days before the election—and the subsequent election results meant that the country had a civilian government. This, therefore, could have proven to be a turning point in the history between the two countries as the new Pakistani government did not project an aggressive intent towards its neighbours.

Despite significant differences on the restoration of judges between the two main constituents of Pakistan's government, the relative ease with which President Musharraf was manoeuvred out of office, and the strong support given to the civilian leadership within the country and internationally, was interpreted as an indication of the potential for change. The new Army Chief, General Ashfaq Kayani was touted as a professional soldier since he withdrew the Army from retail politics, and agreed to brief members of the National Assembly on security issues. Significantly, President Karzai had met with Ms Bhutto just hours before her death, and was the only foreign dignitary at President Asif Ali Zardari's inauguration. The body language between the two presidents was so different from the earlier, poisoned relationships, that it looked that the two countries were poised to enter a new phase of equal and friendly relations. But within a year, the mood was very different; the Pakistan Army had re-emerged as the key decision-maker with Zardari's inability to retain Nawaz Sharif on the Chief Justice issue, diminishing his own authority to take decisions on issues relating to India, Afghanistan or the US. The Army even forced him to sacrifice his Ambassador to the US, Hussain Haqqani, who had to seek asylum in the US to save himself from being prosecuted for sedition; his only crime being that he followed his President's orders.

The second opportunity for Pakistan to change course arose in 2015-16, when President Ashraf Ghani made his controversial outreach to them soon after assuming power. He first went to China, which is the Pakistani Army's only strategic ally, and therefore has unprecedented leverage over the latter. Then he went to Pakistan, meeting with Army Chief General Raheel Sharif at army headquarters even before he met Prime Minister Nawaz Sharif. This was just the beginning, and then Ghani went on to effectively give up all his cards. He withdrew his predecessor's request to India for security assistance, handed over to Pakistan the wanted leader of the Tehrik-e-Taliban Pakistan (TTP), Latifullah Mesud, who had sought asylum in Afghanistan, sent Afghan Army officers to Pakistan Army's training schools, allowed close interactions between corps commanders of the two armies, and, overruling objections of his intelligence chief, agreed on an intelligence-sharing agreement between the ISI and Afghan National Directorate of Security (NDS).

Though criticised by many people within and outside Afghanistan for his naiveté in thinking that Pakistan would deliver on peace, Ghani understood that there could be no peace in Afghanistan without the Pakistani Army being on board. The Taliban would not have become a fighting force post-2001 without the Pakistani Army's active support, including continued sanctuaries, funds flow, training and arms & ammunition. Hence, bringing the Pakistani Army on board seemed the only way out. In the short-term, it seemed that Pakistan was all aboard peace-making efforts. It facilitated contacts with the Taliban, and a round of meetings were held between the Afghan government and Taliban representatives with China and the US in attendance as observers. But before the second round of talks could be held in late August 2016, two developments shook the belief that the Pakistan Army was acting as an honest broker.

One, news broke out that the Taliban Chief, Mullah Omar, who was said to have sanctioned the peace talks, had died in a hospital in Pakistan over three years before. This news knocked the bottom out of the credibility of the talks, as it raised fundamental questions about whether the Taliban rank and file would accept any agreement reached between the sides. Two, there was the eruption of a war of words between Afghanistan and Pakistan at this stage. And though it was Afghanistan which took the lead in this, with President Ashraf Ghani accusing Pakistan of sending out 'messages of war', the Afghans could hardly be blamed for breakdown. That year had been the worst year for civilian causalities in Afghanistan since the United Nations started tracking them. Afghan security forces had also suffered huge casualties with over 4,300 dead and 8,000 injured in the January-August period. But what really upset President Ghani was a string of attacks in Kabul, three on 7 August that led to over 50 deaths, and one on 10 August at the entrance of Kabul airport that killed five persons. That this spike in violence immediately followed the first publicly acknowledged intra-Afghan talks, made Ghani's outreach to Pakistan, untenable.

Key Issues

Most explanations of Pakistan's efforts at controlling the Afghanistan state or at least of having a friendly regime in Kabul relate to the former's desire to obtain strategic depth against India. This view of Pakistan's driving force in its Afghanistan policy is an inversion of theory as strategic depth refers to the space a country has in front of its area of strength. It can then, in the face of aggression by a vastly-superior army, keep withdrawing into its own territory so that the enemy's frontline gets stretched, its supply lines are under strain, and the defender can choose a time and place for a counter-attack. The Russians' tactics against Napoleon and Mao's Long March are classical examples of this. Were Pakistan to choose Afghanistan as its strategic depth, it would imply vacating Lahore, the rest of Punjab and even Islamabad, and then hitting back at the Indian Army only when the Pakistani Army reaches the Hindukush. The control of the territory of Afghanistan would, at best, allow Pakistan to move a limited amount of its strategic assets such as nuclear weapons and aircraft to Afghanistan.

The unfinished agenda of acceptance of the Durand Line keeps the Pakhtunistan issue alive, in a manner of speaking. Throughout the 1950s, the government in Kabul kept encouraging the forces on both sides of the Durand Line to continue putting pressure on the Pakistan Government, culminating in the then-Afghanistan Prime Minister Daud Khan's efforts to use tribal *lashkars* to force the issue. Pakistan reacted by imposing an economic blockade on Afghanistan that was effectively enforced. The episode proved to be a far cry from the present argument extended by Pakistan about the Pakistan-Afghanistan border areas being 'ungovernable spaces'. Even the nomadic Kuchis were not allowed their seasonal movement to Pakistan with their flocks of sheep. The economic consequences of this blockade on Afghanistan that lasted four years, were disastrous—it ended in Zahir Shah's dismissal of Daud and the move to a new Constitution (1964).[4] However, even with a strong pro-Pakistan regime in place, the Taliban did not agree to recognise the Durand Line as the international border between the two countries. In any case, on the ground, the Line is largely fictional, with considerably free egress for tribes and extremists. Consequently, the upsurge in Pakhtun radicalisation—presently on religious but, at some point, not inconceivably on nationalist grounds—could be a major threat to the unity of Pakistan.

Afghanistan has been traditionally friendly with India while, historically, Afghanistan and Pakistan have not been the best of friends other than during the Taliban interlude. In recent decades,

Pakistan's goals have been to not allow the India-Afghanistan relationship to foster and, in fact, to proactively disrupt it. In the period after the overthrow of the Taliban, Pakistan has sought to prevent India making inroads into Afghanistan. It regularly raises such issues as Indian development assistance and the 'opening' of Indian consulates near the Pakistan border. In fact, the Indian consulates in Jalalabad and Kandahar (plus Herat and Mazar) are decades old. The Pakistani position on this issue gained currency and was frequently referred to in the recommendations of think tanks/experts.[5] What these experts do not consider is how, historically, Afghanistan has acted when called upon to choose between India and Pakistan. Afghanistan remained neutral during the 1965 war which began when Pakistani infiltrators were detected in Kashmir, trying to blow up infrastructure and initiate an insurrection against Indian rule. This was soon after the end of the four-year economic blockade against Afghanistan by Pakistan that brought the former literally to its knees. The 1971 war, which was also initiated by Pakistan, but was occasioned by Bangladesh's efforts to free itself from Pakistani rule, once again saw Afghanistan not take any sides. Afghanistan realises, but others often do not, that geography matters a lot and if deep ethnic ties are added to it, then the situation becomes even more complex, at least from the Afghan point of view. President Karzai put it best, but he was misunderstood, when he said that Pakistan and Afghanistan were 'conjoined twins.' This is very true from the Afghan point of view. Many Indians criticised Karzai for saying this, little realising that such a physical relationship can be extremely limiting in that it does not allow either party any agency, and that they can only exist in harmony. Afghanistan's dependence on Pakistan is considerable, but the same is not true for Pakistan, whose location, size, population and resources are extensive.

Key Pakistani Players

As part of the restoration of civilian government in 1988 after the death of General Zia-ul-Haq, the Army made it clear to the incoming Benazir Bhutto government that Afghanistan policy, along with Kashmir and the nuclear policies, would continue to be with its general headquarters in Rawalpindi. This has broadly continued over the years, with the civilian authorities getting involved only when it suited the Army. One example is then-Pakistan Prime Minister Nawaz Sharif's decision to go nuclear post-Pokhran. This is shown in the speed with which General Kayani was able to reassert the Army's dominant role in strategic policymaking, within a year of Musharraf's exit.[6] In fact, Kayani proved to be far more adept and effective than Musharraf in this and the Army's credibility as the only institution holding the country together was quickly re-established, albeit with considerable help from the civilian government's ineptitude. Since then, successive chiefs, Raheel Sharif and Qamar Javed Bajwa, have expanded the Army's ambit to include economic policies, taking the China-Pakistan Economic Cooperation (CPEC) under its tutelage despite the then Prime Minister Nawaz Sharif's best efforts to control it. With its success in the side-lining of the two mainstream parties, the imprisonment of Nawaz Sharif and the 'victory' of Imran Khan's Pakistan Tehreek-i-Insaf (PTI), the promotion of the Army's corporate interests against Pakistan's national interest would be a key determinant of the developing contours of Afghanistan-Pakistan relations.

The Army's allies in this include the religious parties which have spawned thousands of madrassas along the two frontier provinces that have helped create the jihadis required to fight in Afghanistan. The Army's equation with the religious parties is an interesting one in that while they agree on the goal of removing all US troops from Afghanistan and the establishment of a rigid Sharia-based regime in the country, they often disagreed on the details of domestic politics in Pakistan.

There are important sections of the Pakistani political class who are quite comfortable with the idea of an independent Afghanistan. There are also sections of the Army, presently not in strategic positions, which see the current path as a dead-end.[7] Then there are also the old trading and trucking industries whose areas of interest extend all the way across Afghanistan into the fringes of Central Asia. It was their commercial desire for the stability in Afghanistan and the frustration at extensive extortion by local warlords during the worst phase of the Afghanistan civil war that prompted them to work with the Pakistan establishment and create the Taliban.[8] All of such groups and interests would welcome a chance for peace and stability.

There are also groups who are caught in-between, the principal one being the Awami National Party (ANP), for long, the dominant party in the Khyber-Pakhtunkhwa province. It has since been seriously challenged in its home territory by Imran Khan's PTI, which received the Army's active assistance to come to power, under Musharraf and again in the recent (2018) elections. The ANP damaged its own cause when it ran the provincial government, but to be fair, the Army's jihadi proxies in Swat and elsewhere prevented its government from acting effectively. At present, the ANP is on the run and its hopes of being in the middle and to develop as an alternate source of power and legitimacy and, therefore, in a position to mediate conflict without surrendering to the militants, has been severely compromised.

The decline of the ANP as a political force has been somewhat matched with the rise of the Pashtun Tahafuz Movement (PTM), or the Pashtun Protection Movement, under Manzoor Pashteen, primarily in the areas earlier designated as the Federal Administered Tribal Areas (FATA). Though the movement formally began in January-February 2018 with the Long March from Dera Ismail Khan to Islamabad via Peshawar to protest against the murder of a Pashtun shopkeeper and aspiring model Naqueebullah Mehsud in Karachi, its origins go back to the Pakistan Army's operation Zarb-e-Azb that began in North Waziristan in 2014, and lasted three years. The operations were said to target the TTP, Islamic Movement of Uzbekistan, East Turkestan Islamic Movement, etc., which collectively killed thousands of Pashtuns and displaced upwards of 1.5 million people, caught in-between the Army and the out-of-control jihadi groups, which the army had itself created. The PTM has taken up the cause of the people abducted and/or killed extra-judicially by organs of the state. With the integration of FATA in the country's political mainstream, PTM even has two members of parliament. The Pakistan army has accused the PTM of receiving funds from India's Research & Analysis Wing (R&AW) and from the National Directorate of Security (NDS), Afghanistan's intelligence agency. The Pakistani Army spokesperson warned the PTM that it should expect a strong crackdown. The first such action happened when a PTM rally in North Waziristan was shot at, leaving three persons at the rally dead. Paradoxically, two PTM MPs who were present at the rally, were been arrested and charged with inciting armed assault on an army check-post. There was practically no support for the PTM in the Pakistani media or political class, all of who were wary of taking on the Army. The army was not believed in but feared, and its agenda was increasingly being suspected.

However, the key actors within Pakistan, in significant positions of power, who have shaped the Afghanistan strategy, see things quite differently. It is their understanding of Pakistan's troika of strategic issues that drives the country's Afghan policy:

- What is the use of the nuclear deterrent if Pakistan still feels threatened?
- What is the use of investing so much in the asymmetric tactics of Lashkar-e-Taiba, Jaish, Lashkar-i-Jhangvi, etc., in Kashmir if Pakistan sees India gaining in Afghanistan?
- What is the use of creating and running the Taliban to ensure a friendly regime in Afghanistan if Pakistan must give it up under pressure?

The Taliban and FATA

Since 2001, the key fact emerging from Afghanistan's and the region's perspective is that the Taliban insurgency is based not in the NWFP or in the erstwhile FATA but in northeast Baluchistan, stretching northwards from Quetta.[9] The several districts here play host to sanctuaries and training grounds for the Taliban. Both the Jamait-i-Islami of Qazi Hussein and the Jamait-i-Ulema-i-Islam of Maulana Fazlul Haq run several madrassas in this part of Pakistan. As various observers have pointed out, there has not been a single Pakistani Army/Frontier Corps action in this area, something the Pakistani Army should explain.[10] It is clear that, as far as the insurgency/militancy/terrorists are concerned, there is no scaling down or repentance. Regarding their operations in Afghanistan, the Taliban clearly see the landmass of Pakistan as affording them the 'strategic depth' to which they withdraw when pushed by US Special Operations forces or by the Afghan National Army. The area also provides them with recruits and training camps, and acts as a conduit for the assistance they receive from their well-wishers in Pakistan, the Gulf and elsewhere. A lot has also been written about the Taliban's links with the ISI specifically and with the Pakistan Army more generally, which need not be reiterated here.

However, their relationship is not as simple or as straightforward as it seems to be and Pakistan's Afghanistan policy would be increasingly shaped by the growth, or restraint, of the Taliban's freelancing tendencies, as will be discussed later. The Pakistan Army has, therefore, tried to develop a two-track approach to the Taliban. It encourages those groups linked with it, to concentrate their efforts in ridding Afghanistan of the presence of 'infidels' and has made efforts to confront some groups within Pakistan that have challenged the Army's authority, the most notable example being the brutal crackdown in Waziristan and other parts of FATA, which accelerated after the killing of schoolchildren at the Army Public School in Peshawar (December 2014). Initially, the Army lacked the will and inclination to take on the recalcitrant terrorist groups. This contrasted with the state's brutal crushing of the Muttahida Quami Movement's control in Karachi in the 1990s and the Balochis' armed insurrection, or in enforcing the economic blockade of Afghanistan referred to earlier. The Pakistani Army was not above using the then Taliban Chief Mullah Omar, to mediate its differences with local extremists/Taliban. In January 2009, there were reports of Mullah Omar 'sacking' Baitullah Mehsud of South Waziristan and head of the TTP, the main Islamic militant outfit in Pakistan.[11] Later, there were persistent reports of Omar admonishing the TTP and other militant groups in Pakistan for attacking the Pakistan Army ('Muslim brothers'), instead of asking them to join hands in expelling foreign troops from Afghanistan.[12]

Developments in Swat in 2008 show how the Pakistan Army can twist the facts of a situation it itself created, to degrade the credibility of Pakistan's political class, and where possible, bring the India factor into its policy towards Afghanistan. The PPP government of Asif Ali Zardari had in 2008, agreed with Sufi Mohammad and Mohamed Fazlullah ('Radio Mullah') to the enforcement of *Sharia* in the entire Malakand Division, of which Swat and other districts are a part. In fact, it just reiterated an agreement reached with the same Sufi Mohammad in 1994 by Ms Benazir Bhutto's second government. The key issues in the second agreement was that no appeal would lie to the regular judiciary in Peshawar against the judgement of local *Sharia* courts besides the almost complete withdrawal of the formal state constituted under Pakistan's Constitution. The Taliban were then allowed to overrun the valley despite the presence of 15,000 security forces. As part of their offensive, the Taliban used to display the bodies of four to five persons killed by them every day—these bodies were hung at the central square of Mingora, the headquarters of Swat. Paradoxically, the local army units are also based in Mingora. Their complicity or disinclination to tackle the Taliban was obvious. The result was that the federal (PPP) and provincial (ANP) governments came across as weak, thereby adversely affecting their credibility.

This reported inability of the Army in such cases is used as an excuse to sell the idea that if only Pakistan's eastern flank (border with India) was secure, then the Pakistan Army could be fully deployed on its western frontier to handle the jihadi terrorist groups. The key component of this strategy has been to pressurise India by arguing for a resolution of the Kashmir issue. And the Pakistanis seem to lose no opportunity to raise the temperature, witnesses of which are the orchestrated remarks in the aftermath of any terror attack in India, be it Mumbai, Uri, Pathankot or Pulwama. The aim is to portray India as the aggressor, rather than as the victim.

The large-scale flow of Islamic militants and weapons in the Pashtun areas of FATA and Balochistan, consequent on the anti-Soviet jihad and conscious army policies of creating militias, weakened the traditional malik/arbab system, allowing mullahs and assorted power entrepreneurs to emerge. This provided fertile grounds for different jihadi groups to base themselves in.

End-Game—Pakistan Army

The ideal end-game for the Pakistan Army in Afghanistan is a stable and pliable regime, discreetly controlled by the former. The Army is comfortable with distant parts of Afghanistan being unstable or out of its control. Pakistan would not only continue to be Afghanistan's largest trading partner but it would also be its largest foreign investor. Afghanistan would, in effect, become a rentier state. It is this desire that has motivated the Pakistani Army's tactics of supporting extremist groups in Afghanistan such as Gulbudin Hekmatyar's Hizb-i-Islami for a long time. When that did not work, it dumped Hekmatyar and supported the creation of the Taliban as well as its activities.

Afghanistan's View—End-Game

Afghanistan's political elite also has reasonably clear ideas of how it would like bilateral relations between the two countries to be based on their understanding of the ground realities, the strengths and roles of the different players, and how things would take shape.

Once the US-Taliban talks started in 2018, the Afghan political elite was initially looking at what it would take to convince the United States to sufficiently incentivise the Pakistani state, and the Taliban, to move towards a ceasefire and an intra-Afghan dialogue where the government's legitimacy is acknowledged. It was primarily for this reason that the presidential elections were twice postponed; they were eventually held on 28 September 2019.[13] The ostensible reason for this delay was problems with the election law, which was real, but was not a sufficient factor for the postponement, looking at the history of the elections. Taliban intransigence and the US' focus on getting out meant that the former held out and refused to accept the Government of Afghanistan as an interlocutor. The Taliban therefore refused to participate in peace talks where any other Afghan entity or individual was invited to attend. The result has been peace conferences where, other than

President Ashraf Ghani and his administration, Afghan politicians across the spectrum participated, but in personal capacities only. This successful public fracturing of the Afghan democratic forces—not that they were very united to begin with weakened the ability of President Ghani to be seen as a legitimate interlocutor. While the fate of individuals may not be very relevant, the loss of consensus on the centrality of democratic governance to Afghanistan's future was troubling, and in the ultimate, contributed to its collapse as a house of cards.

In Afghanistan, there is almost a universal acceptance that in the Afghanistan-Pakistan relationship, they would be the junior partner as they are militarily weaker, economically smaller, geographically challenged and less central to the world's geostrategic concerns. They also accept that, in such circumstances, they would have to compete for attention/favour from the United States and other international partners and donors. There is also no thought that at any time, Afghanistan, as the weaker country, would resort to the use of asymmetric warfare as Pakistan used in Indian states of Punjab and Kashmir, or in a different way, did in Afghanistan with its patronage of the Taliban.

There are also three clear 'Nos' in the Afghanistan position. There is no question of Afghanistan ever becoming, or being seen as, Pakistan's fifth province. During the Taliban times (1996-2001), international calls to Afghanistan were routed through Pakistan, utilising its country code (+92); trivial as it sounds, this seriously challenges Afghan sovereignty. The recent decision of Pakistan that its trade with Afghanistan would be denominated in the Pakistani rupee, not the dollar, is another manifestation of the design to deny Afghanistan sovereignty. The Afghans would not easily accept any form of common security arrangements between the two countries. And controversially, they rule out ceding any territory which makes the acceptance of the Durand Line as the *de jure* international border impossible. This is not to suggest that any Afghan regime would actually take any step to change the status quo but to indicate that the process of normalisation of relations between the two would necessarily leave behind some unresolved issues for future generations. However, this lack of resolution would not hold up moving ahead bilaterally, if other positive factors (like Pakistan abjuring its attempts to control Afghanistan) are in play.

Going Forward

The most important determinant of the direction and intensity of bilateral relations between these two countries would be the role of the United States specifically and the West in general. Any Afghan state, whether run as an Islamic Republic or as an Emirate would require substantial financial assistance to function, except at a very low level. In the circumstances, where the Afghan regime is dependant for its very existence on Pakistan, how much leverage the United States has over Pakistan and how much of it is prepared to use. However, America's perceived reliance on Pakistan, both for access and intelligence, limits its leveraging capacity since 2001, severely constrained US' options, though to be fair, much of it was self-imposed. American policymakers took their time but ultimately questioned the Pakistan Army's links with the Taliban. At a more structural level would be the United States' ability to hold Pakistan, especially the Army, accountable. Billions of dollars in assistance to the Pakistani Army should have equipped it to wage counter-insurgency warfare effectively. Similarly, the Pakistan Army's continued patronage of the Taliban, seen by them as a strategic asset for which they are prepared to pay a significant price (deaths of hundreds of Army men in operations, international opprobrium and ultimately a threat to the Pakistan state itself), is an issue that the paymasters would have to confront.

President Trump publicly called Pakistan's bluff, tweeting about how that country had taken US$ 33 billion from the US but worked against its benefactor. This was followed by a funding squeeze that rocked the Pakistani economy. But these harsh measures could not continue for long since the US public had become tired of US' longest war and wanted out. Consequently, US' new-found dependence on the Pakistan Army to deliver on peace with the Taliban has only made matters worse for Afghanistan, resulting in the collapse of the Islamic Republic.

Another determinant, though by no means crucial, of how Afghanistan-Pakistan relations would develop in the short- to medium-term is the regional dimension. However, this factor can be over-estimated since most regional powers have limited leverage over either of the countries. The argument that if Pakistan's relations with India improve, it would make the former less interested in Afghanistan, has limited traction, since it ignores the inner dynamics driving Pakistan's Afghanistan policy. Certainly, in the long run, a more integrated neighbourhood would lessen bilateral tensions and would enable both countries to better exploit mutually-beneficial synergies.

Weak states do not make for good neighbours, especially if important sections of the stronger neighbour have developed clearly predatory interests in the other. Peace and stability requires the vital catalytic role of a mutual benefactor with the resources and leverage to reduce the influence of negative factors and promote positive ones, which would have global implications. The US felt that it lacked leverage with Pakistan, which has been happy to accept US aid and use US influence to access international funding from the International Monetary Fund, but whose interests are clearly at odds with that of the US, Afghanistan or of the larger neighbourhood. China is at present happy to free-ride; it's half a century investment in the Pakistani Army, its nuclear programme and its strategic goal is simply too important for it to play the role of an honest broker. Most importantly, Pakistan-Afghanistan relations can really take off and achieve its fullest potential if the former's leadership realises that it would need to re-order its internal mechanisms and drop the use of jihadi extremism as an instrument of state policy in Afghanistan, and that would only come about if Pakistan evolves into a normal state that gives priority to the quality of life of its own citizens.

Disclaimer: An earlier version of this chapter was published by the Institute of South Asian Studies, Singapore as WP 56/ 2009, and 'Prospects for Afghanistan-Pakistan Relations'. Grateful acknowledgement to ISAS and its Director, Dr. C. Raja Mohan for permission to use this piece.

Notes

1. Louis Dupree, *Afghanistan*, Princeton University Press, Princeton, 1973.
2. Ahmad Rashid, *Taliban: Militant Islam, Oil and Fundamentalism in Central Asia*, Yale University Press, Yale, 2001.
3. B.R. Ambedkar, *Pakistan or the Partition of India*, Life Span Publishers & Distributors, 2021.
4. Louis Dupree, n. 1.
5. For example, see Barnett Rubin and Ahmad Rashid, 'From Great Game to Grand Bargain', *Foreign Affairs,* November/December 2008.
6. The United States made clear that even as it engaged the civilian leadership, it continued to maintain direct links with the Army.
7. See, for example, the writings of Lt Gen Talat Masood (retd).
8. Reports that local power entrepreneurs of different types had set up over 100 checkpoints on the 60 miles stretch between Chaman, on the Pakistan-Afghanistan border, to Kandahar, which reflected the total breakdown of authority, and the colossal scope for extortion.
9. William Maley, *Stabilizing Afghanistan: Foreign Policy for the Next President*, Carnegie Endowment for International Peace, Washington DC, October 2008.
10. See, for example, Seth Jones, 'Going the Distance', *Washington Post,* 15 February 2009.
11. http://www.thaindian.com/newsportal/south-asia/mullah-omar-sacks-baitullah-for-fighting-against-pakarmy_10014775.html. Accessed on 15 July 2019.
12. Mazhar Tufail, 'Mulla Omar orders halt to attacks on Pak troops', *Pakistan Defence Forum*, 2009, at http://www.thaindian.com/newsportal/south-asia/mullah-omar-sacks-baitullah-for-fightingagainst-pak-army_10014775.html. Accessed on 15 July 2019.
13. Instead of 20 April, which was the initial date chosen. They were then postponed to 29 July.

SECTION 2

The Armed Forces

8. The Pakistan Army

D.S. Hooda

The Pakistan Army was born out of the division of the British Indian Army following the partition of India in 1947. Units that had fought in the bloody battlefields of Belgium, France, North Africa, Burma, and along the Northwest Frontier, were divided along Hindu-Muslim lines. The initial parting in most units was nostalgic and friendly. Larry Collins and Dominique La Pierre, in their book, *Freedom at Midnight,* describe one such farewell: In Rawalpindi, the Second Cavalry gave an enormous Barakhana, a "good luck" banquet, to their former comrades. Every Sikh and Hindu officer spoke, often with tears in his eyes, to bid farewell to the Moslem Colonel Mohammed Idris, who had led them through the bitterest fighting of World War II. "Wherever you go," said Idris in reply, "we shall always remain brothers, because we spilled our blood together."[1]

However, this feeling of comradeship between the soldiers of a unit did not go beyond this level. There was a bitter fight over the division of military resources, with Pakistan accusing India of depriving it of its rightful share. This was seen as an attempt by India to keep Pakistan weak, and this feeling has been a constant theme in the Pakistan Army's thought process ever since.

Although carved out of the same army, the militaries of the two countries have followed entirely different trajectories. The Indian Army easily slipped into its constitutional role and readily accepted the democratic norm of civilian supremacy. Even during the worst period of civil-military relations in the early 1960s, the primacy of civilian control was not challenged. Despite his intention to resign along with General Thimayya, Admiral Katari acknowledges that

Nehru "quite properly sought to emphasise the supremacy of the civil authority over the military. None of us in the armed force [sic] had the remotest doubts about this, nor was there even any thought of defying it".[2]

On the other hand, the Pakistan Army has regularly overthrown elected governments through much of Pakistan's history. Even when not in power, the army has wielded enormous influence in both domestic and foreign affairs. Despite this, it remains one of the most efficient institutions of the country and one that is most trusted by the people. In a nationwide *Jang Geo News* Poll conducted in October 2017, 82 per cent of those polled named Pakistan Army as the most trusted institution of the country, even as 81 per cent of them, paradoxically, considered democracy as the best form of governance.[3]

Today, when we look at the Pakistan Army, we see an organisation that views India with enduring hostility, uses terror groups to fight its proxy wars in India and Afghanistan, and one that could disrupt democratic norms to retain its dominant status in the country. At a time when Pakistan is facing an economic crisis, a terror backlash at home, and diplomatic isolation, this behaviour of the Pakistan Army appears surprising. However, as Christine Fair explains:

> "The Pakistan Army views its struggle with India in existential terms. For Pakistan's men on horseback, not winning, even repeatedly, is not the same thing as losing. But simply giving up and accepting the status quo and India's supremacy, is, by definition, defeat. As a former chief of army staff explained to me in 2000, Pakistan's generals would always prefer to take a calculated risk and be defeated than to do nothing at all. Pakistan's army will insist on action at almost any cost, even that of presiding over a hollow state."[4]

To understand this attitude, it is important to look at the strategic concerns of the Pakistan Army, its organisational culture, and its warfighting doctrine against India. These three issues combined could give us a glimpse into the future; about whether the Pakistani

Army could move towards a different trajectory that leads to a more harmonious neighbourhood.

Core Strategic Concerns

The Pakistan Army's strategic concerns relate to the defence of its borders, the internal security threats, and its international relations, particularly with the US and China. However, it is the concept of 'strategic depth' in Afghanistan and its enduring hostility with India that has mainly shaped the Pakistan Army's strategic culture and actions.

Afghanistan and 'Strategic Depth'

The Pakistan Army in 1947 inherited the western frontiers of the British Empire. However, while the British-Indian Army was primarily focused on this border, the Pakistan Army could not afford to deploy many soldiers here, facing a more hostile foe along its eastern borders. Pakistan-Afghanistan relations were initially rocky, and Afghanistan was the only country to oppose Pakistan's entry into the United Nations. Afghanistan also refused to accept the legitimacy of the Durand Line, the border with Pakistan, and is yet to officially recognise this as the international border.

Despite these differences, there was no overt hostility between Afghanistan and Pakistan in the initial decades following independence. It was the coup against King Zahir Shah and the installation of the pro-Soviet Mohammad Daoud Khan in 1973 that changed the situation. As explained in Christine Fair's book, Pakistan's support to Afghan Islamists started with the establishment of an Afghan cell in 1973. The earliest recipients of Pakistani support were Gulbuddin Hekmatyar and Ahmad Shah Massoud.[5]

The entry of the Soviet Army into Afghanistan in 1979 brought a hostile superpower at the gates of Pakistan and transformed the country into a frontline state of superpower rivalry. The propping up of the Mujahideen against the Soviets also suited the Pakistan Army's strategic interests, and the Inter-Services Intelligence (ISI) grew in power, becoming the primary conduit for arms supply to the various groups fighting the Soviets. However, the conflict did not leave Pakistan unscathed, as approximately 4 million Afghan refugees poured into the country. These refugees "bred lawlessness in the border regions, undermining the traditional tribal authorities and [the] Pakistan government alike."[6] America and Pakistan's nurturing of the Islamic jihadi groups would later have a deadly impact on both countries.

The Soviet withdrawal from Afghanistan and the victory of the Taliban over the anarchic Mujahideen groups in 1996 was initially seen by the Pakistan Army as a period when their vision of 'strategic depth' in Afghanistan appeared to be coming true. The concept of strategic depth was first enunciated by the Army Chief Mirza Aslam Beg in 1988. However, he later denied having "proposed such a defeatist concept of withdrawal to Afghanistan for territorial depth, against Indian military ingress."[7]

A better understanding of strategic depth lies in General Ashfaq Parvez Kayani's statement to the media in 2010. He said, "We want a strategic depth in Afghanistan but do not want to control it. A peaceful and friendly Afghanistan can provide Pakistan a strategic depth." He admitted that Pakistan's objective of supporting the former Taliban regime in Afghanistan was to gain a 'strategic depth' in Afghanistan.[8] This clearly shows that the Pakistan Army will continue its efforts to install a regime in Kabul that is favourable to its interests.

After 9/11 and the US invasion of Afghanistan, Pakistan's relations with Afghanistan deteriorated, and the Indian presence in that country aroused a great deal of disquiet in Pakistan. India's development efforts in Afghanistan and support for training of the Afghan Army were seen as a strategic encirclement of Pakistan. Indian consulates in Afghanistan were accused of running covert operations and supporting insurgencies in Balochistan and FATA. This is the primary reason for the Pakistan Army's continuing support for the Taliban.

With the US withdrawal from Afghanistan and the swift takeover of the country by the Taliban, Pakistan now finds itself in a favourable position. Although the situation in Afghanistan has the potential for terrorism and instability to spill over across the border, as is indeed happening today, the Pakistan Army will draw satisfaction at the waning Indian influence in Kabul.

India—An Implacable Foe

The Pakistan Army's hostility towards India is strong and deep-rooted. Within months of the soldiers of the two armies waving an emotional goodbye to their comrades on the eve of independence, they were fighting a bitter battle in the mountains of Jammu and Kashmir (J&K). The 1947-48 war left the state divided into two parts, and this division remains the most contentious problem between the two countries.

The Pakistan Army's attempt to resolve the issue of J&K through the use of force led to the 1965 war. The Pakistan Army planned to foment a rebellion in J&K through a massive infiltration of troops into the state, followed by an attack in the Chhamb sector. The objective, as defined in the directive of President Ayub Khan, was "to take such action as will defreeze Kashmir problem, weaken India's resolve and bring her to a conference table without provoking a general war."[9]

This was an incredibly naïve assumption but it reflects an underlying theme of the Pakistan Army's thought process. The Indian Army took the fight across the international border into Punjab. The war ended in a stalemate, but its aftermath contained the seeds that led to the next conflict. As Shuja Nawaz describes in his book, *Crossed Swords,* following the 1965 war, an "alarming gap appeared between East and West Pakistan, as the East Pakistanis, one thousand miles away felt that the West had forsaken them to a potential Indian attack."[10]

Political turmoil broke out in East Pakistan after the 1970 election when Mujibur Rahman won a resounding victory, but Zulfikar Bhutto refused to accept the results. The Pakistan Army's brutal crackdown in East Pakistan led to an exodus of 10 million refugees into India and created conditions for the entry of the Indian Army into East Pakistan.

The Pakistan Army was wholly outnumbered and outfought in the 1971 war, leading to a humiliating defeat and the capture of 93,000 prisoners. It is often said that the devastating breakup of the country in 1971 reinforced Pakistan Army's view that India was intent on reducing Pakistan to an inferior state that could not challenge Indian hegemony. This directly led to Pakistan supporting insurgencies in Punjab and J&K to pay India back in the same coin.

This is not entirely untrue, but it was a later, and more limited conflict, that has shaped Pakistan Army's current military strategy of dealing with the challenge of India. The Kargil War of 1999 showed flashes of tactical brilliance by the Pakistan Army in its execution, but a complete lack of strategic direction. The objectives of the operation showed the same false assumptions as had been made during the 1965 war. In a detailed presentation to Prime Minister Nawaz Sharif on 17 May, the Director-General of Military Operations stated that the Indians did not have the will or determination to take on Pakistan in a fight and would not make any serious effort to regain the heights.[11]

Although the Kargil War was a debacle for Pakistan, its army took some important lessons that define its current strategic thought.[12] The first is that conventional operations to alter the Line of Control would be strongly countered by a superior Indian military and have little chance of success. Such an action would also not be acceptable to the international community. Second, Pakistan's possession of nuclear weapons provided the "permissive condition that made contemplating Kargil possible" and also served to "ward off the worst Indian counter-responses that could be precipitated by Islamabad's attempts at strategic diversion."[13] Nuclear weapons thus limit the chances of an all-out war. Finally, with few options available, the Pakistan Army feels that the only possible means of bringing India to the negotiating table on Kashmir is through the use of jihadi proxies.

Organisational Culture of the Pakistan Army

Organisational culture can be defined as the ideology, values, attitudes, and beliefs that contribute to the unique character of an organisation. It also determines how the members of this organisation will behave. It is therefore important to study the dominant beliefs of the Pakistan Army to understand its organisational culture.

Defenders of Pakistan's Ideology

Pakistan's Army sees itself as the ultimate defender of the state of Pakistan from its main enemy—India. This battle is not only seen in territorial but also ideological terms. As Christine Fair says, "Because the Pakistan Army sees itself as securing Pakistan's ideological frontiers, Islam is an enduring feature of the army's strategic culture."[14] In this role, the Pakistan Army sees itself as the primary actor and brooks no interference from any other institution, including politicians.

Years of military rule and the influence exerted by the army seems to have convinced the officers that Pakistan's security strategy is their preserve. In a study of attitudes of the army officers undergoing the Staff College at Quetta, David O. Smith concludes, "The consistent attitude of virtually all Pakistani students at the Staff College is that the Army is the only remaining state institution that is fully functional, has not become corrupted, is merit-based, and is responsible enough to be trusted with making decisions on key foreign policy and national security matters."[15]

The clearest manifestation of this was in the Kargil War when infiltration for the operation commenced without any political clearance. In an interview to Shuja Nawaz, General Ziauddin stated that "local actions, such as Kargil, are within the army's chain of command' and that there was no need to 'openly bring the prime minister into the plan".[16] This is an absurd comment but reflects the independence of the army in strategic decision-making.

Inflated Sense of Superiority

Underestimating an opponent is perhaps the biggest mistake that a professional army can make. Deriding the Indian soldier, who is classified as a 'Hindu' irrespective of his ethnicity, has been a consistent theme in Pakistan Army's thinking and writings. After studying six decades of Pakistani defence publications, Christine Fair observes that the authors establish Hindus as "dishonorable, meek, pusillanimous, treacherous, and inequitable."[17] The 1965 directive of Ayub Khan, mentioned earlier in this article, also included this line, "As a general rule Hindu morale would not stand more than a couple of hard blows delivered at the right time and place."[18]

Much of this notion was seriously questioned after the 1971 war. In recent years, as the conventional military superiority of India has outstripped Pakistan, there is a more realistic assessment of India's capability. However, the Pakistan Army remains obsessively concerned about appearing weak or inferior to its Indian counterpart. We see this in the smallest of incidents. When the Senate sought details of casualties suffered by the Pakistan Army in firing along the Line of Control, "the military authorities refused to share the details citing security concerns."[19] The real purpose of hiding the details is the inevitable comparisons that will be made with Indian Army casualties, showing the Pakistan Army in poor light. There was similar reasoning behind the army refusing to accept that Indian soldiers had crossed the Line of Control to strike terror camps in September 2016.

Maintaining Dominance in Civil-Military Relations

The asymmetry in the power balance between the military and political leadership is well known. Even when not ruling the country, the military attempts to retain its influence in running the affairs of the nation. In the 1988 elections, the 'ISI assembled a coalition of Islamist and pro-military parties, named the Islami Jamhoori Ittehad (IJI—Islamic Democratic Alliance) to serve as the military's proxy in a controlled political process'.[20] In the 2002 elections, the ISI engineered defections from Nawaz Sharif's Pakistan Muslim League (PML) to create PML (Q), which went on to win the elections.

Pakistan Army officers theoretically support democracy and civilian governance but are extremely critical of the political institutions.[21] Professor Aqil Shah, who interviewed 100 military officers between 2007 and 2013, points out that three-fourths of them viewed a coup as a legitimate form of regime change under 'crisis' conditions and that civilian politicians were incapable of managing national security, while two-thirds of them considered politicians as unfit to rule.[22]

The political leadership of Pakistan has mostly acquiesced to the dominant role of the army, and the judiciary has often supported extra-constitutional acts of the military by quoting the 'doctrine of necessity'.[23] The people of Pakistan also see their army in a very favourable light. Therefore, there is little pressure on the Pakistani Army to correct the current power imbalance in civil-military relations.

Power also brings privileges in the form of post-retirement employment, subsidised plots of land, and a disproportionate share in the country's national budget. The military also runs profitable business ventures, with investments reportedly exceeding $100 billion.[24] With the whole institution profiting, it is difficult to see any internal pressure or motivation for the Pakistan Army to participate in a change that will weaken its influence on the country's political structure.

Use of Proxy Fighters

The use of proxies has always been an accepted form in warfare. However, armies generally use proxies as an adjunct in their strategy while mainly relying on their conventional strength for winning the contest. In the case of the Pakistan Army, the use of terror groups has been the main element of their strategy in contesting stronger neighbours.

In the 1947-48, and the 1965 wars with India, irregular forces preceded the entry of Pakistan Army regulars into battle. When insurgencies broke out in the Northeastern states of India, Pakistan provided active support. In 1956, Phizo, the Naga rebel leader, escaped to East Pakistan and secured help for training and weapons for large groups of guerillas that crossed the border from India.[25]

Pakistan's support to insurgencies in Punjab and Kashmir is well documented, as is its support to extremist groups like the Indian Mujahideen.[26] In Jammu and Kashmir, the calibrated use of terror groups like the Lashkar-e-Taiba (LeT) and Jaish-e-Mohammed

(JeM), and support to the separatists, has kept alive a 32-year-old insurgency.

In Afghanistan, jihadi groups, with Pakistan's support, defeated one superpower, and forced a second into a humiliating withdrawal. Despite enormous American pressure since 9/11, Pakistan never abandoned their support for the Afghan Taliban.

There is no doubt that Pakistan has suffered enormously for the 'snakes in their backyard', as Hillary Clinton famously said. The Lal Masjid siege of 2007 led to the birth of the Tehrik-e-Taliban Pakistan (TTP), and the country descended into bloodshed. Many strategic experts at that time thought that the Pakistan Army would finally realise its folly and break its links with all terror groups. But that did not happen, and they continued to support Kashmir-centric groups and the Taliban.

Looking at the situation today from the Pakistan Army's perspective, they may feel that their approach has succeeded. There has been a significant downturn in terror incidents in Pakistan with fatalities dropping from a peak of over 11,000 in 2009 to 365 in 2019.[27] In Afghanistan, most of the world has tacitly accepted the Taliban rule and recognises the importance of Pakistan in dealing with any fallout of the situation on regional security. Although the security situation has remained under control in Kashmir, there is deep alienation among sections of the population, and local recruits continue to join terror ranks. For the Pakistan Army, all of this may just feel like a success.

Conventional Warfighting Doctrine

There is some concern in strategic circles around the world that a conflict between India and Pakistan could spin out of control and turn nuclear. Due to the growing asymmetry in the conventional capability of the two sides, India's military success in a conventional war could lead to an early breach of Pakistan's nuclear red lines. This impression is also reinforced by frequent references to the nuclear card by Pakistan's military and political leadership. After the recent spike in tensions following the Balakot airstrike on the JeM terror camp, Prime Minister Imran Khan, in an interview to BBC, issued a veiled warning: "Once you respond, no-one can predict where it can go from there."[28]

The stand-off of 2001-02, when India and Pakistan mobilised and massed their armies along the border, led to some deep thinking within the Indian Army on their strategy for the western borders. This resulted in the adoption (though not officially) of the so-called 'Cold Start Doctrine' by the Indian Army. In Pakistan, India's 'Cold Start Doctrine' is seen as aggressive and destabilising, forcing Pakistan to "lower her nuclear threshold in order to address the conventional overmatch enjoyed by the Indian Army."[29]

Pakistan's development of Tactical Nuclear Weapons (TNWs) is largely seen as a response to India's 'Cold Start Doctrine'. A majority of Pakistan's military strategists agree that TNWs complete the full spectrum deterrence and foreclose India's options of fighting a limited conventional war under a nuclear overhang.[30]

This somewhat direct linking of conventional and nuclear war sometimes leads us to believe that the Pakistan Army would threaten the early use of nuclear weapons because it faces a swift defeat from superior Indian land forces. Whether this is true can be assessed by studying the Pakistan Army's conventional warfighting doctrine.

In response to the 'Cold Start Doctrine', the Pakistan Army developed a doctrine named 'New Concept of War Fighting' (NCWF). Pakistani Armed Forces conducted four Azm-e-Nau joint military exercises from 2009 to 2013, after which the NCWF was formally adopted.[31] Although not many details are known of the NCWF, it is designed to blunt India's conventional superiority by adopting the following measures:[32]

- Neutralise India's early launch by faster mobilisation.
- Create additional reserves at all levels to absorb the initial Indian offensive.
- Employ its strategic reserves of Central and Southern Commands for an offensive into Indian territory.

Quite clearly, this strategy is not one that accepts either an early conventional defeat or a quick resort to the nuclear blackmail. Obviously, this requires the Pakistan Army to build up its conventional capability to move beyond only the theoretical underpinnings of a doctrine. Looking at the military procurement in the last few years, and despite its limited budget as compared to India, it appears that Pakistan has been reasonably successful in building up its conventional forces.

As per SIPRI data, there was a 58 per cent increase in military acquisitions between 2010 and 2016 as compared to 2003 to 2009. The sharpest increase was in aircraft, armoured vehicles, and missiles, all of which enhance conventional capability.[33] In the period between 2016 and 2020 Pakistan emerged as the 10th largest arms importer in Asia and Oceania, accounting for 2.7 per cent of major arms imports.[34] Pakistan also has a defence industrial base that appears to be more efficient than India's in producing major platforms.[35]

On the other hand, India's sluggishness in defence procurement and high-revenue expenditure has delayed modernisation that could provide a significant edge over Pakistan's military. Walter C. Ladwig, in his study on conventional deterrence in South Asia, has pointed out that "India's defense procurement continues to underperform, producing far less in terms of military power than its spending would suggest. Conversely, Pakistan—assisted by China and others—has prevented the emergence of sharp asymmetries in the conventional military balance and even narrowed previously existing gaps."[36]

It does appear that the Pakistan Army could be reasonably confident about denying swift military success to India, at least until India substantially enhances its conventional forces. This, in turn, could see the Pakistan Army continuing with its revisionist behaviour.

Future Prospects

Today, there is tremendous pressure on Pakistan, both on the domestic and international fronts. It is facing an economic crisis that has forced it to go in for its 22nd loan from the International Monetary Fund, and it remains on the grey list of the Financial Action Task Force.[37] After the US withdrawal from Afghanistan, the US-Pakistan ties remain strained. Relations with India have hit a new low after the August 2019 decision to dilute Article 370 and bifurcate J&K into two Union Territories.

Despite the crisis that Pakistan finds itself in, it is unlikely that the Pakistan Army will change its behaviour. The suspension of US military aid is not seen as significant, as there had been a steady decline in aid from 2010-11, and Pakistan has diversified its military procurement from countries like China, Turkey, and Russia. Pakistan also feels that its regional role has been enhanced by the Taliban victory. As Kamal Alam writes, "The future, as far as the Pakistan Army is concerned, belongs to them."[38]

India remains the existential threat, and this feeling is unlikely to change. The Pakistan Army will continue with a calibrated strategy of using terror groups to stir up violence in J&K. It feels that it can conventionally hold-off India in any limited conflict and use its nuclear weapons as a deterrence against a major escalation that could result in significant territorial losses. Therefore, it does not see any great danger in continuing with what it views as a reasonably successful strategy to counter its stronger neighbour at a low cost.

The nature of civil-military relations in Pakistan is a primary reason for their poor record in strategic decision-making, as witnessed in its past conflicts with India. Risa Brooks, in her book *Shaping Strategy: The Civil-Military Politics of Strategic Assessment,* opines that the quality of strategic assessment depends on the nature of civil-military relations. In developing her theory, Brooks looks at two key variables—the 'intensity of preference divergence over corporate, professional, or security issues', and the 'balance of civil-military power'.[39]

Looking at the case of Pakistan in the period 1997-99, Brooks finds a "situation consistent with civil-military relations characterised by shared power and high-preference divergence."[40] This combination results in poor strategic assessments, as was witnessed during Kargil. The recent ousting of Prime Minister Imran Khan a result of his fallout with the Pakistan Army Chief shows the continuing infirmities in civil-military relations. It is clear that the Pakistan Army would continue to drive strategic decisions without fully comprehending the political and diplomatic fallout of their actions.

Conclusion

Pakistan has a professional and motivated army, hardened through wars and fighting terror groups within the country. However, the power and political influence that it wields has had a negative impact on Pakistan's development as a nation. The Pakistan Army views its conflict with India in civilisational terms and refuses to accept the growing economic and military disparity between the two countries. It has concretised the role of jihadis as a part of its strategy to destabilise India.

Is there a likelihood of any change in the Pakistan Army's attitudes? Any change will either be due to external or internal pressures. There are limits to the external pressures that can be put on Pakistan as long as it remains a crucial player for exercising a level of control over the Taliban in Afghanistan. China's support also helps ward-off the international pressure, and ties with Russia are growing. Any change from within the army itself appears unlikely. The privileged position that the army occupies in the country incentivises status quo. The political leadership in the country is also too weak and too deferential to the military to be able to force any change.

In January 2022, Pakistan unveiled its National Security Policy (NSP) that seeks to "keep economic security at the core".[41] However, the NSP continues to blame India for "the political exploitation of a policy of belligerence towards Pakistan", and India's "attempts to impose one-sided solutions that can have far reaching negative consequences for regional stability." With little to indicate that there could be a thawing of relations in the near future, India losing patience with Pakistan's support to terror activities, the region remains a flashpoint.

Notes

1. Larry Collins and Dominique Lapierre. *Freedom at Midnight,* 2nd edition, HarperCollins Publishers, London, 1997 (e-pub version).
2. Apurba Kundu, *Militarism in India: The Army and Civil Society in Consensus*, Viva Books, New Delhi, 1998, p. 117.
3. 'Overwhelming Majority of Pakistanis Want Democracy, Trust Armed Forces: Survey', at https://www.geo.tv/latest/168956-overwhelming-

majority-of-pakistanis-want-democracy-trust-armed-forces-survey. Accessed on 26 May 2019.

4. C. Christine Fair, *Fighting to the End: The Pakistan Army's Way of War,* first edition, Oxford University Press, New York, 2014, p. 6.
5. Ibid.
6. Bruce Riedel, *Deadly Embrace: Pakistan, America, and the Future of the Global Jihad,* second edition, Brookings Institution Press, Washington DC, 2012 (e-pub version).
7. 'General Beg Explains His View of Strategic Depth Doctrine', *Daily Times,* 4 July 2017, at https://dailytimes.com.pk/3733/general-beg-explains-his-view-of-strategic-depth-doctrine/. Accessed on 6 June 2019.
8. 'Af-Pak: What Strategic Depth?', Open Democracy, at https://www.opendemocracy.net/en/opensecurity/af-pak-what-strategic-depth/. Accessed on 6 June 2019.
9. Brian Cloughley, *A History of the Pakistan Army: Wars and Insurrections,* Oxford University Press, Karachi and New York, 1999 (e-pub version).
10. Shuja Nawaz, *Crossed Swords: Pakistan, Its Army, and the Wars Within,* first edition, Oxford University Press, Oxford, 2009 (e-pub version).
11. Nasim Zehra, *From Kargil to the Coup: Events That Shook Pakistan,* first edition, Sang-e-Meel Publications, Lahore, 2018 (e-pub version).
12. There is an excellent analysis of the lessons of Kargil Conflict by Ashley J. Tellis, C. Christine Fair and Jamison Jo Medby, 'Limited Conflicts Under the Nuclear Umbrella', 2001, at https://www.rand.org/pubs/monograph_reports/MR1450.html. Accessed on 18 June 2019.
13. Ibid.
14. C. Christine Fair, *Fighting to the End: The Pakistan Army's Way of War,* first edition, Oxford University Press, New York, 2014, p. 66.
15. 'The Quetta Experience: Attitudes and Values within Pakistan's Army', Wilson Center, at https://www.wilsoncenter.org/publication/the-quetta-experience-attitudes-and-values-within-pakistans-army. Accessed on 18 June 2019.
16. Shuja Nawaz, n. 10.
17. C. Christine Fair, n. 14.
18. Brian Cloughley, n. 9.
19. 'Army's Refusal to Share LoC Casualty Stats Irks Rabbani', *The Express Tribune,* at https://tribune.com.pk/story/1429091/armys-refusal-share-loc-casualty-stats-irks-rabbani/. Accessed on 19 June 2019.
20. Ḥusain Ḥaqqānī, *Pakistan: Between Mosque and Military,* Carnegie Endowment for International Peace, Washington, DC, 2005, p. 221.
21. "The Quetta Experience: Attitudes and Values within Pakistan's Army", n. 15.
22. Ḥusain Ḥaqqānī, n. 20.
23. 'Doctrine of Necessity-Application in Pakistan-Cases of Immense Importance-A Critical Review', at https://www.researchgate.net/

publication/268436716_Doctrine_of_Necessity-Application_in_Pakistan-Cases_of_Immense_Importance-A_Critical_Review. Accessed on 19 June 2019.

24. 'Pakistani Army Moves into the Oil Business', *Asia Times,* at https://www.asiatimes.com/2019/03/article/pakistani-army-moves-into-the-oil-business/. Accessed on 20 June 2019.
25. 'Pakistan's Involvement in Terrorism against India', at https://www.satp.org/satporgtp/countries/india/document/papers/Pakistan_report/Anex_G.htm. Accessed on 21 June 2019.
26. Stephen Tankel, 'The Indian Jihadist Movement: Evolution and Dynamics-Analysis', Carnegie Endowment for International Peace, at https://carnegieendowment.org/2014/09/10/indian-jihadist-movement-evolution-and-dynamics-analysis-pub-56588. Accessed on 20 June 2019.
27. "Terrorism in Pakistan - Yearly Fatalities | SATP", at https://www.satp.org/datasheet-terrorist-attack/fatalities/pakistan. Accessed on 24 April 2022.
28. Alessandra Scotto di Santolo, 'India Pakistan Conflict: Imran Khan Issues India Nuclear Warning—"No One Can Predict,"' Express.co.uk, 10 April 2019, at https://www.express.co.uk/news/world/1112264/India-Pakistan-news-Kashmir-Imran-Khan-nuclear-weapons-india-election. Accessed on 21 June 2019.
29. Maj Muhammad Zeeshan Ali, 'Strategic Delusions—The Cold Start Doctrine: Proactive Strategy', at https://apps.dtic.mil/dtic/tr/fulltext/u2/1021787.pdf. Accessed on 21 June 2019.
30. Mansoor Ahmed, 'Pakistan's Tactical Nuclear Weapons and Their Impact on Stability', Carnegie Endowment for International Peace, at https://carnegieendowment.org/2016/06/30/pakistan-s-tactical-nuclear-weapons-and-their-impact-on-stability-pub-63911. Accessed on 21 June 2019.
31. 'Pakistan's New War Strategy', *Daily Times*, at https://dailytimes.com.pk/207360/pakistans-new-war-strategy/. Accessed on 21 June 2019.
32. 'An Integrated Indian Military Strategy-2040: A Perspective', at http://www.indiandefencereview.com/spotlights/an-integrated-indian-military-strategy-2040-a-perspective-part-i/. Accessed on 21 June 2019.
33. Meenakshi Sood, 'The Pakistan's (Non-Nuclear) Plan to Counter "Cold Start"', *The Diplomat,* at https://thediplomat.com/2017/03/pakistans-non-nuclear-plan-to-counter-cold-start/. Accessed on 21 June 2019.
34. "Pakistan Ranks 10th among Largest Importers of Major Arms Globally: Report." *DAWN*, 15 March 2021, at https://www.dawn.com/news/1612678.
35. 'Pakistan Defence Industrial Base Better than Ours: Army Vice Chief', *The Indian Express* (blog), 25 July 2017, at https://indianexpress.com/article/india/pakistan-defence-industrial-base-better-than-ours-army-vice-chief-4766949/. Accessed on 21 June 2019.

36. Walter C. LadwigIII, 'Indian Military Moderniation and Conventional Deterrence in South Asia', *Journal of Strategic Studies*, 38 (5), 29 July 2015, pp. 729–72, at https://doi.org/10.1080/01402390.2015.1014473. Accessed on 21 June 2019.
37. Shahroo Malik, 'Pakistan's Economic Woes: The Way Forward', *The Diplomat*, at https://thediplomat.com/2019/04/pakistans-economic-woes-the-way-forward/. Accessed on 22 June 2019.
38. Kamal Alam, 'The Bajwa Doctrine: The Pakistani Military Has Done More than Enough', at https://rusi.org/sites/default/files/20180216_rusi_newsbrief_vol.38_no.1_alam_web.pdf. Accessed on 22 June 2019.
39. Risa Brooks, *Shaping Strategy: The Civil-Military Politics of Strategic Assessment*, Princeton University Press, Princeton, NJ, 2018.
40. Ibid.
41. Press Trust of India, Islamabad, 14 January, "Pakistan Launches First-Ever National Security Policy; Here's What It Says about India." *India Today*. https://www.indiatoday.in/world/story/pakistan-national-security-policy-nsp-india-war-nuclear-triad-1900251-2022-01-14. Accessed on 30 January 2022.

9. Pakistan Air Force

Amit Aneja

After the partition of India in 1947, the Pakistan Air Force (PAF) was rechristened as the Royal Pakistan Air Force (RPAF). It dropped the prefix Royal in 1956. The PAF today is a force to reckon with as well as any in the world. To understand the true capability and uniqueness of the force though one will have to view it in the context of Pakistan's history and the geopolitical tides that the nation has surfed. It was directly affected by the Cold War influenced by the ambiguity of the last decade of the twentieth century, and then the new global order post-2000. In the context of its immediate neighbourhood India's going nuclear in 1998, had Pakistan follow suit. This opened a new chapter of contiguous nuclear- armed nations who were openly hostile to each other thus impacting its military doctrine and consequently giving a role for the PAF. Post-2000, the world realised the ugly reality of terrorism and sub-conventional warfare. Circumstantially, it shifted the focus of the world to Pakistan and its neighbourhood. That war still continues with all its manifestations in the entire sub-continent. Emerging China with all its global ambitions became an all-weather ally of Pakistan in a new power struggle for dominance against the US. Pakistan's policy of war by other means resulted in a terror strike in Pulwama in south central Kashmir in February 2019. The retaliatory strike at Balakot by the Indian Air Force (IAF) opened yet another dimension of tight-rope engagement between two nuclear-armed nations. It is in this backdrop, that the PAF strives to build its capabilities across the full spectrum of conflict.

History of the Pakistan Air Force (PAF)

Formative Years

The Royal Pakistan Air Force (RPAF) was formed on 14 August 1947 after independence from British India. The RPAF began with a paper share allotment of 2,332 personnel, and a small fleet of aircraft scattered over 7 airbases all over the provinces. Operating these inherited aircraft was far from ideal because of their condition, especially in Pakistan's diverse terrains. However, by 1948 the Air Force acquired better aircraft such as the Hawker Sea Fury fighter-bomber and the Bristol Freighter. These new aircraft gave a much-needed boost to the morale and combat capability of the RPAF.

Although the Royal Pakistan Air Force had little funds to use and markets to choose from, it entered the jet age quite early. In 1957 the Pakistan Air Force received 100 American-built F-86 Sabres under the US aid programme. In 1957 thirty-six-year-old Air Marshal Asghar Khan became the PAF's first commander-in-chief.

Maturing of PAF (1965, 1971 to Kargil Conflict)

During the 1965 Indo-Pak war the PAF fleet comprised 12 F-104 Star fighters, some 120 F-86 Sabres and around 20 B-57 Canberra bombers. The two countries understandably made contradictory claims of combat losses during the war. According to the independent sources, the PAF lost some 20 aircraft while the Indians lost 60-75.[1] Despite intense fighting, the conflict was a stalemate with a lot left for introspection.

After the 1965 war the US placed an arms embargo on Pakistan and the PAF was badly affected. The PAF began searching for new combat aircraft. China was approached and it agreed to supply 72 Shenyang F-6 fighters initially. These were inducted on 30 December 1965. Concurrently; in 1968 the PAF's No. 5 Squadron started converting to the French Mirage IIIEP. As the F-6 was a short-range air defence fighter, the Mirage III became PAF's main offensive weapon. Due to the American arms embargo on Pakistan it became increasingly difficult for them to procure weapons from Western sources. Thus started Pakistan's increasing tilt towards procurement of Chinese equipment and a significant phase in Pakistan's geopolitical realignment.

By late 1971, the intensification of the independence movement in erstwhile East Pakistan led to the Bangladesh Liberation War between India and Pakistan. Hostilities officially ended on 17 December, after the fall of Dacca. India claimed a large amount of territory in West Pakistan, and the independence of Pakistan's East wing as Bangladesh was confirmed. The surrender of more than 90,000 Pakistani soldiers as Dhaka fell was a big blow to their morale and esteem. The dismemberment of East Pakistan was to continue as a thorn in the flesh of Pakistan as far as Indo-Pak relations were concerned.

In 1979, the PAF's Chief of Air Staff, Air Chief Marshal Anwar Shamim, was told by then President and Chief of Army Staff General Zia ul Haq that Pakistan had reliable information of Indian plans to attack and destroy the Pakistani nuclear research facility at Kahuta. ACM Shamim told General Zia that Indian aircraft could reach the area in 3 minutes whereas the PAF would take 8 minutes, allowing the Indians to attack the facility and return before the PAF could defend it. As Kahuta was too close to the Indian border to be effectively defended it was decided that the best way to deter an Indian attack would be to procure new advanced fighters and weaponry. These would be used to mount a retaliatory attack on India's nuclear research facilities at Trombay in the event of an Indian attack on Kahuta. It was decided that the most suitable aircraft would be F-16, which the United States eventually agreed to supply. In 1983, when the first batch of F-16s reached Pakistan, ACM Shamim informed President Zia of PAF's capability to respond to an attack on the nuclear research facilities at Kahuta.[2]

The Soviets invaded Afghanistan in 1979 in support of the pro-Soviet government in Kabul. The situation in neighbouring Afghanistan and the dynamics of the Cold War played out to open the gates for induction of F/16 aircraft into the PAF. The first of these aircraft were flown into Sargodha on 15 January 1983. This aircraft is the spearhead of the PAF ever since.

A blow-hot-blow-cold relationship with America continued to increase the PAF's dependence on China which embraced the situation for its larger long-term geopolitical interests. Thus the F-7P was introduced in 1988 to replace the F-6.

After the Pressler Amendment was passed in 1990, the US placed sanctions and an arms embargo on Pakistan. All eleven Peace Gate III F-16s, along with the 60 Peace Gate IV F-16s, were embargoed and put into storage in the United States.[3] The result was a lost decade with no inductions into the PAF.

The Pakistan Air Force (PAF) did not see active combat during the Kargil conflict between India and Pakistan in 1999, but remained on high air defence alert near the eastern border with India.

As the 20th century came to an end; the situation in Pakistan and the relations between the Pakistani armed forces and powers that be is best described by Air Commodore S. Sajad Haider (Retd) of the PAF in his book *"Flight of the Falcons"* as follows:

> "Every year the 1965 war is celebrated remorselessly to keep under wraps the failures of our leadership at the time. I feel cheated and enraged at the loss of many gallant men who were martyred believing they were fighting for a sacred cause. The 1971 war was a corollary to the 1965 war and the Kargil conflict followed in the same vein. Shallow personal interests were projected as national interests by dictators. All these wars and conflicts proved catastrophic for the economy and security of Pakistan. Were these conflicts avoidable? If not, why were they not planned and directed with professional dexterity? Why were no lessons learnt from each disaster? Such questions have hardly been addressed candidly from fear of retribution by the powers that be."[4]

Post-2001: Modernisation and Acquisitions

In light of Pakistan's significant contribution to the War on Terror, the United States and Western European countries lifted their defence-related sanctions on Pakistan. PAF once again became active in evaluating potential military hardware such as new fighter aircraft, radars and land based air defence systems. However the urgent relief needed in PoK after the earthquake in Kashmir in 2005, forced the Pakistani military to stall its modernisation programme so it could divert its resources for fuel and operations during the rescue efforts.

The modernisation efforts started again in April 2006 when the Pakistani cabinet approved the PAF's proposals to procure new aircraft and systems from several sources, including modern combat aircraft from the US and China. The AFFDP (Armed Forces Development Programme) 2019 oversaw the modernisation of the Pakistan Air Force from 2006 to 2019 and aimed to buy 98 hi-tech aircraft from US and China.[5]

After the 11 September attacks in 2001, the US began to release the F-16 aircraft of the Peace Gate III/IV contract which had been embargoed after the imposition of the Pressler Amendment.

On 19 May 2006, PAF inaugurated a refurbished Sector Operations Centre (SOC) at PAF's Base in Sargodha which had been installed with a Pakistani-developed air defence automation system for command and control. An old air defence system installed in the 1980s was replaced. The TPS-77 radar was introduced into service in April 2008.[6] In December 2009, the PAF's first Saab 2000 Erieye AEW&C was delivered from Sweden and the Il-78MP Midas aerial refuelling tanker/military transport aircraft from Ukraine. The first of the PAF's new F-16D Block 52+ fighters, rolled out on 13 October 2009. According to Air Chief Marshal Rao Qamar Suleman the new fighters would eliminate the PAF's limitations in precision night strike operations. The existing capability was based on around 34 Dassault Mirage V fighters upgraded with new avionics for night-time precision strike missions under the Retrofit of Strike Element (ROSE) project during 1999-2004.[7] Pakistan appears to have been in talks with China to acquire 30 to 40, JF-31 Stealth fighters.

On 7 July 2017 Pakistan Air Force announced its intent to develop a fifth-generation fighter; a medium-altitude long-endurance unmanned aerial vehicle (MALE UAV) and munitions under the Project Azm.

Table 9.1: PAF Force Structure

AIR FORCE									
System	**Inventory**								
	1990	**1995**	**2000**	**2002**	**2005**	**2008**	**2010**	**2015**	**2020**
AIRCRAFT									
COMBAT	380	370	315	310	315	335	347	289	281
5th Generation			..	..	..	..	..	..	..
FGFA	-	-	-	-	-	-	-	-	-
FC-31 [J-31]	-	-	-	-	-	-	-	-	-
4th Generation			..	..	..	..	..	..	..
FC-20 [J-10CE]	-	-	-	-	-	-	-	-	-
JF-17	-	-	-	-	-	2	8	60	125
F-16C/D	-	-	-	-	-	-	1	18	36
F-16A/B	39	34	34	32	32	46	46	48	48
3rd Generation			..	..	..	..	..	..	..
Mirage 5PA/PA2/PA3	54	54	52	52	52	50	50	50	-
Mirage IIIEP	18	18	13	13	13	63	63	63	-
Mirage IIIO	30	30	43	43	43	-	-	-	-
A-5C (Q-5-III)	50	49	45	42	42	41	41	-	-
F-7PG (F-7MG)	-	-	-	-	55	55	54	50	-
F-7P	40	79	77	77	77	77	75	-	-
F-6	150	100	40	40	-	-	-	-	-
RECON									
Mirage IIIR/RP	12	12	11	11	15	15	15	15	15
AWACS									
Saab 2000 AEWC	-	-	-	-	-	-	2	4	4
ZDK-03 Y-8 AEW	-	-	-	-	-	-	2	4	4
EW/ELINT									
Falcon DA-20	-	-	-	2	2	2	2	2	2
Tanker									
Il-78 MIDAS	-	-	-	-	-	-	2	4	4

TRANSPORT									
TRANSPORT - Large Jet									
Boeing 707	3	3	2	2	3	3	3	3	3
Boeing 737	-	-	1	1	-	-	-	-	-
TRANSPORT - Small Jet									
Gulfstream 450	-	-	-	-	-	2	2	2	2
Cessna 560 Citation	-	-	1	1	-	-	-	-	-
Falcon DA-20	1	1	1	1	1	1	1	1	1
TRANSPORT - Large Prop									
An-26	-	-	-	-	1	1	1	1	1
C-130E	7	7	7	7	7	13	11	11	11
C-130B	5	5	5	5	5	-	-	-	-
L-100	1	1	1	1	1	-	-	-	-
CN-235	-	-	-	-	4	4	4	4	4
F-27-200*	2	2	2	2	2	2	2	2	2
Y-12-II	-	-	2	2	1	1	1	1	1
TRANSPORT - Small Prop									
B-200 King Air	-	-	-	1	1	1	1	1	1
Beech Travel Air	1	1	-	-	-	-	-	-	-
Beech F-33 Bonanza	-	-	-	-	1	1	1	1	1
Beech Baron	1	1	-	-	-	-	-	-	-
Cessna 172	-	-	4	4	-	-	-	-	-
TRAINING									
Trainer - Jet									
K-8	-	6	12	12	12	12	12	12	12
FT-7 (JJ-7 / MiG-21)	-	-	13	13	13	20	19	19	19
FT-6 (JJ-6 / MiG-19)	-	-	15	15	15	15	15	15	15
FT-5 (JJ-5 / MiG-17)	30	30	30	30	30	25	25	25	25
T-37B/C	53	44	30	20	20	20	20	20	20
T-33A	10	10	-	-	-	-	-	-	-
MiG-15UTI	6	6	-	-	-	-	-	-	-
Trainer - Prop									

MFI-395 Mashshaq-2	-	-	-	-	-	-	-	-	-
MFI-17/B Mashshaq	45	45	40	40	80	80	80	80	80
CJ-6 (PT-6A)	12	12	-	-	-	-	-	-	-
HELICOPTER									
Mi-171	-	-	-	-	-	4	8	16	16
SA-315B	-	12	-	-	-	-	-	-	-
SA-316 / SA-319	12	12	15	15	15	15	15	15	15
SA-321	4	4	-	-	-	-	-	-	-
MISSILES									
ASM									
AM-39 Exocet	+	+	+	+	+	+	+	+	+
AGM-65 Maverick	-	-	+	+	+	+	+	+	+
AS-30	-	-	+	+	-	-	-	-	-
AGM-84 Harpoon	-	-	+	+	-	-	-	-	-
AAM									
AIM-7 Sparrow	+	+	+	+	-	-	-	-	-
AIM-9 Sidewinder	+	+	-	-	-	-	-	-	-
AIM-9L/P Sidewinder	-	-	+	+	+	+	+	+	+
R-530/Super 530	+	+	+	+	+	+	+	+	+
R-550 Magic	+	+	-	-	+	-	-	-	-
ARM									
AGM-88 Harm	-	-	+	+	+	-	-	-	-
SAM									
Crotale	36	144	144	144	144	144	144	144	144
CSA-1	6	6	6	6	6	6	6	6	6
SA-16	-	-	-	-	-	+	+	+	+

Sources: IISS, The Military Balance of various years, Global.Security.org, at https://www.globalsecurity.org/military/world/pakistan/air-force-equipment.htm

Notes: *According to the IISS Military Balance, one of these aircraft is assigned to the Navy, but still operated by the Air Force.

The PAF operates approximately 450 combat aircraft of four types, which are likely to be reduced to two multi-role types, namely the F-16 and JF-17, by 2025. There are around 20 frontline squadrons. This is however the time to look beyond sheer numbers of platforms as charted above and put the Air Force's operational capability into perspective. The capability of an air force has the following five elements that determine its true potential:

(a) Aircraft
(b) Sensors and Weapons
(c) Tactics
(d) Training
(e) Airman to Airman relations

The PAF presently has a large force of F-16 aircraft that are of early 1980s vintage. With a usual life of an aircraft, the PAF will have to start planning its replacement by about 2025. Added to that are the geopolitical constraints with respect to its relations with the US and other Western powers; replacement of aircraft from a Western source would mean walking a tight-rope walk. China on the other hand will continue to be an all-weather friend for the foreseeable future and therefore most likely to be the main source for induction of aircraft for the PAF in the future. The work-horse of the PAF is expected to be the JF17s.

As for sensors, the induction of AEW&C aircraft in the form of SAAB 2000 from Sweden and ZDK-03 from China has added a significant battle space transparency for the PAF. These along with IL78 AAR would be a force to reckon with owing to its multiplier effect. In addition to the above, a fully automated Air Defence System that has been duly upgraded would make penetration into PAF airspace very lethal. Herein lies the PAF's strength as well as vulnerability as will be discussed later when their tactical vulnerability will be evaluated.

With regard to training the PAF has a robust training system. Its tactics are generally influenced by the US Air Force (USAF). Of late though, because of Pakistan's geopolitical isolation the PAF's access to Western tactics is constrained and consequently, its participation in large and reputed air exercises globally is limited. In the foreseeable future therefore, asymmetric technology and its application may create a gap and become a limiting factor for the development of its capability.

The issue of airman-to-airman a relation is very unique in the PAF and needs to be understood in a wider context. Intra-Air- Force, the relationship is perhaps as is in most of the advanced Air Forces in the world. Between the Services though, the Air Force is considered subordinate to the Army. This has a reflection not only in terms of the status that the PAF enjoys in Pakistan society but also in the doctrine of its employment.

Figure 9.1: Tactical Imperatives

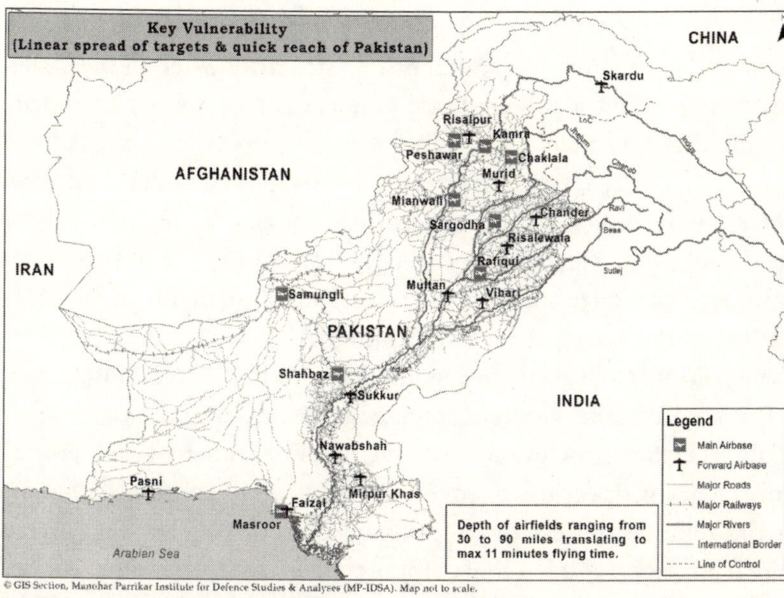

© GIS Section, Manohar Parrikar Institute for Defence Studies & Analyses (MP-IDSA). Map not to scale.

Source: Map outlines with basic data taken from open source. Military information superimposed by the author.

Key Vulnerability (Linear Spread of Targets and Quick Reach)

As can be seen from the maps above in Figure 9.1, the linear disposition of Pakistan brings most of its main and satellite bases within very easy reach of the adversary. Translated in terms of time of flight, no airfield in Pakistan is at a distance of more than eleven minutes flying time from the IAF airfields. Similarly, its communication lines (roads, railway lines, rivers and bridges, electricity grids, etc.) all suffer from proximity vulnerability and hence become easily reachable for targeting. For similar reasons, there is certain predictability about the Pakistan Army's tactical plans and vulnerability in the execution of its RRR (Reorganise, Resize and Reconstitute) strategy designed to counter India's Cold Start Doctrine. Incidentally, the idea of Cold Start owes its origin to *"Operation Parakram"* post the parliament attack. The analysis revealed an operational necessity for quicker deployment and creating an ability to launch a limited offensive at the earliest.

Tactical Compulsion (Playing on the Back Foot)

Pakistan has an unconventional power structure wherein the civilian government plays a subdued role in matters particularly concerning foreign affairs and Defence, with the lead role played by the Pakistan Army. While they have perfected the art of existing under dual power centres, what takes a hit is the conventional wisdom that governs the use of air power. Conventionally in a conflict, Air Forces seek air superiority over the battle space. That pursuit invariably relies heavily on the use of Offensive Counter Air (OCA) in the beginning of the conflict to degrade the enemy Air Force so that its interference in the area of land forces engagement is minimised. Concurrently, a robust Defensive Counter Air (DCA) aims to deny the enemy the same. This proportion changes as the war progresses depending on the relative success of its campaign and gives the Air Force an increasing liberty to act in support of army operations. Greater asymmetry in terms of capability could even permit some parallel operations across the spectrum of conflict right in the beginning.

Because of the power equations defined above and the country's lack of geographical depth, the PAF invariably becomes heavily biased towards the DCA and Close Air Support (CAS) of the land forces prematurely without investing enough in OCA. This strategy could perhaps have been sustainable to some extent in the years gone by, when Airborne Interception (AI) radars were not so versatile,

AWACs had not entered the scene and standoff ranges of Air-to-Air and Air-to-Ground weapons were not so large. Its viability in any future conflict would at best be questionable. The execution of this strategy is best illustrated by the chart given below which shows the proportion of various missions by the PAF during the 1971 Indo-Pak conflict.[8] It must be understood here, that air power is essentially and inherently offensive in nature. Over-emphasis on Air Defence (however offensive) is therefore contradictory to the basic ethos of air power employment.

Figure 9.2: PAF Mission Breakdown (1971 War)

Source: Air Cmde M Kaiser Tufail (Retd) *In the Ring and on its Feet* (Ferozsons Pvt Ltd, Lahore, 2018).

Considering the disproportionate effort (Figure 9.2) that the PAF is forced to devote to Air Defence; it may be pertinent to examine the kind of Air Defence setup the PAF has.

Air Defence of Pakistan

Since its creation, Pakistan's doctrines, strategies and policies have remained Indo-centric and defensive in nature and scope. To this end, Pakistan's Air Defence setup came of age in the late 1980s when it contracted Hughes and Siemens to field integrated Air Defence Control & Reporting (C&R) systems. With little geographical depth, she had no option but to adopt a forward defence posture with all her Air Defence resources. Pakistan Air Defence is a fully integrated, tri-service organisational setup and is rated to be highly efficient. The philosophy of Air Defence has thus been guided by centralised control of all Air Defence weapons.[9]

(a) Concept of area defence.
(b) Achieve air superiority over its own air space and battlefield.
(c) Main weapon likely to be aircraft.
(d) Surface to Air Missiles (SAMs) are likely to be used as inner layer of defence.
(e) In Tactical Battle Area (TBA), low flying aircraft to be engaged by SAMs and Anti-Aircraft Artillery (AAA).

The overall responsibility of the defence of Pakistan's air space is entrusted to the PAF in which it is assisted by the other two services and civil defence organisations.

Air Defence Structure

The importance of Air Defence in Pakistan's doctrine can be gauged from the fact that it has an independent Air Defence Command based at Chaklala, Rawalpindi. The organisation chart is illustrated below

Figure 9.3: PAF Air Defence Structure

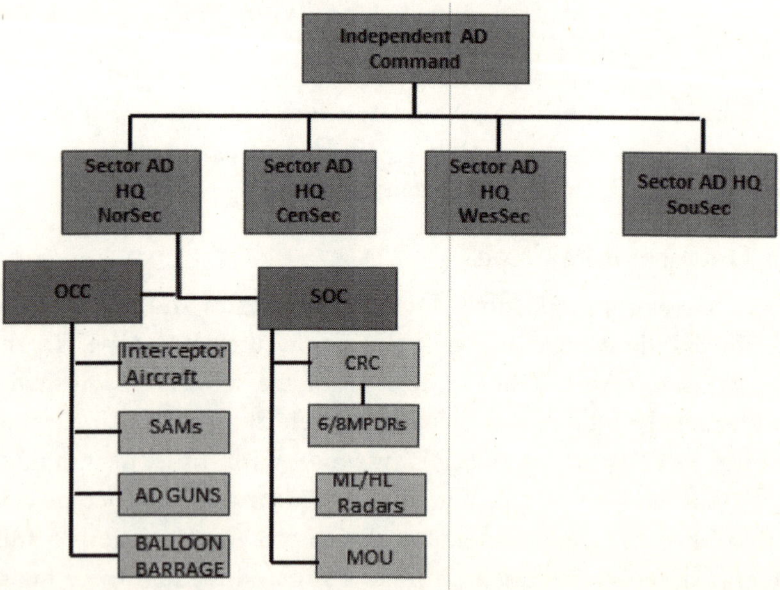

Source: Puneet Bhalla, "Pakistan's Air Defence", *Scholar Warrior*, Spring 2012, p. 78.

Although earlier, the Air Defence Command exercised control over all Air Defence assets; its present role is restricted to coordination, training and induction of new systems and the Air Defence Ground Environment System (ADGES). The operational role is with respective operational commands. There are four Sector Operations Centre (SOC) Headquarters subordinate to, and co-located with, the Air Defence Operation Centres (ADOCs). Early warning is provided in three layers. The first layer is provided by Mobile Observation Units (MOUs), followed by two layers of Mobile Pulse Doppler Radars (MPDRs) and finally AR-1/AR-15 radars providing early warning to Vital Areas (VAs) and Vital Points (VPs). The Control and Reporting Centres (CRCs) are responsible for interception of tracks picked up by the associated radars.

The Operational Control Centres (OCCs) are co-located with the SOCs (Figure 9.3). The role of the OCC is to directly control all Air Defence operations within its own area of responsibility. It is responsible for controlling and initiating tactical action on all tracks that are picked up. It exercises minute to minute control on all Air Defence weapons within its area of responsibility.

There are reports to suggest that the Crotale SAMs have been replaced by SPADA-2000 low-to-medium altitude Air Defence system consisting of radars with a range of 60 km and 4x6 cell missile launchers with ASPIDE-2000 missiles. These missiles can intercept enemy missiles and aircraft at a range of over 20 km.

Pakistan Air Force Strategic Command[10]

The Pakistan Air Force Strategic Forces Command, known as AF Strategic Command, is one of the major commands of the Pakistan Air Force. It is responsible for the Air Force elements of strategic deterrence (Pakistan's nuclear arsenal). The Command is headquartered in Islamabad and directly reports to the Chief of Air Staff (CAS), President, and the Prime Minister of Pakistan.

The unified military combat command structure is intended to give the civilian leadership a unified resource for greater understanding of specific threats to Pakistan's national and strategic assets and the means to respond to them.

History

The need for a Strategic Command was felt in the 1980s. In 1981, Israeli Air Force successfully sabotaged the Iraqi nuclear programme after conducting a successful surprise air strike on Iraqi nuclear installations at Osirak, This played a psychological role in Pakistan as it was a successful operation.

After this incident, the CAS Air Chief Marshal Anwar Shamim decided to form a unified command to protect the nuclear capabilities from outside forces. The 1980s was a decade of modernizing of the Air Force and the PAF inducted and introduced advanced jets in its weaponry. Since the 1990s, the PAF jets are believed to have practiced "toss-bombing"—a method developed by the United States Air Force to deliver nuclear weapons from fighter jets.

The Command was highly active in 1998 when the country, under the leadership of Prime Minister Nawaz Sharif, decided to carry out nuclear test operations at Chagai Hills. The Command flew the nuclear devices from Rawalpindi to Chagai and also carried scientists to the nuclear test sites. The Air Force Strategic Command is one of the most sensitive Commands of the Pakistan Air Force. The Director General, Air Force Strategic Command is also a member of the Development Committee of the Nuclear Command Authority and Chairman, Joint Chiefs of Staff Committee.

PAF in the Context of Nuclear Weapon Delivery

The PAF has had the ability to deliver nuclear bombs by fighter aircraft for a very long time. Probably the F-16s of the PAF were capable of delivering nuclear weapons by the early 1990s. This was a basic capability and was used as a temporary measure while Pakistan acquired/developed ballistic missiles. Using fighter jets for nuclear capability and having no ballistic missiles is not an ideal situation.

However, these gravity bombs and unguided nuclear bombs are a 'dumb' weapon and an unsophisticated way of delivering nuclear devices. The PAF has more recently inducted the Ra'ad Air-Launched Cruise Missile (ALCM), which has a range of 350 km. An upgraded version, the Ra'ad Mark II, has a range of 550 km and can deliver a nuclear warhead.

Pakistan developed and acquired these starting in the 1990s, and today the main burden of nuclear delivery is carried by the ballistic missile inventory and not the Air Force.

To put it into perspective, Pakistan's nuclear weapons delivery capability is as follows:

- Fighter Aircraft:
  - ☐ Unguided gravity bombs (F-16, JF-17, Mirages)
  - ☐ Ra'ad ALCM (Mirages, and JF-17 integration pending)
- Ballistic Missiles:
  - ☐ *Hatf-I*, BRBM(100 km)
  - ☐ *Nasr*, tactical BM, (70 km)
  - ☐ *Abdali-I*, SRBM (200 km)
  - ☐ *Ghaznavi*, SRBM (320 km)
  - ☐ *Shaheen-I/IA*, SRBM (750-900 km)
  - ☐ *Ghauri-I*, MRBM (1500 km)
  - ☐ *Ghauri II*, MRBM, (2000 km)
  - ☐ *Shaheen-II*, MRBM (2000 km)
  - ☐ *Shaheen-III*, MRBM (2750 km)
  - ☐ *Ababeel*, MIRV capable MRBM (2200 km)
- Cruise Missiles:
  - ☐ *Babur-I,* subsonic cruise missile (700 km)
  - ☐ *Babur-II*, upgraded CM, (750 km)
  - ☐ *Babur-III*, submarine launched or SLCM (450 km), this arguably completed the nuclear triad and allowed for second strike capability.
  - ☐ *Ra'ad-I*, ALCM (350 km)
  - ☐ *Ra'ad-II*, ALCM (550 km)
  - ☐ *Harbah*, Sea LACM (450 km)

These systems constitute a full air and ballistic missile capability, and a partial sea capability (SLCM instead of SLBM). So Pakistan has an almost complete nuclear triad. The last piece of the puzzle is the submarine launched ballistic missiles (SLBMs). Pakistan only has submarine-launched cruise missiles (SLCMs) for now.

To summarise, in terms of aerial delivery of nuclear weapons, the F-16s and JF-17s can deliver nuclear weapons, certainly via unguided bombs, and if integrated, by air-launched cruise missiles.

No. 16 and 26 Squadrons have been reported as likely to be tasked with the delivery of nuclear weapons. They were reportedly stationed at the PAF base in Masroor in early 1998. By late 1999 they had reportedly been re-deployed to Peshawar Air Force Base. This deployment however, is neither sacrosanct nor material to employment because of the role flexibility and rapid deployment potential of the aircraft. It is also certain that aircraft are not kept locked for nuclear delivery. It is assumed that certain number of aircraft would have been modified for nuclear delivery but would be in mainstream employment. They could rapidly redeploy and switch to nuclear delivery as and when required however, notwithstanding the capability of the aircraft to deliver the nuclear weapons; Pakistan's real nuclear delivery capabilities exist mostly in the form of other systems, such as Ballistic Missiles and Cruise Missiles.

Use of Air Power under Nuclear Overhang

Having seen the existence of the PAF Strategic Command and its preparedness to have aerial means of delivery of nuclear weapons, it is time to step back and take a macro view of this capability in the correct perspective. Unlike conventional weapons, nuclear weapons are generally perceived not as weapons for use but to signal a recessed, unaffordable destructive capability and hence draw imaginary lines not to crossed by the adversary. In the case

Figure 9.4: The Larger Military Objective

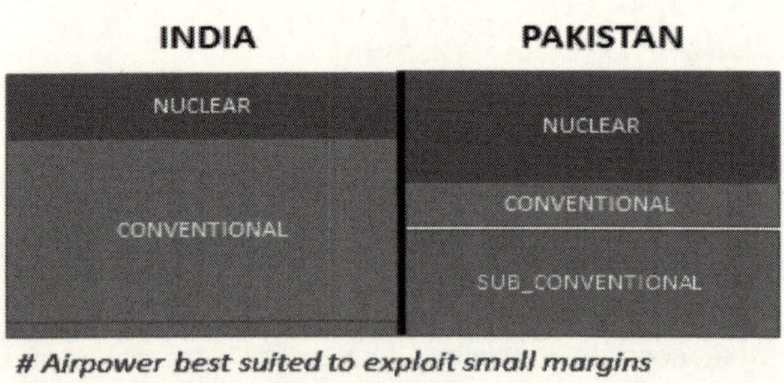

Source: A Figure created by the author to comprehend the larger military objectives of the two adversaries under the nuclear overhang. It indicates how the adversaries would like to appreciate the available window for conventional engagement.

of Pakistan, its nuclear posture is designed primarily as a deterrent against India, particularly because of its relative size and asymmetric conventional military capability. The figure above tries to explain the doctrinal military objectives.

Pakistan would like to make the sub-conventional warfare window of use as large as possible, with its stated first-use policy, lowering the nuclear threshold to the extent that the zone of conventional engagement is squeezed to a very small, risky and ambiguous area. On the other hand, India would wish to minimise/ eliminate the sub-conventional warfare zone and consequently, expand the window covering the conventional engagement in which it has an upper hand. At the top end of the spectrum, both flash a nuclear capability as an ultimate threat and deterrent. Pakistan has its stated policy of first-use as against no-first-use by India but a policy of massive retaliation if attacked.

In the geopolitical context and considering the ethical dimension of the use of sub-conventional means of warfare as a state policy, Pakistan seems to have put itself globally on the back-foot. This has given India greater flexibility for exploitation of the conventional warfare window in a certain geographical area and context, with extreme care in terms of choice of targets. The Balakot strike by the Indian Air Force (IAF) on 26 February 2019 was one such example of exploitation of this limited conventional warfare window. If this window of flexibility in conventional warfare is intelligently exploited by India and the IAF in particular, the terrain imperatives, ethical and geopolitical constraints and domestic public pressure would continue to keep Pakistan and the PAF in particular, in a continued state of dilemma and frustration in terms of choices for retaliation and response. For this to stay in a state of sustainable equilibrium, India would have to show utmost restraint and yet swift and steely resolve to decisively use that capability, when needed.

Attrition Analysis and Projection: Conventional War

The Figure 9.5 below the attrition pattern as it manifested in the 1971 Indo-Pak war. As can be noticed, the attrition percentage in air combat is nearly the same on both sides while losses to Anti-Aircraft

Figure 9.5: Attrition Analysis

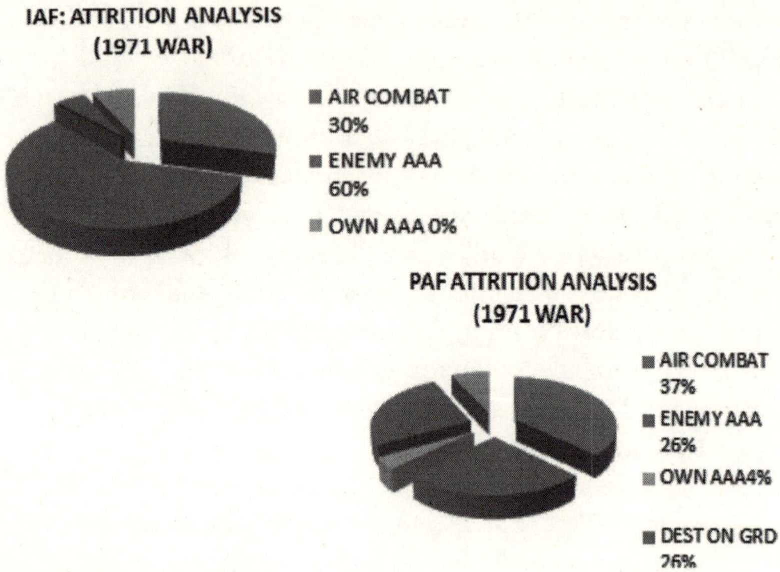

Source: Air Cmde Kaiser M Tufail (Retd), *In the Ring and on its Feet* (Ferozsons Pvt Ltd, Lahore, 2018).

Figure 9.6: AIR Attrition & AIR Superiority in Perspective

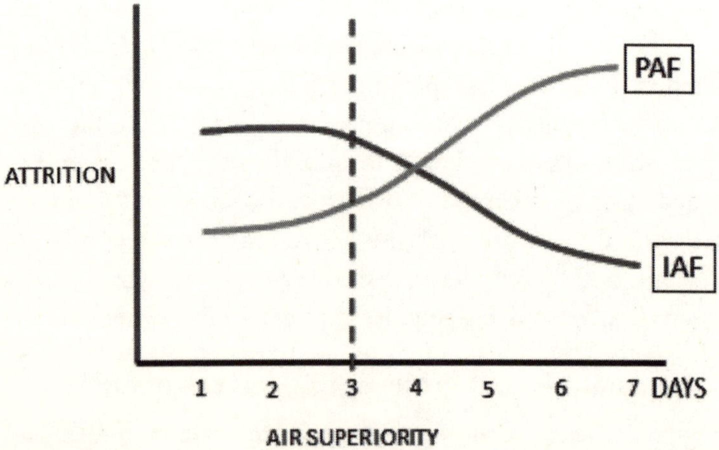

Source: A representative graph created by the author to indicate likely trend. The figures are not absolute in Figure 9.5.

Artillery (AAA) are weighed against the IAF 26:6. The reason is simple. The IAF in pursuit of air superiority carried out a much larger number of Offensive Air Strikes (OCA) in enemy territory while the PAF was largely focusing its efforts towards Defensive Counter Air (DCA). During those days all the strikes in their terminal phase used to be at low levels with very little stand-off capability and hence the vulnerability to AAA. In contrast, if a confrontation takes place now, the pattern is going to vary with air combat losses being the main contributors. Technology will play a big role in determining relative attrition. Better penetration capability is likely for the IAF with greater battle-space transparency assisted by fused data dissemination through discrete Operational Data Link (ODL) and more lethal Beyond Visual Range (BVR) missiles available with the IAF on SU30s and Mirage 2000 Upgrade (UPG). Similarly, large stand-off accurate Air-to-Ground (A/G) weapon capability will further reduce losses. On a day-wise timeline for proportionate attrition, the pattern is likely to remain the same due to unchanged IAF strategy of starting with focus on OCA (refer Figure 9.6). That would entail higher losses for the IAF in the first few days but quickly reverse as the IAF achieves air superiority. Due to the existence of BVRs, the air-to-air losses could be at larger ranges. Greater battle space transparency, speed of decision-making and decision quality data dissemination, along with extensive use of space-based sensors, electronic warfare and exploitation of media for perception management, would make any future engagement unique.

Conclusion

As discussed earlier, the biggest drawback that the PAF has is absence of geographical depth. Most of its airfields and Vital Areas (V/As) & Vital Points (V/Ps) remain within 11 minutes of flying time from its eastern borders. That certainly is inadequate time for an effective defence in ingress mode. Coupled with this is the technology-driven greater penetration capability of the IAF, battle space transparency provided by force multipliers and greater stand-off distances available for the strike aircraft for Precision Guided Munitions (PGM) and smart weapons delivery. The result would be higher attrition of the PAF aircraft and early achievement of air superiority by the IAF. Lack of depth forcing emphasis on Air Defence and the inter-se relationship between the Pakistan Army and the Air Force would force premature and disproportionate commitment of the PAF into Close Air Support (CAS). By conventional air campaign wisdom, this strategy is neither viable nor tenable. That perhaps is the reason why Pakistan keeps flashing the deployment of Tactical Nuclear Weapons (TNWs) in the Tactical Battle Area (TBA).

The internal dynamics of Pakistan's power structure and its undeniable support for the so called Jihadi movement has put the country into geopolitical isolation. As a result, its access to the global market for state-of-the-art aircraft and sensors becomes somewhat constrained and conditional. National interests and political constraints of countries like the US and France would dictate what and under what conditions they would offer state-of-the-art combat platforms to the PAF. In the foreseeable future however, China would remain a steady and all-weather supplier to the PAF. Its next fourth and at some point, fifth- generation aircraft therefore, are likely to be of Chinese origin or co-produced with China. Perhaps Russia could become another active player in the medium term. The other point to note is the faster decision cycle for the acquisition of defence equipment because of dual power centres in the polity of Pakistan. Of late, Pakistan has shown greater appreciation towards prioritising the modernisation of the PAF and the Pakistan Navy as against its usual preference for the land forces. Therefore, notwithstanding the state of Pakistan's economy, their procurement of combat aircraft and supporting assets could get disproportionate priority as per the perceived requirement.

By all accounts and experience, the pilots of the PAF are well-trained, motivated, proud and determined air warriors. Their training is well designed on a building block approach with the pinnacle for the fighter pilots being the Combat Commander's School (CCS) based at Air Force Base Sargodha.[11] The CCS is essentially a fine filter for mid-career officers, namely fighter pilots and air defence controllers and an ultimate badge of being the teeth end of the PAF for those who qualify. It also is responsible for experimenting and devising new tactics for the PAF responding to the changing tactical environment.[12] In a nut-shell, the PAF is a potent and professional arm of the Pakistan defence forces, well trained and motivated to derive the best out of any existing situation. Any engagement with the PAF will be hard-fought and high-paced. It is likely to cause high attrition on both sides. By no means is the PAF a push-over.

Notes

1. Edward V Coggins, (ed.) (2000), *Wings That Stay On,* Turner Publishing Company Padukah, Kentucky, pp. 163-164.
2. Iftikhar A Khan, "Threat to destroy Indian N-plant stopped, attack on Kahuta", *The Dawn*, 28 May 2010. M Anwar Shamim, *Cutting Edge PAF: A former Air Chief 's Reminiscences of a Developing Air Force*, Vanguard Books, Islamabad, 2010.
3. John Pyke, 'F-16 Fighting Falcon', at Globalsecurity.org. Accessed on 3 May 2020.
4. S Sajad Haider, *Flight of the Falcon*, Vanguard Books, Lahore, 2009, p. xiii.
5. https://en.m.wikipedia.org/wiki/History_of_Pakistan_Air_Force, Accessed on 10 February 2020.
6. John Fricker, *Battle for Pakistan: The Air War of 1965*, Littlehampton Book services Ltd, 1979.
7. 'Pakistan Air Force Squadrons', at Globalsecurity.org. Accessed on 2 May 2020.
8. Air Cmde M Kaiser Tufail, *In The Ring And On Its Feet*, Ferozesons (Pvt) Ltd, Lahore, p. 181.
9. Puneet Bhalla, 'Pakistan's Air Defence', *Scholar Warrior*, Spring 2012, p. 77, at https://dokumen.tips/documents/pakistans-air-defence-by-puneet-bhalla.html. Accessed on 20 April 2020.
10. https://en.wikipedia.org/wiki/Air_Force_Strategic_Command_(Pakistan). Accessed on 12 April 2020.
11. www.paf.gov.pk. Accessed on 4 May 2020.
12. http://quwa.org. Accessed on 15 April 2020.

10. Pakistan Navy: Nuclear Ambitions and Arabian Sea Security Dynamics

Vijay Sakhuja

Pakistan's ambition to acquire a sea-based nuclear deterrent has added a new dimension to the already complex and stressed South Asian security environment. It is their belief that constants of geography marked by limited strategic depth make sea-based deterrence against India important. Furthermore, the rapid naval build-up of the Indian Navy including its growing nuclear naval capability has added to Pakistan's security concerns.

This chapter presents a narrative of Pakistan's naval strategic thinking, policy formulations for the development of sea-based nuclear deterrent, and a desire to develop nuclear strike capability 'from the sea' through a hybrid naval platform. The chapter begins by providing a brief overview of the primacy of submarines in Pakistan's naval thought and planning, sources of submarine acquisition, and deployment of submarines during the 1965 and 1971 India-Pakistan wars. Further, an attempt is made in the chapter to highlight naval nuclear dynamics in the Arabian Sea involving regional powers and the established nuclear powers.

Primacy of Submarines in Naval Thought

After the bifurcation of the Indian Navy by the Armed Forces Reconstitution Committee (AFRC) in 1947, a motley collection of ships were handed over by the British to the Pakistan Navy in the ratio of 2(India):1(Pakistan).[1] The primary responsibility of the then Pakistan Navy was to protect shipping lanes and safeguard sea-borne trade.[2] It was quite clear in the minds of the naval planners that the country was unlikely to go to war, but in case of a war with India, the political leadership would seek support from friendly countries and challenge the adversary. Further, if the country was to be involved in a limited war, the Pakistan Navy would carry out the task by itself.[3]

Another important facet of Pakistani naval thinking was embedded in the belief that a submarine is the optimal platform for countries with limited naval power for use against a superior force. It was thus decided to focus on submarines and anti-submarine warfare platforms. Furthermore, these would act as force multipliers and early warning assets for detecting enemy surface ships and submarines.

Pakistan approached the UK, with whom it still had strong naval contacts, but they were constrained due to issues of export, as much of the British equipment had US parts and assemblies. In 1954, Pakistan was a beneficiary of US military aid under the Mutual Defense Assistance Agreement (MDAA) and subsequently joined as a member of the SEATO and CENTO.[4] Its role in the context of NATO strategy was also assessed[5] and "Pakistani naval planners began to mirror most things American as they learned to adapt to US naval hardware and operate in the framework of Western alliance strategy. The Pakistan Navy even contemplated following the American force structure model centered on the aircraft carrier."[6] Several naval platforms originating both in the US and the UK (these were paid for by the US) under the MDAA were inducted into the Pakistan Navy. Among these, a Trench-class diesel-electric fast-attack submarine the *USS Diablo* was given on a four-year lease and was commissioned in the Pakistan Navy as *PNS Ghazi* in 1964.[7]

The Pakistan Navy was also scouting other sources for submarines and in 1963, it approached France for Daphne-class submarines and Atlantique maritime patrol aircraft[8] and these were supplied. The UN embargo on military sales to South Africa resulted in a surplus of Agosta-class submarines with the French and Pakistan did not miss the opportunity and the contract was finally signed in 1966.[9]

PNS Ghazi took part in the India-Pakistan War of 1965 and was deployed outside Bombay harbour to bottle-up the Indian Navy. Vice-Admiral Tasneem (then second in command of *Ghazi*) has recorded that at the commencement of hostilities, the submarine was off Bombay to attack any Indian warship,[10] and other forces were employed in a defensive role along the coastline. Thus, the belief that submarines are the most suitable platforms for countries with limited naval power for use against a superior force, paid off. The primacy of submarines in Pakistan's naval thought was vindicated.[11]

The Pakistan Navy replicated its 1965 strategy of 'offensive defence' in the 1971 India-Pakistan war, although it had distinct advantages in terms of underwater platforms, i.e., four submarines and six midgets. Three Daphne-class submarines patrolled in areas off the west coast of India, and *PNS Ghazi* was dispatched to the Bay of Bengal to attack INS Vikrant; however, the submarine was sunk by the Indian Navy off Vishakhapatnam.[12]

Likewise, Atlantique maritime patrol aircraft from France and later P3C Orion long-range maritime patrol aircraft from the US provided the Pakistan Navy a distinct edge over the Indian Navy. In fact, the Pakistan Navy can be credited as the front runner in acquiring submarines and long-range maritime patrol aircraft in South Asia and putting it to use in both the wars with India.

In 2016, Pakistan placed orders for eight S20 diesel-electric submarines from China. These are based on the Yuan-class (Type 039A-series) design and four of these are under construction in China by the China Shipbuilding Industry Corporation (CSIC) and are likely to be delivered by 2022.[13] The remaining four will be constructed in Pakistan by the Karachi Shipbuilding and Engineering Works (KSEW), and are planned to be delivered by 2028.

Classic to Hybrid: Quest for Nuclear Submarine

The desire to acquire of nuclear submarines has resonated in Pakistan since the time the country came into being in 1947. Pakistan Navy planners were of the belief that nuclear weapons at sea when deployed in a tactical role could be game changers.[14] Many years later, Admiral Sirohey, the then Pakistan Navy Chief, made reference to nuclear submarines in Pakistan's naval thinking and expressed the desire for acquisition of nuclear submarines.[15] He even had plans to train about 200 naval personnel for its operations.[16]

Pakistan approached some countries for possible acquisition of an SSN (Submersible Ship Nuclear)[17] and contacted Canada in 1988 for nuclear technical assistance. By 1990, Islamabad had made inquiries with several other sources[18] including China for possible sale of *Han*-class nuclear submarines.[19] In May 1999, the Pakistan Navy was 'assigned a nuclear role' and in 2012 it constituted a 'Strategic Directorate' at the Naval Headquarters[20] to control shore-based fixed and mobile missiles.

Senior Pakistani naval officers have often argued that a sea-based nuclear capability would provide the Pakistan Navy power projection capability as also counter Indian sea-based nuclear weapon capability. For instance, Admiral Abdul Aziz Mirza, former Chief of Naval Staff, noted that "Any country that has developed a nuclear capability has to then think of the delivery system ... it is obvious that anyone who has that capability will consider a sea-based system along with land-based and aircraft-launched nuclear weapons that form the traditional nuclear triad. It's logical to at least consider sea-basing those weapons". Pakistan was only developing conventional capabilities and not entering into an arms race due to budgetary constraints ($400 million) and preferred "deterrence in certain areas—selective deterrence".[21] In 2001, at a press briefing after the culmination of the annual naval exercise *Seaspark-2001*, Rear Admiral Mohammad Afzal Tahir, the Deputy Chief of Naval Staff (operations) announced that the Pakistan Navy was thinking of equipping its submarines with nuclear missiles for defensive purposes.[22]

In 2012, media reports were rife about Pakistan acquiring a *Han*-class SSN on lease from China and that a Pakistani delegation had rushed to China after India acquired the *INS Chakra* on lease. It was noted that "Pakistan wants to acquire a submarine, initially may be on lease and then build its own one with Chinese help."[23]

However, an Indian commentator was sceptical of Pakistan getting a Chinese nuclear submarine on two counts; "first China itself doesn't have enough to spare one, as their *Han*-class have been unsuccessful and *Jin*-class is under production. Second, Pakistan cannot build a nuclear capability on its own unless China gives it to them. If China does so, it might prove to be too big a transaction for which it will get hostile world opinion."[24]

Since the Pakistan government did not encourage or plan to either build or acquire a nuclear submarine, the Pakistan Navy explored the possibility of fitting nuclear warheads on land attack cruise missiles (LACM) which could be fired from Air Independent Propulsion (AIP) fitted submarines, probably inspired by the Israeli experience (discussed in detail later in the chapter). An Agosta 90B submarine fitted with AIP or a Chinese Yuan-class with AIP can be modified to provide Pakistan a hybrid platform to serve as a sea-based nuclear deterrent. This approach has been labelled as the 'poor man's second strike capability".[25]

It is widely known that torpedo tube-launched nuclear missile capability is a very complex technological achievement; however the Pakistan Navy is striving hard to acquire this capability. This could prove to be a challenge for the Indian Navy, given that the Indian Ocean waters are notorious for unfavourable submarine operations due to high salinity and temperature and other vital bathymetric and hydrological underwater data available to both the navies.

It is also not beyond the realm of possibility, especially with technical help from China, that Pakistan may miniaturise and marry a LACM with a small nuclear warhead. In this context, a claim by Pakistani nuclear scientist Samar Mubarik Mund, who led the team that conducted six successful nuclear tests in May 1998 merits attention, Mund has noted that Pakistan has a "more effective and better" nuclear-powered submarine technology which it developed in 2017."[26]

In December 2017, the Pakistan Navy test-fired *Babur-3*, a Submarine-Launched Cruise Missile (SLCM) with a range of 450 km[27] from an undisclosed location in the Indian Ocean using an underwater mobile platform and reportedly hit the target with accuracy. *Babur-3* SLCM is a variant of *Babur-2* Ground-Launched Cruise Missile (GLCM) and "incorporates state-of-the-art technologies including underwater-controlled propulsion and advanced guidance and navigation features, duly augmented by Global Navigation, Terrain and Scene Matching Systems. The missile features terrain-hugging and sea-skimming flight capabilities to evade hostile radars and air defences, in addition to certain stealth technologies, in an emerging regional Ballistic Missile Defence (BMD) environment".[28]

The commissioning of the nuclear submarine *INS Arihant*, by India has added uncertainty in the minds of Pakistani leadership. In February 2019, Prime Minister Imran Khan convened the National Command Authority (NCA) and the press release stated:

> "NCA took note of the growing conventional and strategic weapons' development in the region. It expressed serious concerns over the adverse ramifications for peace and security on this account. NCA reiterated its determination to take all possible measures to make national security robust; enabling it to effectively respond to the threats to national security without indulging in arms race. Reiterating that nuclear deterrence is the factor of stability in South Asia, NCA expressed the resolve to maintain 'Full Spectrum Deterrence,' in line with the policy of Credible Minimum Deterrence."[29]

There is visible urgency among Pakistani naval planners to develop a powerful submarine force which should include a 'nuclear deterrent at sea' given that "strategic equilibrium in the western Indian Ocean has shifted decisively in India's favour." A Pakistani commentator has noted that the Indian Navy's "carrier force will be backed by five to six Arihant-class nuclear submarines".[30]

Nuclear Submarine Deployments in Arabian Sea

The Arabian Sea is not new to nuclear-propelled underwater platforms and all five nuclear powers have operated SSBNs/SSNs in these waters. During the Cold War, the US and Soviet nuclear submarines shadowed each other in the Indian Ocean.[31] In the case of the former, the US Task Force 74, which apparently included a nuclear submarine, was dispatched in 1971 to coerce India to stop the war against Pakistan (modern-day Bangladesh) by surrounding "India from all four sides and force them to retreat and leave East Pakistan". The Soviet Union, having vetoed a UN Security Council Resolution introduced by the US, directed its forces which included nuclear submarines, to the Indian Ocean and the Soviet Navy Commander ordered to "lift the submarines and bring them to the surface so that it can be pictured by the American spy satellites or can be seen by the American Navy!' It was done to demonstrate, that we had all the needed things in [the] Indian Ocean, including the nuclear submarines."[32]

In recent times, the US and British nuclear submarines were deployed in the Arabian Sea to hit targets deep in the heartland in Iraq in support of *Operation Iraqi Freedom* and against terrorist targets in Afghanistan under *Operation Enduring Freedom*. Three US Navy ships and submarine *Providence* (SSN-719) had fired as many as 80 Tomahawks.[33] They were joined by the British Royal Navy nuclear-powered submarines *HMS Triumph* and *HMS Trafalgar*, deployed in the Arabian Sea which also fired at targets in Afghanistan.[34]

The French Navy maintains a continuous at-sea deterrent posture by its submarines [35] which are part of the French naval task force.[36] They also operate with the US Navy and the British Royal Navy in the Arabian Sea/Indian Ocean in support of *Operation Inherent Resolve* under a tripartite agreement between the three navies.[37] The French nuclear submarines also carry out exercises in the Arabian Sea with other friendly navies such as India.[38]

In recent times, China has begun to deploy nuclear submarines in the Indian Ocean. For instance, a Type-093 attack nuclear submarine was deployed in the Indian Ocean during December 2013 to February 2014.[39] In 2018, at a press conference, the Indian Navy Chief stated that the PLA Navy submarine deployments in the IOR, which started in 2013, had become regular and annually, two deployments of three months duration had been observed.[40] Further, "they alternate between a conventional boat [submarine] followed by a SSN (nuclear-powered attack submarine) and there has been no change in this pattern."

Naval Nuclear Capability of Arabian Sea Littorals

By the end of the lease period of *INS Chakra*, the Indian Navy had gained good knowledge and sufficient proficiency to operate and maintain such platforms. This led to doctrinal conceptualization, refinement of the indigenous design and above all, the ability to showcase that the country could operate technically sophisticated sea-based platforms. It helped formulate a nuclear strategy that has led to a good understanding of the role of sea-based nuclear weapons in national nuclear strategy.

In 2012, India again acquired on lease an Akula II-class attack nuclear submarine on lease for 10 years from Russia and named this also as *INS Chakra*. The submarine was returned approximately ten months prior to the expiry of her ten-year lease. Under the indigenous nuclear submarine programme, in 2009, India launched the 6000-tonne *INS Arihant* which has now been commissioned. It is capable of firing 700-kilometre-range nuclear-tipped SLBM (submarine-launched ballistic missiles) developed indigenously by the Defence Research and Development Organisation (DRDO) and the Defence Research and Development Laboratory (DRDL). India plans to build 3-4 such platforms.

Iran

Iran's naval inventory includes a variety of underwater platforms including three Russian Kilo-class submarines, three indigenously-built submarines, presumably a version of North Korean submarines, and mini submarines. In June 2012, Iran announced that it had drawn plans to build nuclear submarines. According to Iranian Navy sources, "Initial steps to design and build nuclear submarine propulsion systems have begun" and that "All countries have the right to use peaceful nuclear technology, including for the propulsion system of its vessels."[41] Meanwhile, Iran's parliamentary committee approved a bill urging the government to 'design nuclear-powered merchant ships' to overcome sanctions to avoid refuelling. It can serve as a 'justification for producing weapons-grade 90 per cent enriched uranium.'[42]

In 2013, the Iranian Atomic Energy Organisation was quoted saying that "At present, we have no enrichment plan for purity levels above 20 percent, but when it comes to certain needs, for example, for some ships and submarines, if our researchers need to have a stronger underwater presence, we will have to make small engines which should be fuelled by 45 to 56 percent enriched uranium".[43]

In February 2019, Iran launched a 600-tonne submarine and Rear Admiral Hossein Khanzadi, commander of the Iranian Navy announced that "*Fateh* submarine was a leap in building submarines and it completed the defensive chain of our country below waters."[44] The submarine is reported to possess "surface-to-surface systems, torpedo launcher, advanced sonar, electrically-powered propulsion, battle management systems, integrated electronic security and communications technology."[45]

Although there is a strong naval nuclear ambition in Iran, building nuclear submarines or launching nuclear tipped missiles from underwater platforms, requires a strong technological base and a highly trained human resource with appropriate skill sets. Iran is also attempting to exploit the geography of the Gulf waters that are shallow and murky and present enormous operational challenges to foreign nuclear submarines.

Israel

Israel acquired three Howaldtswerke-Deutsche Werft (HDW)-built Dolphin-class submarines (displacement [submerged] 1,900 tonnes; 57-metre long) from Germany. These are fitted with 'six regular tubes for firing 533-millimetre DM2A4 heavyweight fiber-optic-guided torpedoes and Harpoon anti-ship missiles—as well as four 650-millimetre mega-sized tubes, which are rare in modern submarines.'[46] In 2012, the German Newspaper, *Dar Spiegel* disclosed that according to an official of the German government with knowledge of the matter, "From the beginning, the boats were primarily used for the purposes of nuclear capability".[47]Apparently, Popeye Turbo type missiles with a range of around 1,500 km can fit into the expanded sized tubes in the submarine and may even have a miniaturised nuclear warhead.

In June 2009, it was reported that an Israeli submarine sailed through the Suez Canal for the Arabian Sea, prompting speculations that the Israeli Navy may be planning deployment in the Arabian Sea to respond to any adventures by Iran. According to an Israeli military analyst, "The Obama administration should note with satisfaction the passage of an Israeli submarine through the Suez Canal and see it as proof that its efforts to bring regional cooperation to fend off the Iranian threat are beginning to bear fruit."[48]

Reports originating in the US indicated that an Israeli submarine had operated in the Indian Ocean in 2000 and may have even conducted missile firing tests; 'the US Navy observed Israeli missile tests in the Indian Ocean in 2000, and that the Dolphin-class vessels have been fitted with nuclear-capable cruise missiles of a new design'.[49] Further, in October 2003, it reported that 'Israel had successfully modified nuclear warheads to fit its *Harpoon* missiles.'[50]

Arabian Sea Security

India-Pakistan and Iran-Israel represent two distinct security complexes, i.e., South Asia and Middle East or West Asia; yet, their nuclear plans and related developments shape the Arabian Sea security. There are at least four dynamics for the Arabian Sea that are noteworthy. First, Pakistan has unwaveringly endeavoured to match up to India's conventional military power which has been an unsuccessful pursuit till now. This conventional asymmetry encouraged Pakistan to pursue its nuclear weapons programme and Prime Minister Bhutto told the people of Pakistan: "If India builds the bomb, we will eat grass or leaves, even go hungry, but we will get one of our own. We have no alternative."[51] This appears to be the guiding principle for the development of submarines which should be able to carry a nuclear warhead. Pakistan believes that it can achieve nuclear deterrence at sea if not equal to, then at least similar to India, by building/acquiring hybrid naval platform to counter the naval nuclear advantage enjoyed by India.

Second, Iranian threat perceptions are driven by Israel's undeclared nuclear capability. In his address to the 62nd Annual Session of the IAEA General Conference in Vienna in 2018, Kazem Gharibabadi, the Iranian ambassador and permanent representative to the International Atomic Energy Agency (IAEA) 'pointed to the Israeli regime's nuclear weapons and its threatening behaviour towards its neighbours in the Middle East, urging the international community to pressure the regime into joining the NPT as an urgent necessity' and expressed concerns over the "lack of political will" among regional states.[52]

Third, Israel is unsure of Iran rolling back its nuclear programme and according to a former Israeli army chief of staff, "the possibility of a military strike against a nuclear Iran, remain relevant".[53] Further, Israel is concerned about Iranian support for the Hamas group which has regularly conducted attacks against the Israeli military.[54] In March 2019, Prime Minister Benjamin Netanyahu warned the Hezbollah that "Israel will continue to do all that's necessary to defend itself. We will continue to use all means, overt and covert, to block Iran's effort to use Syria, Lebanon and Gaza as forward bases for attacking Israel."[55]

Fourth, the GCC countries are worried about Iran's desire to acquire nuclear capability which would impact on the regional balance of power. Saudi Arabia is perhaps most concerned about Iran's nuclear weapons programme. For instance, according to the former Saudi Intelligence Chief, Turki: "if our efforts, and the efforts of the world community, fail to convince Israel to shed its weapons of mass destruction and to prevent Iran from obtaining similar weapons, we must, as a duty to our country and people, look into all options we are given, including obtaining these weapons ourselves."[56] In 2015, it was noted "Saudi Arabia has been periodically dropping hints that, should Iran's nuclear ambitions go unchecked, it might just have to get nuclear weapons itself".[57]

This is despite the fact that Saudi Arabia had supported Pakistan's nuclear weapon programme through financial aid. A former US defence official observed that, "there has been a longstanding agreement in place with the Pakistanis and the House of Saud has now made the strategic decision to move forward."[58]

Middle East Nuclear Weapons Free Zone

The foregoing nuclear dynamics in the Arabian Sea merit discussion from the perspective of the Middle East Nuclear Weapons Free Zone (MENWFZ). Very briefly, the MENWFZ was first proposed by Iran in 1974, supported by Egypt and includes the territories of all League of Arab states, Iran and Israel. Further, in 1995, a UN Resolution proposed that the Middle East region be free of nuclear and other weapons of mass destruction. Israel has argued that so long as all countries in the region do not publicly recognize and accept it as an integral part of the region, it cannot think of being part of the MENWFZ. There have been calls to include Afghanistan, Pakistan and Turkey in the ambit of MENWFZ, which is still a distant dream. Under the circumstances, north Arabian Sea may emerge as an arena of naval confrontation with a strong nuclear element.

Concluding Remarks

The Pakistan Navy has given primacy to submarines as the main instruments of waging war at sea which is best demonstrated by the fact that these platforms have supported its offensive sea-denial strategy and posed a major threat to the Indian Navy. Furthermore, the Pakistan Navy continues to arm these platforms with sophisticated weaponry and also hopes to 'nuclear tip' land attack cruise missiles. These would provide, if not parity, then deterrence against the fast growing and nuclear-capable Indian Navy.

The Pakistan Navy has internalised the 'offensive sea denial' strategy, a decision which was proven and continues to prevail in Pakistani naval thinking. The offensive component of the strategy aims at attacking high-value enemy naval platforms and destroying key transportation and military facilities, thereby placing the enemy on the defensive. This is now being supplemented by sea-based naval nuclear capability which is under development. It is a natural and a logical choice from the Pakistani perspective, given that the Indian

Navy has grown over the years and has now embarked on a credible second-strike capability with sea-based nuclear platforms.

China can emerge as the primary source of naval hardware particularly submarines, and the PLA Navy the major operational partner for the Pakistan Navy. It may even lease a *Han*-class SSN for training, assist in miniaturising a nuclear warhead and help in marrying it with the land attack cruise missiles. These developments are sure to invite international concern and adversely impact on the security environment in the Arabian Sea, that is already highly unstable.

Notes

1. Jaswant Singh, *Defending India*, Macmillan Press, London, 1999, p. 113.
2. Pakistan Navy Historical Section, *Story of Pakistan Navy, 1947-72,* Elite Publishers, Islamabad, 1991, p. 79.
3. Ibid., p. 109.
4. Murad Ali, 'U.S. Aid to Pakistan during the Tenures of Democrat and Republican Administrations', *IPRI Journal* XVI, No. 2 (Summer 2016): 31-48. Under para 2 of MDA Article I, "The Government of Pakistan will use this assistance exclusively to maintain its internal security, its legitimate self defence, or to permit it to participate in the defence of the area, or in United Nations collective security arrangements and measures, and Pakistan will not undertake any act of aggression against any other nation. The Government of Pakistan will not, without the prior agreement of the Government of the United States, devote such assistance to purposes other than those for which it was furnished."
5. Vijay Sakhuja, 'Pakistan's Naval strategy: Past and future', *Strategic Analysis*, Volume 26, Issue 4, 2002, pp. 493-507.
6. Ibid.
7. 'Submarine Force', at https://www.paknavy.gov.pk/submarine_Force.html. Accessed on 12 April 2019.
8. Pakistan Navy Historical Section, n. 2, p. 209.
9. Ibid.
10. A H Amin, 'Remembering our Warriors: Vice Admiral Tasneem', at http://www.defencejournal.com/2001/may/tasneem.htm. Accessed on 14 April 2019.
11. Vijay Sakhuja, n. 5.
12. Ibid.

13. 'Pakistan Navy modernises Submarine capabilities', at https://asianmilitaryreview.com/2018/11/pakistan-navy-modernises-submarine-capabilities/. Accessed on 12 April 2019.
14. Pakistan Navy Historical Section, n. 2, p. 110.
15. A. Siddiqa-Agha, *Pakistan's Arms Procurement and Military Buildup, 1979-99: In Search of a Policy,* Palgrave, New York, 2001, p. 158.
16. Ibid.
17. Ayesha Siddiqa-Agha, 'Nuclear Navies', *The Bulletin of the Atomic Scientists*, Vol. 56, No.5, September/October 2000, p. 13.
18. A. Siddiqa-Agha, n. 15.
19. Discussions with Indian naval experts.
20. Iskander Rehman, 'Murky Waters: Naval Nuclear Dynamics in the Indian Ocean', at https://carnegieendowment.org/2015/03/09/murky-waters-naval-nuclear-dynamics-in-indian-ocean-pub-59279. Accessed on 16 April 2019.
21. 'Pak should Think of basing nuclear arms at sea: Navy Chief', at https://www.rediff.com/news/2002/jul/31pak1.htm. Accessed on 10 April 2019.
22. Vijay Sakhuja, 'Pakistan Navy and Nuclear Deterrence', at https://ipcs.org/comm_select.php?articleNo=844. Accessed on 5 April 2019.
23. Suman Sharma, 'Pakistan wants Chinese N-sub to counter India', at http://www.sunday-guardian.com/investigation/pakistan-wants-chinese-n-sub-to-counter-india. Accessed on 12 January 2019.
24. Ibid.
25. Tyler Rogoway, 'Pakistan Closer To Nuclear Second-Strike Capability After Sub Missile Test', at https://www.thedrive.com/author/tyler-rogoway. Accessed on 12 April 2019.
26. 'India's nuclear submarine could trigger arms race', at https://www.aa.com.tr/en/asia-pacific/indias-nuclear-submarine-could-trigger-arms-race/1307489. Accessed on 12 April 2019.
27. 'Pakistan conducts first test of submarine-launched cruise missile', at https://www.hindustantimes.com/world-news/pakistan-conducts-first-test-of-submarine-launched-cruise-missile/story-JLSf2adSnvkYpm6rnzUPGJ.html. Accessed on 15 April 2019.
28. 'Pakistan launches first submarine-launched cruise missile Babur-3', at https://defence.pk/pdf/threads/pakistan-successfully-testedbabur-3-cruise-missile-launch-from-submarine-ispr.471649/page-5#ixzz4VI2gdZwA. Accessed on 15 April 2019.
29. 'The "developing strategic depth" and "full spectrum deterrence"', at https://www.thenews.com.pk/print/169366-The-developing-strategic-depth-and-full-spectrum-deterrence. Accessed on 24 April 2019.
30. Ibid.

31. Amnon Sella, *Soviet Political and Military Conduct in the Middle East,* Macmillan Press, London, 1981, p. 57.
32. Sanskar Shrivastava '1971 India Pakistan War: Role of Russia, China, America and Britain', at https://www.theworldreporter.com/2011/10/1971-india-pakistan-war-role-of-russia.html#ixzz1ycKDW6pa. Accessed on 24 April 2019.
33. Gregory Bereiter, 'The US Navy in Operation Enduring Freedom, 2001-2002', at https://www.history.navy.mil/research/library/online-reading-room/title-list-alphabetically/u/us-navy-operation-enduring-freedom-2001-2002.html. Accessed on 24 April 2019.
34. Richard Norton-Taylor, 'Missiles fired from British subs', at https://www.theguardian.com/world/2001/oct/08/september11.afghanistan. Accessed on 24 April 2019.
35. Hans M. Kristensen and Matt Korda, 'French nuclear forces, 2019', at https://thebulletin.org/2019/01/french-nuclear-forces-2019/. Accessed on 12 April 2019.
36. 'French aircraft carrier gets underway for first deployment since 2016', at https://navaltoday.com/2019/03/05/french-aircraft-carrier-gets-underway-for-first-deployment-since-2016/. Accessed on 24 April 2019.
37. 'UK, France, US Sign Trilateral Submarine Agreement', at https://www.navy.mil/submit/display.asp?story_id=100844. Accessed on 24 April 2019. The chiefs of the three navies have noted that they are committed to enhanced interoperability; Vice Adm. Louis-Michel Guillaume, commander, French Submarine and Strategic Oceanic Forces (ALFOST) commented "We thus will have right away in the 5th Fleet area of operations a high-level basis of cooperation to improve our operational results in undersea warfare," and Commander, U.S. Naval Forces Central Command (NAVCENT) Vice Adm. Kevin M. Donegan has stated that the agreement is "a practical framework on how we will operate in the 5th Fleet area of operations when it comes to coordinating anti-submarine warfare operations ... agreement lays the groundwork for executing more operations together and enhancing cooperation in the undersea domain."
38. 'Indo-French naval exercises "Varuna 2018" kick-off at MPT', at https://timesofindia.indiatimes.com/city/goa/indo-french-naval-exercises-varuna-2018-kick-off-at-mpt/articleshow/63372658.cms. Accessed on 26 April 2019.
39. Vijay Sakhuja, 'Chinese Submarines Taste Indian Ocean', at http://cimsec.org/chinese-submarines-taste-indian-ocean/13257. Accessed on 24 April 2019.
40. ShauryaKaranbir Gurung, '14 Chinese navy ships spotted in Indian Ocean, Indian Navy monitoring locations', at https://economictimes.indiatimes.com/news/defence/14-chinese-navy-

ships-spotted-in-indian-ocean-indian-navy-monitoring-locations/articleshow/61882634.cms?from=mdr. Accessed on 24 April 2019.

41. 'Iran "designing nuclear submarine"', at https://www.telegraph.co.uk/news/worldnews/middleeast/iran/9326126/Iran-designing-nuclear-submarine.html. Accessed on 18 April 2019.
42. 'Iranian parliament to consider nuclear powered ships', at https://www.timesofisrael.com/iranian-parliament-to-consider-nuclear-submarine/. Accessed on 17 April 2019.
43. Zachary Keck, 'Iran's Nuclear Submarine Gambit', at https://thediplomat.com/2013/04/irans-nuclear-submarine-gambit/. Accessed on 17 April 2019.
44. Allen Cone, 'Iran unveils submarine that can launch cruise missiles', at https://www.upi.com/Defense-News/2019/02/19/Iran-unveils-submarine-that-can-launch-cruise-missiles/9491550588008/. Accessed on 17 April 2019.
45. Ibid.
46. Sebastien Roblin, 'Israel Might Have as Many as 300 Nuclear Weapons. And Some Are in the "Ocean"', at https://nationalinterest.org/blog/buzz/israel-might-have-many-300-nuclear-weapons-and-some-are-ocean-27011. Accessed on 14 April 2019.
47. 'Israel's Deployment of Nuclear Missiles on Subs from Germany', at https://www.spiegel.de/international/world/israel-deploys-nuclear-weapons-on-german-built-submarines-a-836784.html. Accessed on 14 April 2019.
48. Batsheva Sobelman, 'Israeli warships' use of Suez Canal causes a stir', at https://www.latimes.com/archives/la-xpm-2009-jul-24-fg-suez-warships24-story.html. Accessed on 14 April 2019.
49. 'Israel Submarine Capabilities', at https://www.nti.org/analysis/articles/israel-submarine-capabilities/. Accessed on 14 April 2019.
50. Ibid.
51. 'Pakistan, India and The Bomb', at https://www.nytimes.com/1979/07/01/archives/foreign-affairs-pakistan-india-and-the-bomb.html. Accessed on 14 April 2019.
52. 'Iran says world must pressure Israel into joining NPT', at https://www.presstv.com/Detail/2018/09/21/574749/Iran-Israel-join-npt. Accessed on 14 April 2019.
53. 'Ashkenazi denies blocking Israeli strike on Iran, says option still on the table', at https://www.timesofisrael.com/ashkenazi-denies-blocking-israeli-strike-on-iran-says-option-still-on-the-table/. Accessed on 14 April 2019.
54. Yaakov Lappin, 'Naval arms race between Israel and Hamas picks up steam', at https://www.jns.org/naval-arms-race-between-israel-and-hamas-picks-up-steam/. Accessed on 14 April 2019.

55. 'Israel-Iran exchange threats of aggression', at https://www.tv7israelnews.com/israel-iran-exchange-threats-of-aggression/. Accessed on 14 April 2019.
56. 'Saudi Prince Turki urges nuclear option after Iran', at https://www.reuters.com/article/nuclear-saudi-idAFL5E7N62G920111206. Accessed on 14 April 2019.
57. Fareed Zakaria, 'Why Saudi Arabia Can't get a Nuclear Weapon', *The Washington Post*, 11 June 2015.
58. Rick Moran, 'Saudis in Talks with Pakistan to Purchase Nuclear Weapons', at http://www.americanthinker.com/blog/2015/05/great_news_saudis_in_talks_with_pakistan_to_purchase_nuclear_weapons.html. Accessed on 30 July 2015.

SECTION 3

The Nuclear Dimensions

11. Pakistan's Nuclear Grand Strategy

Rajiv Nayan

An oft-repeated question for each nuclear weapon country is: Does it have a grand strategy? If the answer is in the affirmative, the follow-up question that comes up, is: what is its grand strategy? Like most of the terms in social sciences, the security/strategic studies struggle to provide a precise definition or a set of fixed contours for strategy and quite naturally, for grand strategy. As articulated by a leading writer on the subject, the term is "terra incognita—still awaiting exploration, and understanding".[1] Most writers on the subject do not find any difference between strategy and grand strategy, though another set of writers project grand strategy as 'higher strategy'.[2] There is a general understanding that a universal grand strategy, which all the nations adopt or ought to adopt to promote their national interests with given resources, is not feasible.

Notwithstanding the differences among the nations and writers on the subject, an understanding has evolved over 'a set of core approaches'[3] and broad features of what is dubbed as a grand strategy of a country. A grand strategy is expected to provide cohesion to a country's policy. The grand strategy of a nation or a group of nations guides the political goal or military objective of the country or the group as well as the linking of the objective(s) and required resources. A grand strategy is supposed to give a sense or 'general framework for foreign policy'. Although, of late, strategy has become all-pervasive, used in almost all walks of life, yet predominantly, grand strategy is associated with security and external use of force. It is associated with both war and peace. Thus, grand strategy in IR/ security studies has a wider meaning: from military-related foreign policy to theory and practice of statecraft,[4] to military strategy.

What is nuclear-armed Pakistan's grand strategy: Strategic superiority or parity with India or strategic dominance in its neighbourhood? As nuclear weapons constitute the arsenal of the Pakistan armed forces and Pakistan's anomalous civil-military relationship has been shaping its nuclear weapons strategy from the very beginning, the Pakistani plan to acquire nuclear weapons has led it to devise a unique strategy. Pakistan's acquisition of nuclear weapons is not without any objective and it has a strategy to mobilise resources or means for its acquisition. Keeping the focus on India may help it in the mobilisation of resources and providing the legitimacy to its nuclear bomb in the country and to an extent outside, but the grand strategy of Pakistan's nuclear weapon seems to be, establishing it as a custodian of the Islamic Civilisation, which may facilitate its hegemony over a broad region comprising South, Central and West Asia.

Objectives of Nuclear Weapons

Geopolitical manoeuvre and Survival

What is the real objective of Pakistan's nuclear weapons? Is it to ensure Pakistan's survival? Predominantly, the Pakistani discourse makes the world believe that Pakistan had tried to acquire nuclear weapons for its security, basically to resist external aggression. For its security and survival, it lays claim to several diplomatic experiments. Playing the victim card, Pakistan tells the world that it had sought a nuclear umbrella from the United States (US) but it was not forthcoming. In an interview, Agha Shahi, the former Foreign Secretary of Pakistan, said that despite knowing fully well that the West would not oblige, yet Zulfikar Bhutto had sent Sahabzada Yakub Ali Khan for the nuclear umbrella to the US.[5] However, declassified American documents indicate otherwise. Apparently, the West offered Pakistan a nuclear protective umbrella[6] but it rejected it because it had a plan to manufacture its own nuclear weapons.

Pakistan had signed military pacts with the Western bloc during the Cold War. It entered into a complex relationship with China, based on converging strategic interests, which is now being touted as a time-tested friend. Pakistan fully exploited the period of détente, in which the bipolar world saw some shifts, and China came closer to the Western bloc. The change in the global order suited Pakistan the most; its balancing act between the West and China became easier. However, the Pakistani ruling establishment did not find any security- diplomatic arrangement satisfactory to its needs.

Had the objective been achieving security of the nation, it would have gone in for the American security umbrella. The Western bloc could have extended it to a country that had signed military pacts such as the Baghdad Treaty and South East Asia Treaty Organisation (SEATO). Although Pakistan camouflaged the true purpose behind its nuclear weapons, yet it is evident that it had embarked on the path in the early 1950s. It is true that at that time, it did not have capability but it did have the intention; it later became very evident that it was not peaceful but basically, military in character.

When it comes to its security, Pakistan builds the narrative of India as a threat. So, the question that comes up, is: is it for survival against India that Pakistan has developed its nuclear weapons? If India is accepted as a threat, quite naturally, nuclear weapons figure vis-à-vis its security. The Pakistani ruling establishment and supporting writers have been building a narrative for long that its nuclear weapons are basically India-centric. Nuclear weapons form part of Pakistan's regional security strategy.

The Pakistani strategic community, including the Pakistani state point out a few trigger points to the Pakistani nuclear quest. At times, though superficially, an impression is created that Pakistan became a nuclear weapon state because India went nuclear in May 1998. Some of the official and quasi-official statements and writings have made the world accept this narrative. Some also maintain that its defeat in the 1965 war pushed the idea of a Pakistani nuclear bomb because the war had proven and established India's conventional superiority[7] and the need was felt to develop nuclear weapons as a counterpoise to the erosion of military balance between India and Pakistan. But the dominant Pakistani explanation for going nuclear is India's 1974 Peaceful Nuclear Explosion (PNE).

Pakistanis project that the 1974 and 1998 tests made India militarily more formidable, and already conventionally weak Pakistan, too vulnerable. Now it is established that Pakistan used the events such as India's 1974 PNE and May 1998 tests to justify its nuclear weapons project. The activities of Zulfiqar Ali Bhutto to build the bomb predate the 1974 explosion. The US was also well aware of the fact that the Pakistani programme for nuclear weapons development predates the 1974 nuclear explosion.[8] A number of documents and papers endorse the thinking. The American declassified documents of the 1960s and before, acknowledge the Pakistani nuclear ambition, and most significantly, the limitation of the military treaties like the SEATO in checking Pakistani behaviour.[9] The US, for several years, made efforts to curb Pakistan's reprocessing and enrichment capability[10] and worked with the major "reprocessing" states as well.[11]

A section of the Pakistani strategic community sees a role of nuclear weapons in countering India's 'hegemonic designs' in South Asia and the Indian Ocean.[12] For them, nuclear deterrence may prevent India's military domination over Pakistan.[13] Pakistan repeats the security rationale time and again, predominantly in the regional context. South Asia is deceptively projected as the region of its focus but it is much networked in other regions of Asia as well. By acquiring nuclear weapons, Pakistan may project the aspiration of a weak power to contain a stronger power like India, while in reality, it pushes its own devious agenda. The creation of Bangladesh was a product of the contradictions in the construction of Pakistani nationalism and the nation-state; Pakistan basically created an imaginary Indian nuclear threat in particular and an overall Indian hegemonic threat in general.

Containing India and other countries in its neighbourhood is one of Pakistan's objectives through its nuclear arsenal. It is not the only objective, as Pakistan would like the world to believe. Its idea is not to alleviate the risk of any nuclear attack, but to project the scenario of nuclear escalation, and use this situation as a tool of containment. Pakistan maintains that it is indispensable for overcoming the asymmetrical power relationship in the subcontinent. It tries to justify its nuclear arsenal by pitching the idea that asymmetrical power in South Asia increases vulnerability of a small state like Pakistan. Pakistan has openly stated that balance of power is the objective of its nuclear arsenal.[14] Pakistan in fact is pushing strategic uncertainty through nuclear weapons.

From time to time, the statements of the Pakistani ruling establishment indicate that its objective is other than security or survival vis-à-vis India. Then comes the question: is it a survival against nuclear armed great powers? A section in Pakistan maintains that it joined the two Western military pacts without properly ascertaining the mood of the country, which had tilted or was tilting towards Afro-Asian solidarity.[15] Pakistan had joined the military pacts even before the Non-Aligned Movement (NAM) came into being.

However, Pakistan's membership of these pacts kept coming in the way of its joining the NAM. Pakistani writers maintain that Pakistan joined the pacts to ensure security vis-à-vis its stronger neighbour, India. Although Pakistan joined the NAM as a full member in its sixth summit in 1979, it spoke the language of NAM whenever it suited its purpose. After joining NAM, it drew attention to 'threats and pressures' from the great powers. This was yet another instance of misrepresentation of the rationale for Pakistan's development of nuclear weapons.

Like other NAM countries, it wants to project that its security lies in a world without nuclear weapons. Now, it speaks the language of disarmament in NAM's meetings and elsewhere and also supports the resolutions for nuclear disarmament. A former member of the military alliance finds fault with nuclear-armed alliances for Pakistan's insecurity. For example, the following statement made by a Pakistani representative at the UN underscores another dimension of Pakistani thinking on security relating to nuclear weapons.

> "Progress on nuclear disarmament remains stalled. Some Nuclear Weapon States are neither willing to give up their large inventories of nuclear weapons nor their modernization programmes, even as they pursue non-proliferation with messianic zeal. And, some

> thirty non-nuclear-weapon States—members of nuclear-armed alliances—continue to rely robustly on nuclear weapons while advocating abstinence by other States facing real security deficits, some of which are exacerbated by extravagant arms exports and nuclear cooperation."[16]

However, in reality, Pakistan's design of nuclear disarmament as a tool for its international security or Nuclear Weapons Free Zones contradicts its argument that it needs nuclear weapons to counter India's conventional superiority. Here, too, the Pakistani proclamation on nuclear disarmament is basically yet another instance of deception.

The Pakistani leadership, at times, reveals the real objective of the nuclear bomb. It searches for a pretext to keep its nuclear weapons for its regional dominance, including leadership of the Islamic world. Its ambition of becoming the leader of the Islamic world has been a key factor ever since it came into being. It roped in some of the West Asian and other Muslim countries with the false promise of delivering to them an Islamic Nuclear Weapon. For example, Zulfikar Ali Bhutto, in order to see "the Islamic civilization at par with the Hindu, Christian and Jewish civilizations", had planned to develop 'full nuclear capability'.[17] This thinking existed before and after Bhutto. Even Ayub Khan, who is projected as an opponent of the nuclear programme, was not against the idea of acquiring nuclear weapons to dominate the adversary.

In effect, it was nothing but an instrument to exercise power in the Islamic world. This has been acknowledged by some leading Pakistani authors on nuclear weapons. For example, one of the prominent Pakistani writings on the subject notes: "Pakistan's sense of national identity has a complex relationship with its Islamic identity. The perception that Pakistan is a victim of discrimination—that the world is opposed uniquely to an 'Islamic bomb' became a source of pride. Of the Muslim polities, only Pakistan has managed to cross the nuclear threshold. This nuclear accomplishment gave Pakistan certain pre-eminence in the Islamic world."[18] Actually, it is a newly-constructed proud Pakistani nationalism, which uses Islam to give the civilisational angle to its nuclear bomb.

Defining Grand Strategy: War or Peace

Samuel Eliot Morrison stated: "Grand strategy or higher strategy is simply national foreign policy continued in time of war."[19] Sir Basil Liddell Hart, in his classic work, expounds grand strategy "is to coordinate and direct all the resources of a nation, or band of nations, towards the attainment of the political object of the war."[20] However, he also stated that grand strategy needs to take 'a long view' by attaining peace. More or less, the same thinking is echoed in Edward Meade Earle, "The highest type of strategy—sometimes called 'grand strategy'—is that which so integrates the policies and armaments of the nation that the resort to war is either rendered unnecessary or is undertaken with the maximum chance of victory."[21]

Thus, Earle and Hart both consider grand strategy in terms of war and peace. In Earle's idea of grand strategy, war is 'rendered unnecessary'; this guides us not merely towards the absence of war, but also toward deterrence. In general, writers on grand strategy argue that the tools of statecraft for war and peace could be different. However, nuclear weapons have introduced a great deal of complexity in a country's grand strategy. In the 1950s, the US accumulated nuclear weapons, and the emboldened Eisenhower Administration began to think about possible nuclear weapons' use in a battlefield.

Gradually, better sense prevailed. The taboo to use nuclear weapons became the dominant norm in the international community. The nuclear weapon, a tool for war, became a factor of prolonged but tense peace in the bipolar world during the Cold War. This idea of peace was mainly defined by the concept of deterrence. The threat to use nuclear weapons very much stayed on the horizon. The nuclear arms race supported by credible nuclear threat or credible nuclear deterrence bolstered this tense peace.

After discerning the primary objective of the nuclear bomb's acquisition, a related question comes up: how does Pakistan envision using its nuclear weapons? Does it want to use them as tools of war or of peace? Like other nuclear weapon countries, it does talk about peace and stability, mainly regional. When it has to target India, it begins talking about South Asia and its stability. It projects concepts such as Nuclear Weapons Free Zone or Strategic Restraint in South Asia. Any nuclear energy development initiative for India as well as joining of any forum or body, is projected as destabilising South Asia's regional stability. But it underplays its role in destabilising not merely South Asia but also West and East Asia through multiple means.

Pakistan also officially espouses nuclear deterrence; it comes from the entire spectrum of the Pakistani decision-making system. In almost every document or statement on Pakistan's nuclear policy, the phrase—credible minimum deterrence—is engraved. Pakistan avows to pursue the 'policy of Credible Minimum Deterrence as a responsible nuclear weapons state.'[22] When the National Command Authority makes the statement about credible minimum deterrence, it underlines both the elements: security and safety of Pakistan's nuclear weapon and its delivery programmes and facilities, and more significantly, the operational readiness of Pakistani nuclear weapons. Pakistan basically possesses an extortionist nuclear deterrence. The entire idea behind it is nuclear blackmail.

For Pakistan, the nuclear weapon has no 'peace-inducing qualities'; for sure, it is not designed as a weapon for peace. It is a weapon, which is to be used in a non-nuclear or conventional conflict situation. Does the Pakistani notion of nuclear deterrence mean preventing a nuclear war? As Pakistan does not subscribe to the "no-first-use" doctrine, it relies on warfighting role for its nuclear arsenal. So, for Pakistan, the nuclear weapon is primarily a tool of war. As Pakistan has a warfighting role for its nuclear weapons, its nuclear deterrence may eventually trigger a nuclear backlash—a full-fledged nuclear war. What is pushing Pakistan to employ battlefield weapons has been discussed by scholars all over the world, though no one could be sure which theory or analysis matches the thinking and strategy of the Pakistani nuclear establishment. Yet the effort to dissect the strategy is on.

Pakistan envisages two kinds of war with the help of nuclear weapons: a direct war in the conventional mode and proxy war. Though Pakistan is accumulating nuclear weapons, yet it is nowhere near what the US was in the 1950s. Pakistan has been projecting nuclear pre-emption through *Nasr/Hatf-IX* in a battle. It is emphasising its counter-force strategies. In recent years, it has been openly stating that India, whose conventional weapons capability is superior to Pakistan, is the principal target of its nuclear weapons. In fact, in a number of conflict situations, the Pakistani leadership threatened to use nuclear weapons. During the Kargil War, Pakistan threatened to use nuclear weapons when it stared defeat in the face. However, seemingly, India's retaliatory signal made it understand the implications of introduction of nuclear weapons in a battlefield/conflict scenario.

Yet, Pakistan's public posturing of using nuclear weapons continues. Later, on several occasions, too, Pakistan threatened to use nuclear weapons. For example, when India exerted pressure to enter into Pakistan after its Parliament had been attacked in December 2001, Pervez Musharraf threatened to use nuclear weapons.[23] Samar Mubarakmand, a key figure in the Pakistani nuclear establishment, stated in an address that Pakistan would have been punished after the November 26, 2008 Mumbai terror attack had it not possessed nuclear weapons.[24] Quite disturbingly, Imran Khan, the current Prime Minister of Pakistan, threatened to use nuclear weapons after India had abrogated Article 370 in Jammu and Kashmir in 2019.[25] Such threats are not rare and have been appearing quite frequently. Now and then, it threatens to use nuclear weapons to put pressure on India to settle the boundary issue. As the target for its nuclear weapons may remain confined to India, the same warfighting policy could be applied to other countries as well.

Pakistan uses nuclear weapons to wage a proxy war, especially against India. The entire exercise is conducted as a dexterous strategy. The spectre of a nuclear exchange is relayed globally. A section of the global non-proliferation community is roped in to further spread this terrifying scenario. Admittedly, some in the global non-proliferation community inadvertently fall prey to this propaganda, while its sponsorship of global terrorism is now well recognised. The Pakistani nuclear arsenal is devised to provide a shield to Pakistan-sponsored terror activities. Sponsoring terror or fanning insurgency is a low-cost proxy war for Pakistan. The moment a victim country like India makes any move to intervene through conventional weapons after confirming Pakistan's involvement, a statement emerges from one of the Pakistani officials or its political leaders.

Does Pakistan want 'a great premium on resolve, on risk-taking, and perhaps ultimately on recklessness?'[26] Yes, if Pakistan's nuclear behaviour is an indication, it may be asserted that it has not gone for a risk-averse strategy to promote its grand design of regional dominance. By all means, a rational section of its decision-making body ought to be aware of the cost involved in such a risky venture. If this kind of strategy is adopted against a nuclear weapons country, quite naturally, the consequences are going to be disastrous. For India, which relies on a robust nuclear deterrence and massive retaliation capability, the possibility of almost total annihilation of Pakistan exists. Already, the world had a glimpse of the possibility of the use of conventional force when India had undertaken some restrained action against Pakistan to punish it for its acts of terror.

The Proliferation Network: Means or End

Pakistan's proliferation network involving a number of number of state and non-state actors has been stealing the global limelight for decades. Is the proliferation network that has been feeding the Pakistani nuclear weapons acquisition and manufacturing, part of its grand strategy? The answer is, yes; ever since Pakistan decided to acquire nuclear weapons, it adopted the strategy of "beg, borrow, or steal".[27] The proliferation network was used as a means but later it became a goal of the Pakistani nuclear arsenal. The sustained existence of the proliferation network became a necessity for the actors involved in it. This sustained existence acquired the shape of an alliance of these nuclear black/ grey market actors.

One of the declassified American papers of 1966 notes that Pakistan had the intention to develop nuclear weapons but badly lacked the capability to do so.[28] One Pakistani nuclear scientist maintains that Pakistan began its nuclear weapons hunt in an 'ocean of ignorance'.[29] Another former official who manned an important position in the nuclear establishment, wrote: "Early on, Pakistan['s] scientific leaders identified the lack of trained physicists and engineers as a crucial deficiency that its nuclear programme would have to rectify."[30] Pakistan sent people to European and American institutions for short- and long-term courses. These people, after their return, tried to set up infrastructure for bomb-making. The host scientific institutions were by and large kept under the dark.

Some of the joint collaborations, in which Pakistan was a partner, and which were signed for peaceful uses, were used for Pakistan's nuclear weapons development. The secret network transacted all the services and procured all the items for building Pakistani nuclear weapons. The transacted items have been documented and written about several times. As a result, several books, articles and reports describing multiple dimensions of the proliferation network are available in the public domain.[31] Pakistan also diverted funds, which had come for other purposes . In the initial years, apparently, Pakistan ran 'three parallel secret programs simultaneously'. However, as discussed, none of them succeeded. This forced Pakistan to reorient its strategy and look outwards, to procure key technologies for its nuclear weapons.

Does flexibility or rigidity matter in a nation's grand strategy? If yes, how does it matter vis-à-vis nuclear weapons? Pakistan has been showing enormous flexibility in its nuclear posture/policy, if not in the intent. To shield its nuclear weapons, it has been engaging in a complex relationship with non-proliferation. On the one hand, it is involved in the proliferation network for decades, and on the other, it has been projecting several meaningless non-proliferation initiatives such as the South Asia Nuclear weapons Free Zone and Strategic Restraint Regime as a cover for its murky business. After the AQ Khan network stormed the world in the beginning of the twenty-first century, it made extra efforts to showcase its hollow commitment to non-proliferation by enacting new laws and regulations for export controls. It is a well-known fact that in a clandestine proliferation network, a legal arrangement is overlooked, not followed.

An impression is generated that it was AQ Khan who was responsible for running the proliferation network, and the Pakistani state or Government had nothing to do with it. To reiterate the point that the Pakistani establishment has nothing to do with the proliferation network, Pakistan has been frequently making statements. The statements for the purpose come from the entire Pakistani establishment. In 2004, even AQ Khan was forced to own up 'unauthorised proliferation activities' as his personal venture.

As a matter of fact, the proliferation network had existed for a long time and more significantly, it had existed even before AQ Khan actively entered the Pakistani nuclear weapons business. Over the years, credible evidence has surfaced indicting the complicity of the Pakistani Government in the proliferation network. The complicity of the Government has been deep and even ugly. The role of the Government at the highest level in the illegal procurement of goods and items from the global nuclear black/gray market has been traced. Even the role of leaders like Benazir Bhutto is well documented. The network adopted an ugly method of assassinating a diplomat's wife and using the coffin for transporting nuclear and missile items.

The question that comes up now is: why did Pakistan choose the strategy of developing a proliferation network to procure nuclear weapon related items? The answer is very simple: Pakistan had an ambition to acquire a nuclear weapon but it did not have the capacity/capabilities to develop nuclear weapons indigenously because of its weak industrial and engineering base. Even its scientific and technological infrastructure was less than sufficient to support nuclear weapon-making at that time. AQ Khan's arrival on the nuclear weapon-making scene became possible because the older nuclear establishment had failed to deliver the desired results.

Initially, Pakistan opted for the plutonium route to develop nuclear weapons. It struggled in the beginning, and despite the recent reinforcing of the plutonium route by adding a number of reactors and a reprocessing centre, it is still struggling. AQ Khan came with the promise of delivering nuclear weapons through the enriched uranium route. The deficiency in capability affected the enriched uranium route. Since AQ Khan was the head of the laboratory and the establishment for undertaking uranium enrichment, he had to take the lead in approaching the proliferation/procurement network he had developed, using his employment in the nuclear lab in the Netherlands. Such an active leadership role is used to project the proliferation network as the AQ Khan Proliferation Network, in order to shield the Pakistani state.

An informed Pakistani work notes:

> "Pakistan's strategy was to keep its procurement activities within the limits of commercial law of the country, and if necessary, operate within the legal grey areas ... When individuals were caught, Pakistan would at times officially deny US allegations and disassociate itself from any illegal activities. At other times it would privately explain to the United States that it had to do what was in its national interest. Pakistan would then use diplomacy to mitigate the damage, especially during critical periods of the Cold War when Pakistan's role was strategically significant to US security objectives. This cat-and-mouse game of sorts would last for three decades."[32]

The US was aware of the growing nuclear proliferation nexus existing for decades but was hoodwinked into adopting a state of self-denial.

Alliance for Hidden Extended Deterrence

The role of alliance in a nation's grand strategy is extremely significant, though a question is asked: whether the nuclear proliferation network could be called an alliance. In strategic studies, an alliance is normally a formal grouping of countries explicitly spelling out expectations and obligations. The proliferation network is, at times, understood as a coalition in which the member-countries are united informally by common interest. However, there is no single definition or understanding of an alliance; the idea of alliance is evolving. The nations are united in a grouping for both shared objectives and shared risks. Stephen M. Walt, an authority on alliance defines it as "a formal or informal relationship of security cooperation between two or more sovereign states".[33] Different alliances may have different faces and contents. An alliance helps in counter-balancing adversaries of the participating countries as well as dissuades the member-countries from excessive self-reliance.

The proliferation network is a kind of alliance of nations willing to acquire or refine their nuclear weapons clandestinely. The unity of command, considered significant for an effective grand strategy, is generally absent in such a grouping. Normally, the political factor enjoys primacy in comparison to the technological or military factor but in the proliferation network, technological acquisition enjoys primacy. It may have security considerations but collective security parameters are certainly missing. The partners of the proliferation network may not share the single objective of conquering any particular country. Yet, they share some responsibility to mutually assist each other.

That Pakistan wanted its own a fleet of nuclear weapons became evident even before 1974, but the question emerged about the alliance that would procure this fleet of nuclear weapons. Pakistan opted for a more circuitous path. Its clandestine collaboration with China was reported for some decades[34] even before it overtly went nuclear. The nuclear connection between China and Pakistan in fact shaped the proliferation network that flourished in the later years. Pakistan supported China's nuclear weapon tests in the 1960s even if the US or the West did not approve of Pakistan's direct and indirect support to Chinese nuclearisation.[35]

Various factors seemingly made the international community look the other way. In the 1960s, it was the Pakistani alliance with the US, which made the US hesitate in taking any drastic action. In the 1970s, the open official statements and declassified documents both indicated that the US had strategised to prevent Pakistan from testing as well as transferring nuclear items to other countries, basically China. However, the US and its allies were unwilling to impose sanctions or use a 'stick'.[36] The Western bloc dangled all kinds of carrots to influence Pakistan. But Pakistan carried on. In the late 1970s, Soviet involvement in Afghanistan gave Pakistan an opportunity to manipulate the Western bloc.

Even if it is accepted that the Chinese had the capability to manufacture and transfer nuclear weapons to other countries, the problem in openly transferring nuclear weapons was a stark reality. Since the late 1960s or the détente period, even China had developed a close and complex relationship with the Western world. It gradually became a beneficiary of high- technology weapons as the Western world had started easing technology restrictions for it. China began working to convince the Western world that it would also become an important stakeholder in the non-proliferation order. China finally joined the Nuclear Non-Proliferation (NPT), which made the official nuclear collaboration between Pakistan and China more difficult.

As open nuclear weapons collaboration with China was becoming increasingly difficult because of non-proliferation, Pakistan started working with China to refine and broaden the clandestine route. If China was the first ally, many others joined the proliferation network led by Pakistan and China with time. Moreover, the lack of Chinese nuclear capacity to manufacture weapons for other countries in the initial years seemingly had a coalition of non-NATO and non-Warsaw Pact countries interested in developing nuclear weapons. This extended relationship expressed in terms of a clandestine proliferation network, has evolved into a new alliance system with unique characteristics.

Though China had not extended its protective nuclear umbrella to any of its close or friendly countries, yet an overt extended deterrence would have put several restrictions on Pakistan, and the most important restriction was on acting independently to use its nuclear weapons. However, the countries involved in the proliferation network have developed a different kind of extended deterrence relationship. This network has its own operational procedures, different from open extended deterrence. All the countries keep their national nuclear identities intact. This possibly serves Pakistan's strategic objective better than the formal extended deterrence relationship. However, Pakistan has always been stretching its strategic or security imperatives. Could this alliance have a 'pre-determined target list accompanied with authority to use nuclear weapons' as found in the classical alliance systems? The answer is no, though in the future this possibility is not ruled out.

The common objective of this alliance was and is, to develop nuclear capabilities of individual participating countries. The network primarily transacted denied/prohibited items. The network sought to facilitate 'strategic substitutes' for an item denied by the West. The partners of this unique alliance used collective expertise to reverse-engineer whatever Western technology they had got hold of. They also sought help from joint expertise in disabling restrictive clauses generally incorporated to prevent stealing or reproducing designs or other proprietary issues by the supplier countries in the contracts.

Unlike the dominant Cold War alliance system which was based on ideology, the proliferation alliance has no ideology, though some commentators do point out that the 'socialist leaning'[37] of Zulfiqar Ali Bhutto, the so-called political father of the Pakistani nuclear bomb, helped Pakistan in gaining proximity to North Korea and China. In fact, Pakistan's proximity to China or even North Korea is because of mutual interests, less because of any ideology. For Pakistan, this alliance provided external balancing against a formidable India.[38]

The presence of China and North Korea negate the Islamic character of the alliance, but considering the flexible nature of the proliferation network and alliance, Pakistan did use the Islamic connection to bolster its nuclear weapons acquisition goals. Interestingly, Pakistan's relationship with both the countries is strong, despite its Jihadi activities and sponsoring Islamic terrorism all over the world.

The Islamic civilisation card was played; Pakistan projected that it had become the target of the non-proliferation regime because it wanted to build an 'Islamic bomb'. Many believe that Pakistan succeeded in playing the "victim card" in the Islamic world. Apparently, Saudi Arabia, Libya, the United Arab Emirates and Iran supported the Pakistani nuclear weapon quest.[39] Of all these countries, the support from Shia Iran became critical in running the network. Saudi Arabia and, other rich Islamic countries, most likely, provided financial support to the Pakistani nuclear weapons programme.

As discussed, in the future, the partners of the proliferation network or alliance may agree to work together but as of now, there is no common security goal. China may share the Pakistani strategy of India's containment, but other countries may not have any interest in it. Most of the countries have their strategic goals set in their regional contexts. They could be basically interested in increasing their regional influence. The principle of assurance is operational only for maintaining the supply chain of proliferation, not any joint military action.

Does the alliance share best practices for nuclear safety and security as well? The members of the alliance are encouraged to participate in the regional, global and various multilateral forums like Nuclear Security Summits to understand the appropriate practices for nuclear safety and security. Yet, the members of the network may be learning from each other's experience in managing nuclear safety and security of their arsenals as well, though all the members of the network boast of possessing robust nuclear safety and security systems.

For example, the Pakistani establishment keeps highlighting the institutional framework it has developed over the years. The Pakistan Nuclear Regulatory Authority (PNRA) and Pakistan Atomic Energy Commission are projected as the institutions enforcing nuclear security and safety. The National Command Authority gives the assurance statement that it will keep conducting 'the safety review' of all the current and future civil nuclear facilities. Pakistan assures proper management of "various aspects of command, control, safety and security of nuclear weapons in Pakistan."[40]

Grand Strategy Post Balakot Strikes

On 26 February 2019, the Indian Government authorised the attack on a terror centre in Balakot. This was considered retaliatory action against the terror attack which had killed around 40 Central Police Forces. Earlier, on 28 September 2016, India had also launched a surgical strike in retaliation against the loss of its soldiers in Uri. How do these two strikes impact Pakistan's nuclear grand strategy? The two strikes seem to have demolished the narrative Pakistan built around its nuclear weapons. Its bluff of using nuclear weapons in an event of a conventional strike seems to have been called. Yet, some argue that Pakistan has a position that when its survival is at stake, it may use nuclear weapons; so, a non-response to the limited strikes should not mean that Pakistan has changed its position. To an extent, this argument may appear to be true.

However, both the Pakistani posturing of frontline deployment of the so-called battlefield nuclear weapon, *Nasr*, and the threat to use it in the early stage of war, have lost credibility. What Pakistan calls its survival is vague and undefined. In the contemporary world, the war is generally limited in nature and thus, a country has to determine the crossing of the line that may adversely affect its survival. Pakistan now has better understanding of the danger of threatening or using nuclear weapons in an event of a crisis. The Government of Pakistan may still maintain a brave face by not precisely defining the survival line which is to be saved by nuclear weapons.

Pakistan's grand strategy of providing a nuclear shield to its proxy war against India will certainly come under tremendous pressure. The calling of Pakistan's nuclear bluff has targeted Pakistan's nuclear blackmail. India also challenged the Pakistani attempt to control the escalation ladder. Later, Pakistan did try limited skirmishes through air power but finally preferred to de-escalate by returning the captured Indian pilot. Pakistan may have to recalculate the cost and benefit of launching any terror attack on India. Whether Pakistan will indeed end the proxy war or stop sending terrorists to strike in India is too early to say. But the Indian strikes, abandoning its long-practised restraint of crossing the border, have definitely disturbed Pakistan's calculation of bringing in the nuclear factor in its proxy war.

For sure, in the future, Pakistan would not like to miscalculate[41] as it knows that India may not hesitate to escalate if Pakistan does so. If Pakistan breaches the sacrosanct nuclear threshold, now it knows a "New India" will no longer be restrained. The analyses of Western scholars have somehow become better and more realistic, yet it looks difficult for them to shed the archaic paradigm and terminology which is highly unrealistic and arrogant.[42]

Will Pakistan maintain its alliance? As the strategy behind erecting the alliance was to mutual enhancement of joint and individual capacities to build the individual national bomb, not sharing common security threat management, Pakistan may remain involved in the alliance and keep feeding the proliferation network which is the backbone of the alliance. Of course, the operational refinement of the alliance or the network will continue. Except China no other partner may think of militarily engaging India in a conflict.

Conclusion

Pakistan has devised a grand strategy with flexible goals to be achieved with its limited resources in terms of both material and human resources. Its acquisition path follows a combination of indigenous programmes and reliance on the clandestine proliferation network. The failure of one route made Pakistan search for an alternative route. The failure of the indigenous plutonium-based nuclear weapons development programme made way for enriched uranium- based nuclear weapons through the proliferation network. However, Pakistan is still pursuing the plutonium-based route, as it has set up several reprocessing facilities in recent years.

This strategy is of neither post-1974 nor post-1998 origin. This predates not only both the years but also the 1965 war. When it conducted its nuclear tests in 1998 after India's Shakti series of tests, the elements inside and outside Pakistan may have projected that the Pakistani response was merely a reaction to the Indian nuclear weapons tests. Needless to say, it is an over-simplistic understanding of Pakistan's nuclear weapons acquisition. Now it is well documented that Pakistan had planned for its nuclear weapons procurement for a long time. Zulfikar Bhutto's rhetoric—"Eating Grass But Building a Bomb" was merely an outburst of an old existing, partly open and partly hidden, nuclear weapons acquisition plan.

Pakistan weaves the survival narrative to win the sympathy of the international community. For this purpose, it has been projecting a formidable enemy in India. As merely the projection of formidable enemy would not be sufficient to push the agenda, Pakistan also painted the picture of an aggressive India which enjoys superiority vis-à-vis Pakistan in terms of conventional forces. The Pakistani strategy of projecting this narrative helps it in providing legitimacy to its nuclear weapons. The Art of Deception that Pakistan has developed for nuclear weapons acquisition is applied to the rationale of managing this arsenal as well.

Pakistan's grand strategy may make it appear that its nuclear weapons is India-centric, yet the Pakistani Government does not restrict its objective only to counter India but has projected itself for a larger role in the region as well. Pakistan's meddling in Afghanistan is well-known now. The clandestine nuclear acquisition process drew it closer to the West Asian countries. These countries were relevant for Pakistan for funding its nuclear weapons programme; Iran may have had some technological collaborations, whether they fructified or not is a different matter. Pakistan sold the idea of 'a Nuclear Bomb for the Islamic civilisation' to these countries. The apprehensions surrounding a race for Sunni and Shia bombs is growing in West Asia. Pakistan may play its game with both the sects. It shall try to hegemonise in Asia.

The Indian conventional strikes deep inside Pakistan may not affect major changes in terms of Pakistan's strategic posturing. The rhetoric and linkage to survival will continue. India, a nuclearised world, Islamic identity and so on, may continue to appear as the security rationale for its nuclear weapons. As for providing the nuclear shield to terrorists, the strikes may force Pakistan to recalibrate its strategy. India's resolute stances backed by international public opinion, may bring about a long-term change in its terror strategy. Pakistan would continue to target India through its regional disarmament rhetoric. More significantly, Pakistan's grand strategy for regional dominance and hegemony in South, Central and West Asia, may remain unchanged.

Notes

1. Basil H. Liddell Hart, *Strategy: The Indirect Approach, 1941*, Faber and Faber, London, 1967.
2. Ibid., p. 335.
3. Steven A. Yetiv, *The Absence of Grand Strategy: The United States in the Persian Gulf, 1972-2005*, The Johns Hopkins University Press, Baltimore, 2008.
4. Colin S. Gray, *The Strategy Bridge: Theory for Practice,* Oxford University Press Inc., New York, 2010.

5. Adrian Levy and Catherine Scott-Clark, *Deception: Pakistan, the United States and the Global Nuclear weapons Conspiracy,* Penguin Books, New Delhi, 2007, p. 12.
6. "Note: A.S. Gonsalves to Ministry of External Affairs, 'Nuclear Guarantee', 6 July 1965", Digital Archive, International History Declassified, Wilson Center, at https://digitalarchive.wilsoncenter.org/document/123924. Accessed on 14 January 2021.
7. For example, Mahmud Ali Durrani, 'Pakistan's Strategic Thinking and the Role of Nuclear Weapons', Occasional Paper 37, Cooperative Monitoring Center, Sandia National Laboratories, SAND 2004-3375P, at https://www.sandia.gov/cooperative-monitoring-center/_assets/documents/sand2004-3375p.pdf. Accessed on 14 January 2021.
8. The National Security Archive, 'Memorandum to Holders, Special National Intelligence Estimate, Prospects for Further Proliferation of Nuclear Weapons', SNIE, 4-1-74, 18 December 1975, the George Washington University, 2 March 2010, at https://nsarchive2.gwu.edu/nukevault/ebb333/doc01.pdf. Accessed on 14 January 2021. The National Security Archive, 'Personal Memorandum for Director of Central Intelligence, July 21, 1965', The George Washington University, 29 May 2003, at https://nsarchive2.gwu.edu/NSAEBB/NSAEBB114/chipak-1.pdf. Accessed on 14 January 2021.
9. The National Security Archive, 'Personal Memorandum for Director of Central Intelligence, July 21, 1965', no. 8.
10. Gerald R. Ford Presidential Library & Museum, 'Memorandum for the President on Nuclear Policy, September 15, 1976', Nuclear Policy Statement (3), Box 24, James M. Cannon Files, at https://www.fordlibrarymuseum.gov/library/document/0039/16988096.pdf. Accessed on 14 January 2021.
11. Gerald R. Ford Presidential Library & Museum, 'Memorandum for Brent Scowcroft, Jim Cannon, Jim Connor from Bob Fri on Dealing with the Subcommittee, White House, August 4, 1976', Box 60, Folder '1976/08/06 - Bob Fri' of the James M. Cannon Files, at https://www.fordlibrarymuseum.gov/library/document/0039/1535225.pdf. Accessed on 14 January 2021.
12. Javid Husain, *Pakistan and a World in Disorder: A Grand Strategy for the Twenty first Century*, Palgrave Macmillan, New York, 2016, p. 190.
13. Ibid., p. 191.
14. Director General, Inter-Services Public Relations, Twitter page @officialDGISPR, 28 May 2020, at https://twitter.com/OfficialDGISPR/status/1265985677600206850. Accessed on 14 January 2021.
15. Naveed Ahmad, 'The Non-Aligned Movement and Pakistan', *Pakistan Horizon*, 32 (4), 1979, pp. 79-91.

16. Maleeha Lodhi, 'Statement at the 2015 Substantive Session of the United Nations Disarmament Commission', Pakistan Mission to the United Nations, New York, 7 April 2015, at https://pakun.org/statements/First_Committee/2015/04072015-01.php. Accessed on 14 January 2021.
17. Zulfikar Ali Bhutto, *If I am Assassinated*, Vikas Publishing House, New Delhi, 1979, p. 21.
18. Feroz Hassan Khan, *Eating Grass: the Making of the Pakistani Bomb*, Foundation Books, Delhi, 2013, p. 10.
19. Samuel Eliot Morrison, *Strategy and Compromise*, Little Brown, Boston MA, 1958, p. 6.
20. B. H. Liddell Hart, no. 1, p. 322.
21. Edward Meade Earle, (Ed.), *Makers of Modern Strategy*, Princeton University Press, Princeton, NJ, 1943, p. viii.
22. Inter-Services Public Relations, 'Press Release', No PR-166/2011-ISPR, Rawalpindi, 14 July 2011, at https://ispr.gov.pk/press-release-detail.php?id=1796. Accessed on 14 January 2021.
23. Rediff.com, 'Pak was ready to nuke India on breaching border', Press Trust of India, 30 December 2002, at https://www.rediff.com/news/report/pak1/20021230.htm. Accessed on 14 January 2021.
24. Rediff.com, 'Without nukes, Pak won't have "survived" post-26/11', Press Trust of India, 30 May 2009, at https://www.rediff.com/news/report/without-nukes-pak-wont-have-survived/20090530.htm. Accessed on 14 January 2021.
25. 'Pak PM issues nuclear threat to India after Modi-Trump meet', BusinessToday.in, 27 August 2019, at https://www.businesstoday.in/videos/news-reel/pak-pm-issues-nuclear-threat-to-india-after-modi-trump-meet/375624.html. Accessed on 14 January 2021.
26. Marc Trachtenberg, *History and Strategy,* Princeton University Press, Princeton, 1991.
27. Mahmud Ali Durrani, no. 7.
28. The National Security Archive, 'The Likelihood of Further Nuclear Proliferation, National Intelligence Estimate, 4-66, January 20, 1966', The George Washington University, at https://nsarchive2.gwu.edu/nukevault/ebb423/docs/1.%201966%20NIE.pdf. Accessed on 14 January 2021.
29. Feroz Hassan Khan, no. 18, p. 10.
30. Ibid., p. 28.
31. For example, Adrian Levy and Catherine Scott-Clark, *Deception: Pakistan, the United States and the Global Nuclear Weapons Conspiracy,* Penguin Books, New Delhi, 2007; Bruno Gruselle, 'Proliferation Networks and Financing', Fondation pour la Recherche Stratégique, Paris, 2007. Gordon Corera, *Shopping for Bombs: Nuclear Proliferation, Global Insecurity, and the Rise and Fall of the A.Q.*

Khan Network: Nuclear Proliferation, Global Insecurity and the Rise of the A.Q. Khan Network, Oxford University Press, New York, 2006; Rita Grossman-Vermaas, 'Proliferation and development—Exposing the Link', Autumn 2007, at https://www.nato.int/docu/review/2007/issue3/english/art3.html. Accessed on 14 January 2021; Alexander H. Montgomery, 'Ringing in Proliferation: How to Dismantle an Atomic Bomb Network', *International Security*, 30 (2), Fall 2005, pp. 153-187; Richard P. Cronin, K. Alan Kronstadt and Sharon Squassoni, *Pakistan's Nuclear Proliferation Activities and the Recommendations of the 9/11 Commission: U.S. Policy Constraints and Options*, CRS Report for Congress, 24 May 2005.

32. Feroz Hassan Khan, no. 18, p. 127.
33. Stephen M. Walt, *The Origins of Alliances*, Cornell University Press, 1990, p. 1.
34. 'Intelligence Note 506 from Thomas L Hughes to the Secretary, "Will Communist China Give Nuclear Aid to Pakistan" August 12, 1966', Digital Archive, International History Declassified, Wilson Center, at https://digitalarchive.wilsoncenter.org/document/134064. Accessed on 14 January 2021.
35. National Security Archive, 'Personal Memorandum for Director of Central Intelligence, July 21, 1965', n. 8.
36. 'Note from Anthony Lake Director Policy Planning Staff to Secretary of State Vance, "the Pakistani Strategy and Future Choices," documentcloud.org, September 8, 1979', at https://www.documentcloud.org/documents/347013-doc-2-9-8-79.html. Accessed on 14 January 2021.
37. Feroz Hassan Khan, n. 18, p. 68.
38. Ibid., p. 24.
39. Ibid., p. 162.
40. Inter-Services Public Relations, 'Foreign Media Briefed at Strategic Plans Division', Press Release, No PR-45/2008-ISPR, 26 January 2008, at https://ispr.gov.pk/press-release-detail.php?id=488. Accessed on 14 January 2021.
41. Sameer P. Lalwani, et al., 'From Kargil to Balakot: Southern Asian Crisis Dynamics and Future Trajectories, February 2020, at https://www.stimson.org/wp-content/uploads/2020/02/2020-2-SA-Crises-Consequence-PolPaper-1062.pdf. Accessed on 14 January 2021.
42. Ibid.

12. Pakistan's Full Spectrum Deterrence: Efforts to Expand Options

Shalini Chawla

Pakistan relies on nuclear weapons for deterrence, war prevention, image build-up and very importantly, to conduct its strategy of sub-conventional war against India without fear of Indian retaliation. Nuclear weapons remain central to Pakistan's strategic posturing and are proudly seen as an ultimate guarantee of safety and sovereignty of the state. Islamabad has long tried to balance its domestic vulnerabilities with nuclear weapons. Its nuclear history and thinking explicitly explains its nuclear behaviour and brinkmanship that we see today.

Pakistan started its nuclear weapon programme in the early 1970s after the humiliating defeat in the India-Pakistan war of 1971 resulting in the disintegration of Pakistan. After its third defeat against India the Pakistani leadership was convinced that acquisition of nuclear weapons would neutralise India's conventional superiority. In the initial years, from the early 1950s to 1971, Pakistan's official policy was to build-up the nuclear programme for the development of nuclear energy. Starting from the 1970s under the leadership of Zulfikar Ali Bhutto, and subsequently, in the decades that followed, the development of the nuclear programme was shaped by increasing militarisation of Pakistan's state polices and its strategic alliances. Bhutto's conviction for nuclear deterrence strengthened after the 1971 war, when Pakistan did not receive Chinese and US assistance, and thus, any international norms and treaties restricting Pakistan's nuclear weapon development were unacceptable to him. He was convinced that Pakistan needed to acquire the nuclear bomb to match India's defence capability. Pakistan claimed to achieve the capability of a nuclear bomb in 1987.[1] The unwritten nuclear doctrine it opted for, has been outlined by policy makers and talked about *Minimum Nuclear Deterrence*. In May 1999, Prime Minister Nawaz Sharif distinctly highlighted the key elements of Pakistan's nuclear policy at the National Defence College:

> "Nuclear restraint, stabilisation and minimum credible deterrence constitute the basic elements of Pakistan's nuclear policy."[2]

Pakistan's nuclear and missile programme continued to build up and expand with clandestine Chinese assistance. Support from North Korea was extended when the US sanctions tightened their control over China. The effort from Pakistan has been to build a capability and have a doctrine which it thought was sufficient to deter an Indian military response (to its covert war). In the initial years of its nuclear weapon programme, Pakistan's nuclear positioning centred around the projection of *Credible Minimum Deterrence*. The need for *Full Spectrum Deterrence* was strongly felt within Pakistan after India made its stance clear regarding a possibility of a conventional war under the nuclear overhang. India's position on the possibility of a conventional war did challenge Islamabad's conviction about New Delhi's strategic restraint and hesitation in responding militarily to a Pakistan-sponsored act of terror.

In 2011, Pakistan tested its short-range surface-to-surface multi-tube ballistic missile *Hatf-9* (NASR). According to Pakistani military officials, *Hatf-9* belongs to the category of tactical nuclear weapons (TNW) and is a low-yield battlefield deterrent, capable of inflicting damage on armed brigades and divisions.[3] Pakistan claimed that it is developing a sea-based nuclear force to be able to match India's nuclear triad. Pakistan is seemingly proud of the full-spectrum deterrence and it conveniently claims to have developed the nuclear capability to be launched from all three platforms—land, air and sea.

Pakistan's *Full Spectrum Deterrence* is not limited to just spectrum of platforms (land, air and sea) but to the wide range of spectrum of scenarios. This can be well understood with the three Ps of its nuclear dimension which drive each other:

1. The Premise—on which Pakistan built its weapons and expanded consistently over the last four decades.
2. The Perception—that drives Pakistan's nuclear weapons programme and the perceptions Pakistan intends to generate and sustain (through the nuclear weapons).
3. The Projection—Pakistan has adopted based on the perceptions it intends to generate.

The Premise

Parity with India

Pakistan's perceived security threat from India which emerges from its geographical and structural weaknesses, has largely shaped its strategic posturing. The perceived security threats prompted the nation for its first aggression and war for Kashmir in 1947-48 under the umbrella of a tribal revolt and then again in 1965. Pakistan's defeat in the wars against India did deepen the desire for military modernisation, and the military's expanding political role did facilitate the military acquisitions from the major powers.

Although, Pakistan has repeatedly blamed India's peaceful explosion at Pokhran in 1974 for the acquisition of its nuclear weapons, facts suggest that Pakistan started to think about the nuclear weapons very seriously after the 1971 India-Pakistan war. Feroz Hassan Khan, in his explicit study of Pakistan's nuclear programme stated the objectives of the famous Multan Conference in 1972:

> "Bhutto had two clear-cut goals for the meeting. The first was to provide support for the nuclear program and its Pakistani scientists and engineers. But the second and probably more important goal was to announce publicly the new PAEC chair."[4]

The humiliation of the defeat in 1971 and the disintegration of the country was a turning point for Pakistan in terms of its strategic thinking and posture. The leadership in Pakistan was convinced that the country needed to explore an option to neutralise India's superior military capability. The nuclear weapons clearly were the potential answer to deal with Pakistan's "enemy number one", even though Bhutto admitted that the cost of building a bomb would be stressful for Pakistan's weak economy. In the Multan conference in 1972 Bhutto said:

> "We are fighting a thousand-year war with India, and we will make an atomic bomb even if we have to eat grass."[5]

Lt. Gen. Sardar F.S. Lodhi, clearly stated the need for the nuclear weapons in the wake of Pakistan's weak conventional build-up as compared to India:

> "During any future Indo-Pak armed conflict India's numerical superiority in men and conventional arms is likely to exert pressure beyond endurance. In a deteriorating military situation when an Indian conventional attack is likely to break through our defences or has already breached the main defence line causing a major set-back to the defences, which cannot be restored by conventional means at our disposal, the government would be left with no other option except to use Nuclear Weapons to stabilize the situation. India's superiority in conventional arms and manpower would have to be offset by nuclear weapons. The political will to use nuclear weapons is essential to prevent a conventional armed conflict, which would later on escalate into a nuclear war."[6]

Guarantee Ultimate Security

The basic rationale for Pakistan acquiring nuclear weapons has been its expectation to neutralise India's perceived conventional military superiority and the way it was employed by it in the 1971 War. Former Foreign Minister Agha Shahi referred to it as the "Sword of Damocles" hanging over Pakistan's head, and he talked about the objectives of Pakistan's nuclear weapons:

> "to equalise, to compensate our military imbalance that hangs like a sword of Damocles over the head of the nation which cut our country into two in 1971."[7]

G. Parthasarthy, former Indian ambassador to Pakistan expressed a similar view:

> "Pakistan decided to acquire nuclear weapons not because India had nuclear weapons, but because its ruling elite believed that after the dismemberment of the country during the Bangladesh conflict, it needed such weapons because of India's size and conventional superiority."[8]

Stephen Cohen talked about the value of nuclear weapons for Pakistan and quoted Samar Mubarakmand:

> "Nuclear weapons are as valuable to Pakistan as they are to North Korea—they constitute survival insurance for both. As Samar Mubarakmand, one of the leaders of the Pakistani weapons designs team, reminded the world ... Pakistan, like North Korea, is too nuclear to fail."[9]

In this respect Pakistan adopted a doctrine and strategy not very different from that pursued by the North Atlantic Treaty Organisation (NATO) against the USSR. Pakistan envisioned nuclear weapons as the sole guarantor of its national pride and national survival, and thus started to seek Chinese assistance clandestinely, for its nuclear weapon programme in the late 1960s in the aftermath of US sanctions.

Nuclear weapons were also seen as a currency of power for Pakistan which could enhance its importance in the strategic world and Muslim nations in particular. Bhutto in his death cell testimony stated:

> "... We were on the threshold of full nuclear capability when I left the government to come to this death cell. We know that Israel and South Africa have full nuclear capability. The Christian, Jewish and Hindu civilisations have this capability. The Communist powers also possess it. Only the Islamic civilisation was without it; but that position was about to change."[10]

Pakistan's appeal to the Muslim world for financial assistance was facilitated with the need to build an "Islamic Bomb". By the mid-1970s, Pakistan started receiving significant financial support from the Arab world. By mid 1976, five Arab countries and Iran had provided grants and loans worth nearly $1,000 million. In a matter of three years (between 1973-74 and 1976-77), the Muslim countries ranked first in the list of aid donors to Pakistan.[11] Pakistan did have the financial support of Saudi Arabia and Libya, and eventually it did share nuclear technology with Iran, Libya and Iraq. Being a leader of the Islamic World also ensured Pakistan smoother access to oil in return of the technically skilled manpower it offered to the various nations of the Muslim world.

Hamas leader Shaykh Ahmad Yassin hailed Pakistan's capability as an "asset to the Arab and Muslim nations."[12] Although, many Pakistani leaders have expressed their discomfort with the use of the phrase 'Islamic Bomb', the fact remains that Pakistan's nuclear weapons capability is projected and seen as an *Islamic bomb* throughout the Muslim world, which would be potentially used in the interest of Islam.

As Pakistan's nuclear weapon programme expanded, it did serve the purpose of deterring the major powers (the United States post-9/11) from taking military action against it. Post-9/11 Pakistan became the frontline state of the US and subsequently, on multiple occasions, the US frustration and harsh stance surfaced on account of Pakistan's continued strategy of supporting the Afghan Taliban and the Haqqani network in Afghanistan. But the US pressures were restricted to issuing warnings, cutting off of the military assistance, while military action against it was not an option. In Pakistan's mind, the nuclear weapons did save it from any probable US military action.

To Conduct Sub-Conventional War Without Fear of Indian Military Retaliation

Pakistan opted to use sub-conventional war against India as early as 1947 when it launched the war under the umbrella of a "tribal revolt". Pakistan has been consistently engaged in a covert war in pursuit of establishing its illegal hold over Jammu and Kashmir (J&K).

Pakistan in its aggressive approach, has fought four conventional wars with India, and three have been for Kashmir. Each of the three wars (1947, 1965 and 1999) have been launched in a covert manner, and later took the shape of full-fledged conventional war. Pakistan's covert war was accelerated in the Valley (in the 1980s and 1990s) and other parts of India (Punjab-fuelling the Khalistan movement). Covert war was a deliberate choice, as from Pakistan's point of view, it was a cheaper option and provided it with an option of defiance.

The acquisition of the nuclear capability enhanced Pakistan's ability to wage and escalate the covert war in Kashmir, as nuclear weapons were believed to deter India from responding militarily in a conventional manner. Policy makers in Pakistan carried a conviction that they can continue and accelerate the covert war in the Valley with the threat of nuclear weapons and this would restrain India's strategic moves.[13] Pakistan certainly felt more confident of conducting the covert war under the nuclear umbrella. There is a clear correlation between progress in the acquisition of nuclear weapons and the launch of the covert war in the last forty years. In 1987, Pakistan claimed that it has the capability to build a nuclear bomb. The much-desired and sensational revelation from Pakistan was made in AQ Khan's famous interview conducted by, Kuldip Nayar. There were aggressive efforts from Pakistan to send a strong message to India, deterring it from any conventional military action and AQ Khan said:

> "Mr Nayar, if you ever drive us to the wall, we will use the bomb. You did it to us in East Bengal. We won't waste time with conventional weapons. We will come straight out with it."[14]

The revelation which was intended to generate global uproar was timed with *Operation Brasstacks*. The Operation was seen by the Pakistan military and analysts as a threatening display of India's conventional capability. The interview and the revelation were arranged to warn the Indian leadership about the consequences of militarily attacking Pakistan.

Pakistan claimed that it had the capability to build a nuclear bomb in 1987 and in the 1980s and 1990s the terrorist activities became more organised and significantly intensified, challenging the Indian security forces. Pakistan's grand strategy was to use the nuclear card for conducting militancy in Kashmir in the 1990s and eventually in other parts of India. In 1989, the then Army Chief, General Aslam asserted that Pakistan lost the previous wars with India due to "lack of clear strategic vision". He announced that Pakistan had a coherent strategy now:

> "One aspect of the strategy was launching of the militant proxy war in J&K from July 31, 1988; and the other was the achievement of nuclear deterrence {to provide 'defence' in the offensive-defence strategic doctrine, while irregular war was used for the 'offensive' component} by 1987."[15]

It is noteworthy that Pakistan became more vocal about its nuclear weapons in the late 1980s and 1990s. Pakistan's former Prime Minister Nawaz Sharif during his visit to Kashmir on 23 August 1994 declared Pakistan's possession of a nuclear bomb, conveying a message to India that a conventional attack would possibly lead to nuclear retaliation from Islamabad.[16]

Nuclear weapons were aimed to not only blackmail India but also to send a message to the international community in anticipation that international pressure could potentially deter India from a military response to Pakistan's acts of terror. Trends in terrorism-data/numbers in the Valley (and other parts of India, notably Punjab) clearly indicate that Pakistan's reliance on covert war escalated after it claimed to have acquired nuclear weapons in 1987.

Perception

Low Nuclear Threshold: First Use Doctrine

Pakistan claimed to have acquired nuclear weapons in 1987 and since then the effort has been to build a perception of Pakistan's low nuclear threshold. In 1987, when AQ Khan announced that Pakistan has a bomb, the message regarding Pakistan's readiness to use the nuclear bomb was intentionally conveyed. Pakistan has long held the belief that being a weaker state, it can compensate for that weakness by taking bold initiatives—preferably with strategic surprise—to attack the Indian military capability and thus, reduce the adverse margin of capabilities. This was the military strategy it practiced in all its wars it waged against India. Seen in this context, it is not surprising that it adopted the nuclear doctrine of 'First Use'. Islamabad often claimed that it would/could use nuclear weapons at the beginning of the war, if the Indian military crossed the international border.

The *First Use* doctrine was evidently spelt out by Lt. Gen. Sardar F.S. Lodhi (Retd.) in the *Defence Journal*:

> "The political will to use nuclear weapons is essential to prevent a conventional armed conflict, which would later on escalate into a nuclear war.... Pakistan's Nuclear Doctrine would, therefore essentially revolve around the first-strike option. In other words, we will use nuclear weapons if attacked by India even if the attack is with conventional weapons."[17]

Pakistan also, rejected India's proposal for a joint no-first pledge and held the position that it would opt for nuclear weapons first:

> "India's offer of a treaty to be signed by the two countries, agreeing not to be the first to use nuclear weapons against each other is one-sided and would benefit India only, as it has a superior conventional force. It may be more apt for both countries to sign a mutual test ban treaty to start with, followed by a no-war pact."[18]

Statements from Pakistan's policymakers also indicated that Pakistan wanted to keep an option open for "pre-emptive nuclear strikes" against India. Islamabad seems to be carrying a conviction that the pre-emptive strikes would lead to the destruction of India's retaliatory capabilities and also paralyse India's decision-making.

Pakistani elites did spell out the scenarios in which Pakistan would opt for nuclear weapons first. Lt. Gen. Khalid Kidwai, former head of the Strategic Planning Division (SPD) in Pakistan's Nuclear

Command and Control System, in 2002, in an interview to Italian journalists, claimed that, "nuclear weapons would be used only "if the very existence of Pakistan as a state is at stake". But he went on to state that Pakistan would definitely use nuclear weapons in case the deterrence fails and:

1. If India attacks Pakistan and conquers a large part of its territory (space threshold);
2. If India destroys a large part either of Pakistan's land or air forces (military threshold);
3. If India proceeds to economically strangle Pakistan (economic strangling);
4. If India pushes Pakistan into political destabilisation or creates large-scale internal subversion (domestic destabilisation).[19]

The first two scenarios highlighted by Kidwai can be identified and measured to an extent, but the pronouncement of the third and the fourth scenario are intended to include a vast spectrum of scenarios (rather undefined and vague!) which could be a potential trigger for Pakistan to use nuclear weapons against New Delhi.

Pakistan's objective has been to deter any form of Indian military response and thus, the assertion on first use was rather frequent by Pakistan. Islamabad tried to project a low nuclear threshold which, in its view, helped the crisis situation by averting the war. Air Commodore Tariq Mahmud Ashraf in his study supported the low nuclear threshold:

> "A nuclear deterrent should not be able to avert a war in first place, it should be able to avert an abject defeat in the event of a war materialising and not going well. Pakistan's nuclear threshold must keep these considerations in mind. If the war is not going well, Pakistan could well threaten to employ her nuclear weapons in an effort to avert an abject defeat."[20]

In recent times, Pakistan tried raising the threat of nuclear weapons multiple times after India's decision to revoke Article 370. Prime Minister Imran Khan and Foreign Minister Shah Mahmood

Qureshi did not hesitate to build a war hysteria raising the threat of a possibility of a nuclear war in the region. The need for Pakistan to assert on first use has been further exacerbated after India pronounced that the possibility of a conventional war is not ruled out, even though both India and Pakistan are nuclear weapon states and Pakistan has a First Use Doctrine. India's position has been proven during the Kargil War and with India's military retaliation in the form of the Uri surgical strikes and the Balakot air strikes.

Rapid Expansion of the Nuclear Arsenal

Pakistan considers nuclear weapons as the ultimate guarantee of security and expansion of the nuclear arsenal has been a priority for the state despite economic pressures. The highlighted threat perceptions by the military and civilian leadership did help to justify the diversion of national resources towards the nuclear build-up, despite the fact that country has been under a constantly rising debt burden. This has been reflected in diverse Pakistani writings. Air Commodore Tariq Mahmud Ashraf wrote:

> "The Pakistani populace has been led to believe by the ruling elite that it is only by developing a viable nuclear capability that Pakistan can thwart Indian hegemonic designs."[21]

The 'actual' control of the nuclear weapon arsenal, doctrine and strategy remains primarily with the military and any interference by the political leadership in the nuclear weapons domain has never been acceptable to the army. Propagation of the criticality and indispensability of the nuclear weapons by the leadership convinced most Pakistanis that diversion of national resources for the build-up of the weapons is in the best interest of the nation. Expansion of the nuclear arsenal has always been welcomed at the domestic level, owing to two factors:

1. The weapons are seen as the ultimate protection against India and eventually against the United States (post-2001). The dominant belief has been that the US could not push Pakistan against the wall despite severe drifts in the relationship, because Pakistan possesses nuclear weapons. Also, the fear of nuclear

weapons falling into the hands of non-state actors in Pakistan and jihadi elements, did play a role in the cautious US position towards Pakistan.

2. Second, Pakistan realised that it will be tough for it to match India's conventional capability and possessing and expanding the nuclear arsenal would reduce the pressure of modernising its conventional forces. The perception was strengthened that having nuclear weapons is actually viable for Pakistan's economy, as it needs to spend less on the conventional capability build-up. However, the defence acquisitions in the last 20 years project a different thinking and reality.

It is noteworthy that significant developments in Pakistan's missile programme took place in the 1990s with Chinese assistance, when the economy was struggling with a heavy debt burden. It received M-9 and M-11 missiles from China. The M-9 SRBMs, capable of carrying nuclear and conventional warheads, were delivered to Pakistan in early 1991. Pakistan received the M-11 missile (which the Chinese refer to as the Dong Feng-11) in 1991, when US intelligence discovered their transfer along with the accompanying transporter-erector-launchers to Pakistan.[22] The *Hatf-1* entered service in 1992 and the *Hatf-1A* in 1995. The production for the *Hatf-2* started in 1987; the programme was reportedly delayed, in all probability due to the acquisition of the M-11 in the early 1990s. A new programme was later commenced in 1997 by the Pakistan National Development Complex (now NESCOM) with a reduced range of 180 km and was called the *Hatf-2* or *Abdali*.[23] The *Hatf-4* or *Shaheen-1* is believed to be a scaled-up version of the M-11 missiles supplied to Pakistan in 1991. The development programme for the *Hatf-5* or *Ghauri* commenced in 1993 at the Khan Research Laboratories and was publicly announced in 1997. An engine test was carried out in January 1998, and the first flight test was made in April 1998.

Missile development has continued with consistent pace despite the fact that the 1990s was marked by declining growth, large fiscal imbalances, rising inflation, declining public sector investment, deterioration in physical infrastructure and a deplorable state of the social sector. The delivery systems have been developed significantly in the last two decades. The Pakistan Air Force is in the process of rapid modernisation of its combat fleet, with a clear focus on building up the numbers as well as the quality of the aircraft. Pakistan conveniently claims to have developed the nuclear capability to be launched from all the three platforms—land, air and sea.

Projection

Ambiguous and Irrational

Since Pakistan's nuclear weapons were aimed at deterring an Indian military response and avoid a conventional war with India, Pakistan's adoption of an unambiguous and irrational posture facilitated its strategic objectives. Pakistan opted for an unwritten doctrine and the statements made by the policy makers in Pakistan have outlined the basic elements of its nuclear doctrine. There is an unofficial code adopted by the Pakistani leadership, based on *Indo-centricity, credible minimum deterrence, strategic restraint and first use*. Very interestingly and rather ironically, the code emphasizes the principles of a peaceful programme revolving more around maintaining a balance against the Indian force build-up; but it includes making a first strike in response to not only a conventional attack by India but also a posed threat from India. Pakistan has maintained a posture of ambiguity and kept the various options open in terms of: (i) when to use the nuclear weapons; and (ii) what to use, keeping its options open, from Tactical Nuclear Weapons (TNWs)—*Nasr* to long-range ballistic missiles like *Ghauri* and *Shaheen III*, besides aircraft and possibly a warship (for sea-launched missiles). The leadership in Pakistan, declared on various occasions (especially, before overt nuclearisation in 1998) that Pakistan would be ready to use nuclear weapons at the slightest trigger from the Indian side, projecting a low nuclear threshold. The SPD head Lt. Gen. Khalid Kidwai's interview published in 2002,[24] outlined that Pakistan's nuclear red lines created ample pandemonium globally. The projection of a low nuclear threshold has been a strategy to deal with a crisis for

Pakistan. Ironically, during the same time when Pakistan's threshold was being projected as low, Pakistan's declaration of using nuclear weapons as a "last resort" began to surface,[25] before Pakistan started to portray a posture of a "restrained and responsible" nuclear weapons state. In 2006, Lt Gen. Khalid Kidwai in his address to the Naval Postgraduate School, Monterey, said that Pakistan has dealt with formidable challenges by developing a nuclear policy based on 'restraint and responsibility' with four silent features:

> "(1) deterrence of all forms of external aggression; (2) ability to deter a counter-strike against strategic assets; (3) stabilization of strategic deterrence in South Asia; and (4) conventional and strategic deterrence methods."

Pakistan did make an effort to adopt a posture of a 'restrain and responsible nuclear power' in 2006-2007. This posture was necessary from Pakistan's point of view as the leadership was trying to convey the message to the West and the international community that its nuclear arsenal is safe and not threatened by a potential jihadi takeover.

The option of nuclear weapons as weapons of last resort and then restrain and responsibility projected a high nuclear threshold. On the other hand, Pakistan continued to issue nuclear threats during the Kargil War in 1999 and *Operation Parakram* in 2002. Even though Pakistan's stated position has varied, the ultimate strategic objective that nuclear weapons are expected to serve is to guard against India's conventional moves and provide Pakistan an ultimate weapon of security.

Full Spectrum Deterrence

For decades policymakers in Pakistan held a conviction that they will be able to carry on, or rather accelerate their acts of terror in India, with the threat of the use of nuclear weapons. However, India's stance on the probability of a conventional war under the nuclear overhang challenged Islamabad's conviction about New

Delhi's consistent restrain and hesitation in responding militarily to a Pakistan-sponsored act of terror.

On 19 April 2011, Pakistan tested its short-range surface-to-surface multi-tube ballistic missile *Hatf-9* (*Nasr*). The official press release for *Nasr* said:

> "[The *Nasr* Weapon System] has been developed to add deterrence value to Pakistan's Strategic Weapons Development programme at shorter ranges. *Nasr* with a range of 60 km, carries nuclear warheads [emphasis added] of appropriate yield with high accuracy, [and] shoot-and-scoot attributes. This quick response system addresses the need to deter evolving threats."[26]

The *Nasr* provides Pakistan with short-range missile capability in addition to the long-range ballistic missiles and cruise missiles. Pakistan has repeatedly claimed that *Hatf-9* is the counter to India's Cold Start Doctrine which envisions limited conventional response from the Indian side in response to the sub-conventional attacks on India originating from Pakistani territory. This belief reflected in Lt. Gen. Khalid Kidwai's statement (2015):

> "I strongly believe that by introducing the variety of tactical nuclear weapons in Pakistan's inventory, and in the strategic stability debate, we have blocked the avenues for serious military operations by the other side."[27]

Kidwai justified that *Nasr* was born to fill in the 'deterrence gap':

> "*Nasr*, specifically, was born out of a compulsion of this thing that I mentioned about some people on the other side toying with the idea of finding space for conventional war, despite Pakistani nuclear weapons ... we figured out that what was driving this particular concept on the other side was that they were looking at certain gaps in the, on the nuclear weapon inventory of Pakistan."[28]

Pakistan claimed that it is developing a sea-based nuclear force to be able to match India's nuclear triad. The Naval Strategic Force Command was announced in 2012. In January 2017, Pakistan conducted the first test of its submarine-launched cruise missile (SLCM), the *Babur-3* from a submarine. It is estimated that *Babur-3* has a range of 450 km and will be carried on Pakistan's diesel-powered Agosta 90B submarine.

Pakistan has been keen on achieving a sea-based deterrent mainly because of two factors. First, Pakistan believes in maintaining uncertainty and enhancing deterrence. Sea-based nuclear capability does fulfil the objective of enhancing deterrence for Pakistan by achieving a nuclear triad. Second, Pakistan does not seem to believe India's No-First-Use (NFU) and maintains a perception that India, even with a NFU doctrine, could use nuclear weapons against Pakistan. Given this assumption, sea-based nuclear capability in Pakistan's view provides it with a survivable deterrent.

Pakistan's ballistic missile programme is evolving at a consistent pace and in January 2021, Pakistan tested *Shaheen III* surface-to-surface ballistic missiles with a range of 2,750 km. In March 2015, the missile was tested for the first time and has not been operationally deployed.[29] The *Shaheen III* test was much applauded, as given its extended range, it is "capable of reaching the farthest point in India's northeast and Andaman and Nicobar Islands" according to the Pakistani media.[30] Pakistan has been anxious to cover the Andaman and Nicobar Islands and talking about the logic of *Shaheen III*, Kidwai said:

> "What we are counting on also is not just the main Indian landmass, the peninsula, the eastern dimension, the southern dimension. There is, of late, there have been reports of the Nicobar, and the Andaman Islands in the Bay of Bengal, being developed as bases, potentially as strategic bases. And if those bases are not covered by Pakistan, and *Shaheen III* does that, with 2,750 km.... Pakistan will be allowing, so to say, a second strike capability to India within its land borders."[31]

Pakistan conveniently claims to have developed the nuclear capability to be launched from all the three platforms—land, air, and sea. The aim of full spectrum deterrence is to deny New Delhi any space for a conventional military retaliation. Pakistan's nuclear posture before and after the overt nuclearisation indicates that full spectrum deterrence for Pakistan also implies full spectrum of scenarios, since Pakistan believes in maintaining a projection of a low nuclear threshold and also an element of uncertainty. The nuclear posture seems to rely on the threat of use of nuclear weapons to deal with a wide range of crisis vis-à-vis India. After the overt nuclearisation Pakistan's nuclear redlines drew vague parameters trying to accommodate any potential punitive action by India as a possible trigger for Pakistan to opt for nuclear weapons. Later, even though Pakistan talked about using nuclear weapons as a *last resort,* it continued to use the threat of nuclear weapons frequently to deal with a crisis vis-à-vis India. It talked about the last resort but also simultaneously took pride in projecting reliance on TNWs, leaving the basic question unanswered: *What is last resort for Pakistan?*

Full spectrum deterrence for Pakistan implies: *Full spectrum of platforms*—land, air and sea; *Full spectrum of scenarios*—keeping a low threshold and maintaining ambiguity provides flexibility to Pakistan; and *Full spectrum of targets*—counter-value and counter-force.

Conclusion: What does it Mean for India?

Pakistan acquired the nuclear weapons with an objective of neutralizing the Indian conventional capability; build an image of a dominant and important power of the Islamic world; have an answer to India's perceived hegemonic ambitions; guard its 'sovereignty and survival'; and attract global attention on Kashmir. Stephen Cohen aptly highlighted military's conviction in seeking advantage in Kashmir through nuclear weapons:

> "Pakistani officers suggested to me that once they got the nuclear weapons, they could again open up the Kashmir issue, as well as protect themselves against India's larger conventional force. Thus,

> nuclear weapons were not merely another way of countering Indian power; they could also give Pakistan a decisive strategic advantage in the struggle over Kashmir."[32]

The threat perceptions of Pakistan were often exaggerated to justify and rationalise the indispensability of the nuclear arsenal despite Pakistan's economic woes and worrisome social indicators. Pakistan's strategy of using covert war through terrorism was facilitated with the acquisition of nuclear weapons and the proclaimed doctrine of the first-use doctrine. Pakistan believed that an ambiguous nuclear posture and a first-use doctrine would deter India's conventional response to a Pakistan-sponsored terror attack. The central strategic assumption of Pakistan's nuclear strategy has been that India cannot impose a conventional war on Pakistan, leave alone achieve a decisive victory without the risk of catastrophic consequences of Pakistan's nuclear attack. This belief was challenged with India's position of a possibility of a conventional war under the nuclear overhang. Pakistan launched *Nasr* in 2011 and projected the TNWs as an answer to an Indian conventional military response. However, India's position on a conventional military response has been clarified by India only in response to a Pakistan-sponsored terror attack.

There are contradictions in Pakistan's nuclear posture with the lowering of the nuclear threshold and the talk about the last resort and restraint and responsibility. Pakistan expresses its willingness to have peace with India but never misses an opportunity to raise the nuclear threat. The effort has been to talk peace and stability under the nuclear overhang. It continuously talks about the dangers of a nuclear war but has been creating war hysteria, especially in the last two years. Pakistan has very *rationally adopted a posture of irrationality.*

Pakistan's nuclear posturing did suffer to some extent with India's airstrikes in Balakot on 26 February 2019 in retaliation to the terror attack in Pulwama on 14 February 2019, claimed by Jaish-e-Mohammed (JeM). But its reliance on using the threat of nuclear weapons seems to be unaltered. Pakistan's efforts to use the nuclear card in the past spasmodically stems from its basic insecurity as a state and its failure to develop its strengths. Its excessive reliance on the threat of use of nuclear weapons and its assertion on "first use" grew with the growing asymmetry between India and Pakistan.

India needs to continue to focus on modernising its missile capabilities with greater range and accuracy. The conventional military build-up needs to continue and clear nuclear signalling needs to be emphasised in India's strategic posture towards Pakistan. Looking into Pakistan's nuclear posture for the last four decades, some interesting conclusions can be drawn:

- Pakistan is likely to continue to raise the threat of nuclear war to justify the enormous nuclear build-up to its people and to attract international attention on Kashmir.
- There might be a pause of nuclear blackmail and threats of a nuclear war from Pakistan, owing to its strategic compulsions (from time to time), but, the basic tenets of its nuclear posturing—uncertainty, ambiguity and projection of irrationality are unlikely to change.
- Pakistan will continue to build-up a second-strike capability.
- The focus of the conventional military build-up (post-Kargil War) has been modernisation of the air force and aerial maritime strike capabilities of the navy. This trend is likely to continue, primarily with Chinese assistance.

Disclaimer: Parts of the chapter have been published in author's work *Nuclear Pakistan* (KW Publishers, New Delhi, 2012), and "Pakistan's Nuclear Brinkmanship: Continued Reliance on Nuclear Weapons", in Tilak Devasher (ed.), *Pakistan Insights 2020* (Pentagon Press, New Delhi, 2021), pp. 103-111.

Notes

1. '"If you drive us to the wall, we will use the bomb"—In December 1986, India launched the largest war game ever. Pakistan responded with a message of its own', *The Telegraph*, 4 November 2007, at https://www.telegraphindia.com/7-days/if-you-drive-us-to-the-wall-we-will-use-the-bomb-in-december-1986-india-launched-the-largest-war-game-ever-pakistan-responded-with-a-message-of-its-own/cid/1534921. Accessed on 20 June 2021.

2. 'Remarks of the Prime Minister of Pakistan, Nawaz Sharif, on Nuclear Policies and the CTBT', National Defence College, Islamabad, 20 May 1999.
3. 'Pakistan successfully test-fires nuclear capable *Hatf-9*', *The Express Tribune,* 20 April 2011.
4. Feroz Hasan Khan, *Eating Grass: The Making of the Pakistani Bomb*, Cambridge University Press, New Delhi, 2013, p. 85.
5. Sultan Bashiruddin Mahmood, interview by author, Islamabad, 14 December 2006, cited in Ibid., p. 87.
6. Lt. Gen. F.S. Lodhi, 'Pakistan's Nuclear Doctrine', *Defence Journal,* at http://www.defencejournal.com/apr99/pak-nuclear-doctrine.htm. Accessed on 10 May 2011.
7. Former Foreign Minister of Pakistan Agha Shahi in Fasahat H. Sayed (ed.), *Nuclear Disarmament and Conventional Arms Control Including Light Weapons,* Friends, Rawalpindi, 1997, p. 421.
8. G. Parthasarthy, 'The Nuclear Doctrine—For Ensuring Global Strategic Stability', *The Hindu Business Line,* 22 September 2005.
9. Stephen Cohen, *Shooting for a Century: The India Pakistan Conundrum,* Brookings,Washington DC, 2013, p. 103.
10. *Transcript of Testimony before the Supreme Court of Pakistan*, in reply to Pakistan Government White Papers, as cited in *From Surprise to Reckoning: The Kargil Review Committee Report,* Sage, New Delhi, 1999, p. 185.
11. Maj. Gen. D.K. Palit and P.K.S. Namboodiri, *Pakistan's Islamic Bomb*, Vikas Publishing House, New Delhi, 1979, p. 36.
12. Ibn Warraq, 'The Islamic Bomb', at http://www.secularhumanism.org/library/shb/warraq_14_3.html.
13. See, Shalini Chawla, *Pakistan's Military and Its Strategy*, KW Publishers, New Delhi, 2009, p. 199.
14. *The Telegraph*, n. 1.
15. General Mirza Aslam Beg, *The Nation*, 13 December 1993, as cited in 'The Army in Pakistan', in Air Commodore Jasjit Singh (ed.), *Kargil 1999: Pakistan's Fourth War for Kashmir*, KW Publishers, New Delhi, 1999, p. 47.
16. Tim McGrik, 'Pakistan has a bomb, ex-PM admits', *The Independent*, 23 August 1994, at https://www.independent.co.uk/news/pakistan-has-bomb-expm-admits-1385374.html. Accessed on 19 June 2020.
17. Lt. Gen. F.S. Lodhi, n. 6.
18. Ibid.
19. As cited in Paolo Cotta-Ramusino and Maurizio Martellini, *Nuclear Safety, Nuclear Stability and Nuclear Strategy in Pakistan,* Landau Network—Centro Volta Report, January 2002.
20. Air Commodore Tariq Mahmud Ashraf (Retd.), *Evolving Dynamics of Nuclear South Asia,* KW Publishers, New Delhi, 2014, p. 166.

21. Ibid., p. 5.
22. Bill Gertz, 'Missile Deception', in *Betrayal: How the Clinton Administration Undermined American Security,* Regnery Publishing, Inc., Washington, DC, 1999, p. 159, as cited in 'Pakistan Profile: Missile Overview', *NTI,* at http://www.nti.org/e_research/profiles/Pakistan/Missile/index.htm. Accessed on 10 January 2011.
23. *Jane's Strategic Weapons Systems*, Issue 48, 2008, p. 109.
24. Paolo Cotta-Ramusino and Maurizio Martellini, n. 19.
25. See, Agha Shahi, Zulfiqar Khan and Abdul Sattar, 'Securing Nuclear Peace', *The News* (Islamabad), 5 October 1999.
26. Rodney W. Jones, 'Pakistan's Answer to Cold Start?', *The Friday Times,* 13-19 May 2011.
27. 'A Conversation with Gen. Khalid Kidwai', Carnegie International Nuclear Policy Conference 2015, 23 March 2015, p. 5, at https://carnegieendowment.org/files/03-230315carnegieKIDWAI.pdf. Accessed on 13 April 2016.
28. Ibid., p. 8.
29. 'Another Successful Test of *Shaheen III* carried out', *The News*, 21 January 2021, at https://www.dawn.com/news/1602683. Accessed on 1 February 2021.
30. Ibid.
31. 'A Conversation with Gen. Khalid Kidwai', Carnegie International Nuclear Policy Conference 2015, n. 27, p. 10.
32. Stephen Cohen, n. 9, p. 103.

13. Ballistic and Cruise Missiles of Pakistan

Rajaram Nagappa

Introduction

There is commonality among the technology building blocks of rockets for space and atmospheric studies and for missile applications. In that sense, Pakistan got an early start in flight testing of sounding rockets, when it established the Space and Upper Atmospheric Research Commission (SUPARCO) on 16 September 1961. The SUPARCO functioned under the Pakistan Atomic Energy Commission with the well-known Physicist Abdus Salam as its Director and Administrative Head. Pakistan launched its first sounding rocket—a Nike-Cajun rocket supplied by NASA and renamed as Rehbar-1 in Pakistan on 7 June 1962. After initial years of sounding rocket flights, rocket development activity did not gather any momentum for scientific purposes nor was there a spin-off into development of missiles. With the nuclear weapon development programme gathering momentum in the 1980s, Pakistan initially focused on air delivery platforms, but soon recognised the efficacy of missiles. Realising that an indigenous missile development programme will involve long gestation time, Pakistan decided to procure ballistic missiles and missile technology from countries which had scant regard for proliferation issues. A few US ship-launched cruise missiles against terrorist targets in Afghanistan malfunctioned and fell in Pakistani territory. Pakistan gleaned enough knowledge from these to reverse-engineer its own cruise missiles. Today Pakistan has ballistic missiles of diverse range capabilities, ground, air and submarine-launched cruise missiles and a short-range battlefield missile. In the absence of demonstrated testing of their miniaturised weapons, their performance and 'deterrence' value remains questionable.

Pakistan took the initial steps in rocketry in the early 1960s, with the SUPARCO taking up studies in atmospheric science using US supplied sounding rockets. A Nike-Cajun rocket flight on 7 June 1962 was the first rocket flight from the SUPARCO's launch station at Sonmiani. During 1967, both US and French sounding rockets were launched from the SUPARCO's Sonmiani launch site. In 1973, two British-made Skua rockets took to the skies from Sonmiani, after which the sounding rocket flights seem to have been discontinued. During these years a total of 82[1] sounding rockets were flown from Sonmiani, comprising both single-stage and two-stage rockets. Indian sounding rocket activity from the Thumba Equatorial Rocket Launching Station near Trivandrum (now Thiruvananthapuram) started about the same time. While sounding rocket activity in India formed the nucleus of a civil space programme, the SUPARCO's activity proceeded neither in the direction of a civil space programme nor was it harnessed for development of missiles during this period. The loss of East Pakistan in 1971 and the Indian Peaceful Nuclear Explosion on 18 May 1974, prompted Pakistan to seriously consider their own nuclear option.

It is outside the purview of this chapter to discuss the details of the Pakistani nuclear programme but suffice to say based on design details of the Chinese Chic-4 nuclear weapon and their own modifications, Pakistan had by May 1995 an aircraft deliverable bomb design.[2] A ballistic missile with its long standoff distance and appropriate range is a more desirable platform than an aircraft and Pakistan took the initial steps towards acquiring this capability in the late 1980s. However, the major thrust towards acquiring missile capability was given only in the late 1990s.

Early Missile Development Effort

India had obtained from Sud Aviation of France, the manufacturing licence for the 2-stage Centaure rocket comprising a 94 kg Venus propellant block for the first stage and 208 kg Belier propellant block for the 2nd stage. Available information[3] points to Pakistan also getting the same rocket manufacturing licence from Sud Aviation, and the beginning of rocketry in Pakistan can be traced to this.

India used Centaure technology as a stepping-stone to develop significant capability in solid propellant rockets, diversified into other space technology development areas and went on to establish a civilian space programme. The development in the civil space provided spin-offs which could be used for missile development. A similar trend was not seen in the case of Pakistan and the sounding rocket initiative did not provide impetus either for the development of a space programme or for the development of a missile programme for quite some years. The reason for this could be the frequent change in the management structure,[4] the relatively low priority for space activity and possible funding constraints. The SUPARCO, since December 2000, is part of the National Command Authority. It is perhaps, no surprise that indigenous development efforts of longer range ballistic missiles and cruise missiles have taken place in the years after 2000.

Pakistan's missile development efforts can be broadly classified under the following categories:

(i) Missiles derived from sounding rocket programme
(ii) Solid propellant rocket missiles procured from PRC
(iii) Liquid propellant rocket missile procured from DPRK
(iv) Indigenous development of solid propellant rocket missiles

In August 2005, Pakistan surprised the world by carrying out a successful flight test of subsonic land attack cruise missiles with a range of 500 km. Two years later an air-launched version was tested. From the very beginning, realisation of a submarine-launched version was viewed by Pakistan as a necessity.

In April 2011, Pakistan flight-tested a battlefield missile with a nuclear warhead. The introduction of this weapon added a new and unforeseen element in the missile employment and deployment schemes. For the purpose of this chapter, Pakistan's development of tactical nuclear weapon will be treated as an additional category of ballistic missiles.

The Pakistani nuclear posture is India-centric and consequently, the design of the missiles has been carried out with the goal of reaching distant Indian locations. Naturally, this capability achievement has spawneda period of three decades and to quite some extent the evolution is a response to launch vehicle and missile-related developments in India. This facet in the initial years is captured in Table 13.1.

Table 13.1: Initial Sounding Rocket, Launch Vehicle and Missile-Related Activities

Date	Event (Indian and Pakistani events in grey and black fonts respectively)
7 June 1962	Pakistan launches Rehbar-1 sounding rocket from Sonmiani Range. Rehbar is the Pakistani name for the US Nike-Cajun rocket carrying a sodium vapour payload
21 November 1963	India launches Nike-Apache from Thumba Equatorial Rocket Launching Station carrying Sodium vapour payload
1 January 1969	Flight test of RH-200—a two stage rocket capable of carrying chaff payload to 70 km for carrying out meteorological studies.
18 July 1980	Successful flight test of SLV-3. SLV-3 was a 4 stage launch vehicle; all stages employed solid propellant. Liquid propellant systems were used for vehicle control purposes
1981	Formal establishment of Space and Upper Atmosphere Research Commission
26 July 1983	Government of India accords approval for the Integrated Missile Development Programme (IGMDP)
25 February 1988	Maiden flight of Prithvi missile
25 May 1988	Pakistan tests nuclear capable ballistic missile[5] from Thar Range. Mumbai and Delhi are claimed to be in the range of the missile

Missiles based on Sounding Rocket Technology

It is seen that sounding rocket flights from the Sonmiani were carried out routinely till 18 April 1973 using sounding rockets of other countries as well as sounding rockets licence-produced in Pakistan. Starting in May 1967 and till April 1972, Belier, Centaure-1 and Dragon sounding rockets of Sud Aviation origin took to the skies from Sonmiani. The features[6] of these sounding rockets are as follows:

Table 13.2: Characteristics of Sud Aviation Sounding Rockets

Sounding Rocket	No. of stages	Performance	
		Payload	Apogee
Belier	1	30 kg	85 km
Centaure	2	60 kg	130 km
Dragon	2	60 kg	475 km
Dauphin	1		
Eridan	2	250 kg	300 km

Notes: • Belier was 305 mm in diameter and used 280 kg of propellant.
• Centaure was also 305 mm in diameter and used a booster with 94 kg propellant and Belier for the 2nd stage.
• Dragon booster was 560 mm in diameter and used 686 kg propellant and
• Belier as 2nd stage. The same booster with a different propellant was used in the single-stage Dauphin.
• Eridan employed two stages of Dauphin.

The first flight of a French sounding rocket from Sonmiani took place on 3 May 1967 using a two-stage Centaure rocket. Two more flights, one using a Dragon rocket and the other Centaure, took place in 1967. In 1968 also, two flights of Centaure and one flight of Dragon was launched.

It is believed that the sounding rocket technology transfer from Sud Aviation must have occurred during this period. The propellant plant connected with the above agreement is located about 10 km west of Karachi. The earliest Google Earth imagery is of 25 February 2000 and is shown in Figure 13.1 below. The separation between the buildings and mounded structures of some buildings is a give away of the hazardous nature of processes being carried out at the plant. The hardware is probably manufactured elsewhere and then brought to the plant for subsequent operations. Under the technology transfer agreement, Pakistan would have obtained the following technologies:[7]

- PVC plastisol propellant composition and processing details
- Related propellant systems like PVC restrictor tube, inhibition
- 15CdV6 steel motor case fabrication and heat treatment
- Propellant charging into hardware
- Nozzle fabrication and thermal protection system
- Fin shroud and fin fabrication
- Nose cone and payload deck fabrication
- Stage ignition and Ordnance system
- Assembly and integration
- Quality control and inspection

Figure 13.1: Propellant Plant Layout

Source: Google Earth imagery of 25 February 2000.

Even though the Centaure is a simple and reliable rocket, as an integrated system it can pose problems. Apart from the mechanical, thermal and payload-related issues, one has to pay attention to aerodynamic and alignment-related issues. It is believed that the by late 1968/early 1969, Pakistan rolled out the indigenous version of the Centaure rocket. Three rockets were flight-tested in February and March 1969. The two rockets flown in February were failures[8] and achieved apogee of respectively 55 km and 12 km against the design value of 130 km. The failures could be due to early developmental teething problems. The third test seems to have achieved the target apogee. However, close to three years from March 1969, there were no flights of Centaure and all the scientific sounding rocket flights used US and British rockets. It appears that this period was used in investigation of the problem and troubleshooting the problem issues and conducting necessary tests for improving the system quality. The result was that the Centaure rockets reappeared on the scene in April 1972 with two successful launches in the same month; there was also a flight of the Dragon rocket, which could have been manufactured in Pakistan. There were three more sounding rocket flights in 1973, using British sounding rockets, Skua and Petrel, following which, there was a literal closure of sounding rocket activities. With the advent of satellites, the interest of research scientists in using rockets for their experiments was waning and Pakistan, suffering from the after-effects of the Bangladesh War and possible resource constraints, was in no position to revive the activity.

Pakistani nuclear efforts had started after the Indian Peaceful Nuclear Explosion (PNE) of 1974 and for quite some time Pakistan was satisfied with modified PAF aircraft as the strategic weapon delivery system. However, the initiation of Integrated Guided Missile Development Programme (IGMDP) in India and the test of the *Prithvi* missile in February 1988, accelerated the Pakistani missile development response. It was not difficult for Pakistan to fashion a missile based on its sounding rocket technology knowledge and this is exactly what Pakistan did for the maiden launch of its missile. Their response with *Hatf-1*, flight-tested in February 1989, was essentially the French sounding rocket Dauphin rechristened as *Hatf-1*. The launch angle and trajectory were adjusted to provide range as opposed to attaining altitude required for scientific flights. Figure 13.2 shows the *Hatf-1* in flight, and its close resemblance[9] to Dauphin is evident.

Figure 13.2: Image of Hatf-1 and Dauphin

The range of the missile was of the order of 80 km with 500 kg payload. *Hatf-2*, a 2-stage missile with a range of 280 km was also tested in February 1989. *Hatf-2* was called Shadoz and had a range of 280 km with a 500 kg payload. It is possible that borrowing the 2-stage idea of Eridan, two *Hatf-1* stages were stacked to realise *Hatf-2*. *Hatf-2* and Eridan are shown in Figure 13.3. Some change in the 2nd stage fin geometry is seen.

Figure 13.3: Hatf-2 (Shadoz) missile and Eridan Sounding Rocket

With *Hatf-1* and *Hatf-2* Pakistan felt it had engineered a response to India's Prithvi launch in 1988 as evident from the statement of Pakistan's Army Chief of Staff General Mirza Aslam Beg.[10] In an Address at the National Defence College in Rawalpindi in February 1989, General Beg announced that two indigenously-manufactured surface-to-surface missiles had been tested. General Beg further claimed that the *Hatf-1* and *Hatf-2* missiles "are extremely accurate systems" that can carry 500-kg payloads to ranges of 80 and 300 km respectively. However, the situation was not so rosy and there were technical problems with *Hatf-2*. Issues with staging as well as guidance were suspected,[11] resulting in the halting of further development on *Hatf-2*.

Need for Longer-Range Missiles

The sounding rocket technology transfer from Sud Aviation involved the low-energy polyvinyl chloride (PVC) fuel-based propellant system; the rockets were fin-stabilised and did not carry any control system; As such, they were not suitable for direct adaptation, as precision missile systems. For missile application, improvements in propellant energetics and related properties, thermal protection, separation of warhead, control and guidance systems were disciplines which had to be mastered. An indigenous development route would have involved considerable time and this would have meant a larger distance from Indian capabilities as well as a large deterrence gap. This is the reason, Pakistan started scouting for technology-transfer from established players.

The range of *Hatf-1* had to be multiplied many times over in order to reach targets deep in India. Though some leading countries had missiles with ranges of interest to Pakistan, they were constrained from selling missiles capable of reaching range of 300 km with a payload of 500 kg or related technology under the stipulations of the Missile Technology Control Regime[12] (MTCR). Among the missile exporting countries, the United States and France were founder members of the MTCR and hence could be ruled out for missile sale/transfer. Russia had adopted the MTCR guidelines before formally joining the MTCR in 1995. Moreover, Russia would not have helped Pakistan overriding Indian security concerns and hence could be ruled out. Considering Israel as a potential source was out of the question for an Islamic country and that left only North Korea and China as possible providers of missiles/missile technology of appropriate ranges. In addition, the North Korean economy, on account of the US sanctions was in bad shape and China (not a member of MTCR) could afford to disregard MTCR guidelines when it suited its political and strategic interests. The distances to major Indian cities from Islamabad are indicated in Figure 13.4 and Pakistan necessarily wanted missiles, which could traverse these and more distances.

Figure 13.4: Distance from Islamabad to Indian Cities

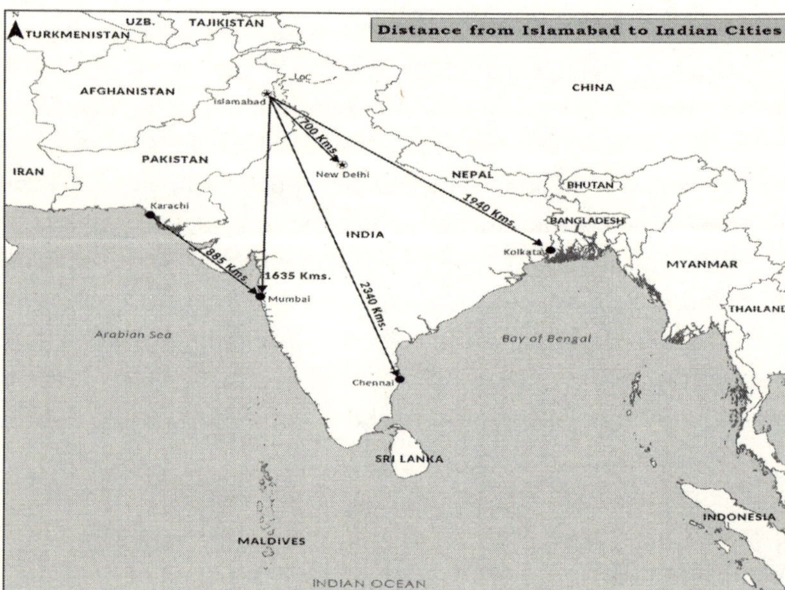

© GIS Section, Manohar Parrikar Institute for Defence Studies & Analyses (MP-IDSA). Map not to scale.

General Mirza Aslam Beg in his capacity as Chief of General Staff had established the Combat Development Directorate, which became operational in 1985. The Directorate was tasked to examine emerging missile technologies[13] for induction into the Army. While, solid propellant rockets are preferred for missile applications, the search must have looked at what was available on offer. According to Feroze Hassan Khan, the Combat Development Directorate "conducted a comprehensive analysis and recommended that the Army Chief seek both liquid fuel and solid fuel ballistic missile platforms of varying ranges for its nuclear weapons".

The Chinese had developed the DF-15 and DF-11 missiles with range of 750 km and 300 km respectively. The first flight of DF-15 had taken place in January 1988 and that of DF-11 in January 1990. The export versions of these were designated M-9 and M-11 respectively and were in the active procurement list of Pakistan. The M-11, in terms of range, fell within the MTCR guideline number of 300 km, but in terms of payload did not meet the criterion.

The other candidate system was the Scud-derived No Dong missile of North Korea. This missile employs liquid propellant and has a range higher than the Chinese solid propellant missiles under consideration. The longer range of No Dong and procurement of missile/missile technology from diverse sources were managerially prudent. The intense rivalry between the AQ Khan-led Khan Research Laboratories (KRL) and the Pakistan Atomic Energy Commission (PAEC), also helped in cementing this approach.

Jane's Defense Weekly in its 20 May 1998[14] issue, stated that Prime Minister Benazir Bhutto supports the acquisition of missiles from China and extending bilateral ties between Pakistan and North Korea in the nuclear and missile fields. Pakistani powers that be, wasted no time in transforming Benazir Bhutto's statement into action. Over the course of two years starting from early 1991, China is reported to have supplied to Pakistan M-11 missiles, M-9 and M-11 missile launchers, sub-assemblies, components and subsystems, production plants and machinery, and control and guidance systems. China also trained Pakistani engineers and technicians in the processing, integration and testing aspects of missile subsystems and complete units.[15] It would appear from a reading of the Nuclear Threat Initiative's (NTI's) Pakistan Missile Chronology that the US' restraining efforts were half-hearted. China repeatedly renegaded on its promise to halt missile transfers and on occasions misrepresented the missile range information. With this initial help, Pakistan appears to have assimilated the technology and internalised it adequately to embark on modifications, develop variants and new capabilities.

Ballistic Missiles

It is mainly the Chinese connection, which has helped Pakistan in achieving a credible missile capability based on solid propellant motors. China has helped Pakistan with full missile assemblies, setting up of production facilities and training. The four main missiles of the Chinese arsenal—*Abdali, Ghaznavi, Shaheen I* and *Shaheen II* are based on, or are similar to, a Chinese equivalent.

Ghaznavi (*Hatf-3*) is the indigenised version of M-11. The M-11 is a single-stage, short-range ballistic missile, which China developed in the 1980s, completed the flight tests in 1990 and deployed it in 1992. The M-11 is a road-mobile missile and can deliver a 500 kg warhead to a range of 280 km and has been configured to conform to the MTCR stipulations. The missile comes with its 8x8 WS2400 Transporter-erector-launcher (TEL). China supplied about 30 of these missiles to Pakistan in 1992 and the crated missiles were picked up by US spy satellites. When confronted by the US, China agreed to stop further shipments of assembled missiles. They however, continued to provide the missiles in dissembled condition and set up assembly facilities in Pakistan. They also trained the Pakistani missile crew in the assembly, checkout and testing procedures. The technology learning from M-11 were used by Pakistan to modify the earlier *Hatf-1* design to improve accuracy and range. The new missile was christened *Abdali* (*Hatf*-2).

Apparently, a Chinese pedigree is traceable for the Pakistani ballistic missiles as shown below:

- *Ghaznavi* (*Hatf-3*) is derived from M-11[16]
- The M-11 inputs/training has helped in the redesign of *Abdali* (*Hatf-2*) missile
- *Shaheen I* (*Hatf-4*) is derived from M-9[17]
- *Shaheen II* (*Hatf-6*) is indicated by some observers as a derivative of M-18 missile. There is no active M-18 missile in the Chinese list of missiles and no images of the missile are available in the

open literature. However, Norbert Brugge[18] provides one image of the missile (conceptual) and one image of a motor which is 1.4 m in diameter, 7.15 m long and having a thrust rating of 594 kN. The dimensions are close to that of *Shaheen II*.

Resulting from the technology transfer, Pakistan would have gained missile system design insights and capabilities in the major missile disciplines. This would include, in addition to the basic design tools, the working of different elements of the missile system, establishment of facilities, facility operation, quality control, test and evaluation. Most importantly, Pakistan would have got trained in the overall mission planning and implementation.

All the missiles derived from Chinese pedigree use solid propellants for the main stages. In recent times, Pakistan sources have talked about the employment of "post-separation attitude control system".[19] Such a system will be based on liquid propulsion-based small rockets which have either been developed in the country or procured from outside. The details of Pakistani solid propellant-based missiles is shown in Figure 13.5.

Figure 13.5: Abdali, Shaheen I, Shaheen IA, Shaheen II, Shaheen III and Ababeel Missiles

In addition to the missile series explained above, Pakistan also has the *Ghauri* missile, which is derived from the North Korean No Dong missile. The No Dong missile itself is based on the Russian Scud missile technology which has been modified by North Korea and proliferated to Iran and Pakistan. North Korea reverse-engineered Scud missiles into the *Hwasong* series. The improved variant, equivalent to Scud C, was known as *Hwasong* 6, which was further scaled-up as the No Dong missile, and had a range of 1500 km. The missile in Pakistan goes under the name of *Ghauri* or *Hatf-5* and is shown in Figure 13.6. There are similarities with the No Dong missile in terms of physical dimensions, fins and jet-vane control system. The No Dong missile is pictured along with *Ghauri* in the Figure 13.6.

Figure 13.6: Ghauri and No Dong Missiles

The characteristics of the Pakistani ballistic missiles are shown in Table 13.3 below:

Table 13.3: Pakistani Solid Propellant-based Ballistic Missile Characteristics

Missile	Stages	Length (m)	Diameter (m)	Range (km)	Remarks
Abdali (Hatf-2)	1	6.5	0.56	80-100	Originally Hatf-1; modified and improved based on technologies from M-11
Ghaznavi (Hatf-3)	1	8.5	0.8	300	Indigenous version of Chinese M-11 missile
Shaheen I	1	12.0	1.0	750	Based on Chinese M-9
Shaheen IA (Hatf-4)	1	12.0	1.0	900	RV is modified and uses PSAC system
Ghauri (Hatf-5)	1	15.9	1.35	1300	Based on North Korean No Dong missile
Shaheen II	2	17.2	1.4	1500	Based on Chinese DF-18. Range originally claimed 2500 km
Shaheen III	3		1.4	2750	Essentially modified *Shaheen*-2 with an additional liquid stage
Ababeel	3	22.1	1.4 / 1.7	2200	The missile is said to carry MIRVs. The *Shaheen III* stages + PBCV

Discussion

- The range indicated is for payload in the range 700-1000 kg. The *Abdali* is able to carry a 500 kg payload and the payload for *Ababeel* with MIRV will be higher. Our estimate of the

MIRV with mounting platform and post-boost-control-system, is 4,000 kg.

- All Pakistani missiles from security and strategic considerations have been designed to be road-mobile. TELs are of Chinese origin but are being produced indigenously.
- Missiles are capable of fielding both conventional and strategic warheads. As a confidence-building measure, India and Pakistan exchange pre-launch notifications of ballistic missiles.
- Pakistan has a 'first-use' policy, but has an elaborate procedure for authorising a nuclear strike. It is also stated to store the missile and the warhead in demated condition.
- The *Ghaznavi,* on account of its Chinese antecedents, is a qualified system and operational. No visible design or performance improvements have been carried out from the Chinese version of the missile.
- The *Shaheen I* similarly is a qualified system based on its derivation from the Chinese M-9 missile. Its first flight in April 1999 was not successful but subsequent flights, carried out at a frequency of approximately one flight per year till 2004, have been successful. The test frequency has dropped, with flights conducted sporadically in 2008 and 2012. More significantly, *Shaheen IA* seems to be replacing *Shaheen I* with a higher range and claimed higher target accuracy. *Shaheen IA* was first flight-tested in April 2012. As per the ISPR notification accompanying a *Shaheen IA* flight, "the missile incorporates series of improvements in range and technical parameters of the existing missile. It is capable of carrying nuclear and conventional warheads to a range of 900 km."
- The stated range of 900 km is equal to an improvement of 20-28 per cent over that of *Shaheen I*. An examination of the *Shaheen I/IA* flight images does not show any discernible difference in physical dimensions of the missile body. However, a change in the Re-entry Vehicle (RV) can be observed. The RV's are compared in Figure 13.7. The major difference is that the *Shaheen I* RV has aerodynamic surfaces while the *Shaheen IA* RV is aerodynamically clean and the aerodynamic fins have

been replaced by liquid propellant reaction control engines for stabilising the RV and providing axial direction acceleration as well as range increment. This is borne out by the media report[20] that the missile is equipped with "post-separation attitude correction system, which provides accuracy and maneuverability to evade missile defences". This is a significant technology improvement and can be adapted for other RV designs also.

Figure 13.7: Shaheen I and Shaheen IA RV

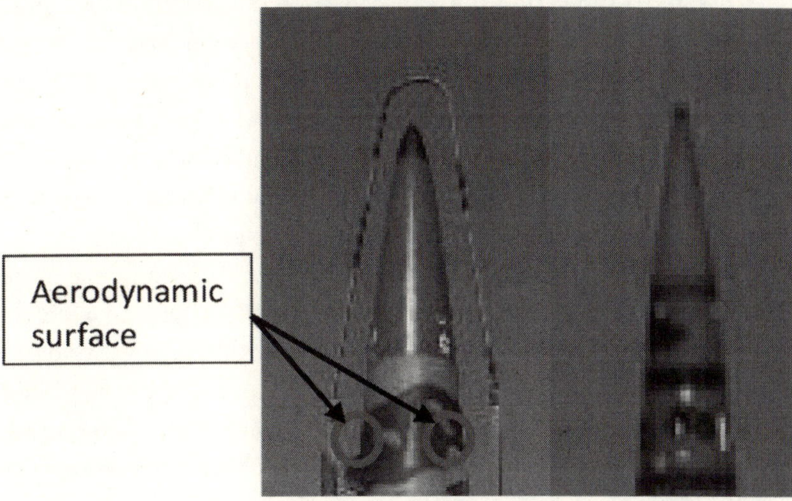

- *Ghauri* is the only missile in the Pakistani arsenal based on liquid propellants and based on technology developed by North Korea. Pakistan manufactures this missile based on know-how as well as supply of plant and equipment from North Korea. An impression is created that different variants of the missile under the nomenclature of *Ghauri 1*, *Ghauri 2*, etc. are available. However, the missile range of most flights have been reported as 1300 km and hence it is safe to presume that only one version is flying. (It must be noted that higher propellant loading and increased range is possible by extending the propellant tanks keeping structural and aerodynamic design parameters in mind.)

- The *Ghauri* has been routinely flight-tested and seems to have performed normally. However, a flight test[21] carried out overland on 28 December 2012 has failed and debris fell in Dadu village of Sind province and was retrieved by security forces. Subsequent flight tests in 2015 and 2018 have been successful.
- *Shaheen II* is the first two-stage long-range missile engineered by Pakistan. From an examination of the frequency of flight tests as well as other data, there seem to be some development issues with this missile. The maiden flight[22] was carried out in 2004 and a range of 2,000 km was claimed. Seven further flights of the missile were carried out between 2005 and 2008 with the same claimed range. The ISPR statement associated with the 2008 test stated that the flight objective was validation of technical improvements. For a significantly long period of six years, there were no flight tests of *Shaheen II*, indicative of some technical issues, which took time to resolve.
- Flight test was resumed on 13 November 2014 and the stated objective[23] was "revalidation of different design and technical parameters of the weapon system". Obviously a design shortcoming had been corrected and had to be "revalidated" in the flight test. Also, there were some minor dimensional changes in the 2nd stage and the RV. More importantly, the range of the missile was trimmed to 1,500 kg from the earlier stated 2,000 km. This would mean that the design modifications needed subsequent to the 2008 flight-test, resulted in trading off performance in favour of reliability.
- *Shaheen III* is a missile with a longer range, claimed to be 2,750 km and has been flown in March 2015 and December 2015. It is derived from *Shaheen II* with an additional third stage. The changes include longer propulsion stages of *Shaheen II* and addition of a third liquid stage, housed in the lower portion of the RV.
- It appears that a *Shaheen III* launch was planned for January 2018 as NOTAMs/NTMs covering missile range safety zones between 28 January and 1 February 2018, had been issued. Measurem1ent of the extreme points of the range safety corridor showed that it was

at a distance of 2850 km, indicating that the planned flight was that of *Shaheen III*. Google Earth imagery of 28 January 2018 showed the missile erected in readiness of launch. It is speculated that the missile flight was not successful[24] as there was no subsequent media content regarding the flight. Absence of Google Earth imagery for the next day, prevented any corroboration in this regard.

Figure 13.8: Google Earth Imagery

- In view of technology commonalities between *Shaheen II/ Shaheen III/Ababeel* missile stages, this failure must have affected the test and development schedule. A repeat flight of *Shaheen III* has not yet occurred. However, after a lull of nearly sixteen months, a training launch[25] of *Shaheen III* took place on 23 May 2019. This flight could even be to study the efficacy of the modifications introduced for *Shaheen III*. One can expect further flights of *Shaheen III* in 2019.
- *Ababeel* is a missile with multiple independently targetable re-entry vehicles (MIRVs). *Ababeel* augments the *Shaheen III* propulsive stages with the addition of a third stage. The post-boost control system (PBCV)—part of the MIRV platform acts as a final stage with multiple start capability. The body diameter of the missile is 1.4 m and the heat shield on top of the missile is of a larger diameter of 1.7 m to house the MIRVs. The estimates indicate that four MIRVs of the size of US Mk-12 RV, which has a diameter of 0.53 m and height of 1.83 m, could fit into the

1.7 m diameter fairing. The question is, has Pakistan managed to miniaturise nuclear warhead to this size? Another pertinent question would be: in the absence of test of a plutonium-based weapon in its 1998 tests, with what confidence is Pakistan fielding such a weapon system?

- Though the claimed range is 2,200 km, in the flight of January 2017, the range was clipped to 1,100 km. The reason for this could be to confirm the release and subsequent performance of the MIRVs from a closer distance.
- All the Pakistani ballistic missiles use the jet-vane control system for the booster stage. This is a legacy from the early Chinese and North Korean designs and Pakistan has not switched over to current and more efficient control systems. This could be due to non-availability or non-development of such technology.

The Pakistani ballistic missile range is captured in Figure 13.9. *Shaheen II* of 2004 is replaced by a modified but lower-range version in 2014. This range is close to the *Ghauri* range. *Ghauri* being a liquid-propelled system, is not best suited for missile application and will in all probability be replaced by *Shaheen II*, which has a similar range. *Ghauri* however, will be continued for possible future satellite launch vehicle application. *Abdali,* with a short range of 80-100 km, is not shown in the graph. *Abdali* does not add much to the strategic content, as it has to be fielded close to the border.

Figure 13.9: Range of Pakistani Ballistic Missiles

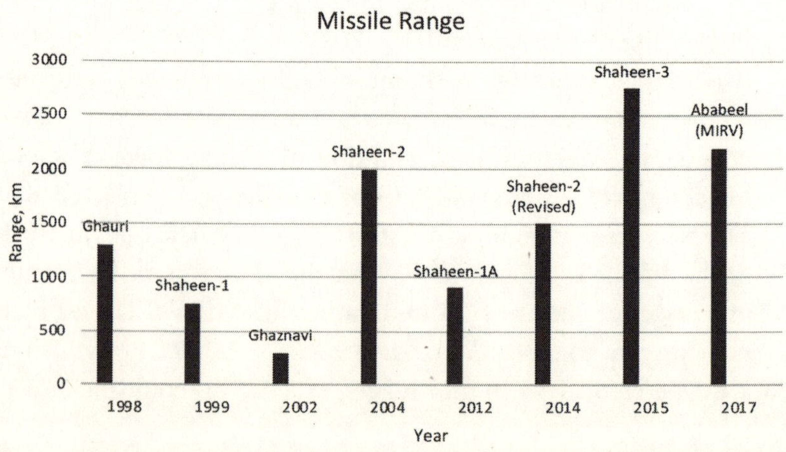

Nasr (Hatf-9)

In April 2011, Pakistan added a new dimension to counter India's conventional superiority with the introduction of a nuclear-tipped battlefront weapon named *Nasr/Hatf-9*. The missile originally had a range of 60 km and the ISPR press release[26] accompanying the launch stated that "Nasr with a range of 60 km carries nuclear warheads of appropriate yield with high-accuracy shoot-and-scoot attributes. The quick response system addresses the need to deter evolving threats." The missile is shown in Figure 13.10 and can be fired in salvo mode.

Figure 13.10: Nasr TNW Emerging from Launch Tube

The estimate of the missile dimensions are as follows:

- Diameter 360 mm
- Length 5400 mm
- Power plant length 3800 mm
- Warhead section 1600 mm (940 mm cylindrical + 660 mm conical)

It is within the technological capability of Pakistan to design and develop a missile of this characteristic. The nuclear warhead is another issue. A survey of US tactical nuclear warheads indicates that linear implosion-based devices like W-42, W-44, W-48, W-79 could fit into the envelope of the *Nasr* missile warhead section. The question is the ability of Pakistan to miniaturize the weapon to this extent and reliability issues in the absence of a test. Further, higher quantity of plutonium is required for linear implosion devices and this is a premium for a country with fissile material resource constraints.

Pakistan has gone on record[27] to say that *Nasr* is developed as a deterrence to India's cold-start doctrine (India has not publicly admitted to the existence of such a doctrine) and the deployment of such a weapon system could be upsetting the deterrence equation between the two countries. Feroze Hassan Khan[28] has alluded that the short range of the missile introduces destabilising parameters, as: (a) the missile has to be fielded close to the border; (b) the concept of a field weapon is compromised if the command and control is centrally administered; and (c) there is increased scope of misinterpreting the signals and triggering a premature or pre-emptive response. Major departures in pre-delegation practices can be expected between what the rules state and what will be practiced.

There is ambiguity in the missile warhead whether it is high-explosive or strategic. This ambiguity also could lead to a premature or a pre-emptive response. The missile is comparatively small and can be stolen or hijacked. Fear of non-state actors and rogue elements calls for extra physical security and vigilance—how much attention can be paid under conflict conditions will always remain a point of concern.

Pakistan claims to have improved the accuracy of the missile[29] and increased the range to 70 km. The improved missile was flight-tested for the first time in 2017. These incremental improvements don't change the overall picture in any significant manner. In an earlier study[30] done at the National Institute of Advanced Studies, it was pointed out the introduction of *Nasr* brings about a doctrinal issue and possibly signifies a shift from 'first use' policy to 'first strike' policy. This, in turn, could translate to nuclear weapon use threats even in unwarranted situations. The Indian nuclear doctrine does not make a difference between a strategic or a tactical nuclear weapon and India's response in case nuclear weapons are used against it or its forces anywhere, would be massive. In short, with the introduction of *Nasr*, Pakistan signalled a lowering of its nuclear threshold to counter conventional military operations by India and this can pose major challenges to the robustness of nuclear deterrence between the two countries. Having said that, it must be noted that recent conventional operations by India have not elicited a deterrence-breaking response from Pakistan.

Cruise Missiles

Cruise missiles are precision weapon systems which operate within the atmosphere like aircraft. They can be designed for achieving different range requirements; can be launched from ground or from air, sea or sub-surface platforms; possess good manoeuvrability and their flight path can be configured to go around known air defence locations; can fly at low altitudes to evade observation by enemy radars; are designed with stealth features; and are very economical. From these considerations, cruise missiles form an important weapon system in any country's offensive and deterrence postures.

Subsonic cruise missiles, as the name indicates, operate at subsonic speeds and consequently longer travel time over the adversary country with associated vulnerabilities are involved. Most currently, operational cruise missiles in the world are of the subsonic variety, with cruise speeds of M 0.8 when powered by a turbojet or turbofan power plant. They provide the advantage of useful stand-off distance, which can be further enhanced by the platform from which they are launched. Cruise missiles, because of their stand-off distance advantage together with low cost and being unmanned, are referred to as the poor man's air force.

Pakistan was an early starter in the development of cruise missiles—having taken advantage of captured US *Tomahawk* cruise missile[31] which had malfunctioned and crashed near Kharam, close to the Pakistani nuclear test site (the missiles had been fired from a ship towards a terrorist camp in Afghanistan). It is reported that examination of the crashed missile hardware, probably with the help of Chinese experts, provided insights to Pakistani engineers to craft their own cruise missile. Pakistan has made good progress in the development of cruise missiles and is in a position to field ground, air and submarine-launched versions.

Babur/Hatf-7 Ground-Launched Cruise Missile (GLCM)

The first reported flight-test of this subsonic cruise missile was carried out in August 2005. The missile is boosted initially by a solid rocket, which separates after this function is over and the cruise phase is powered by a turbojet/turbofan engine. The circumstances of missile development have been elaborated in the preceding section and as can be seen from Figure 13.11, the missile has a close resemblance to the *Tomahawk* cruise missile.

Figure 13.11: Babur and Tomahawk Cruise Missiles

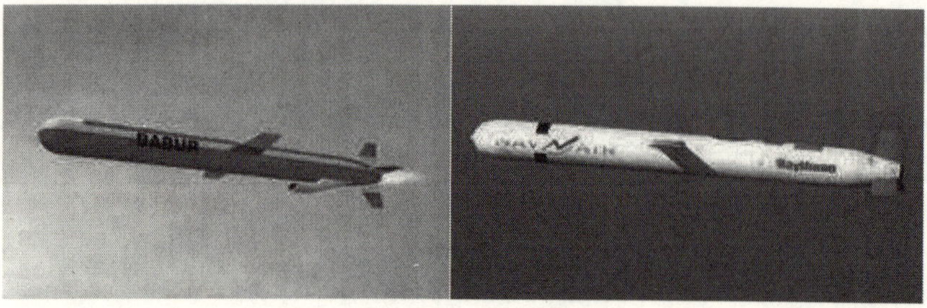

During launch, the main wings as well as the air inlet for the missile power plant are in a retracted position and are deployed after the rocket boost phase is over and during the cruise phase of flight. The *Babur* cruise missile, purportedly equipped with stealth features, has a terrain-hugging capability and a range of 700 km. The missile is claimed to be equipped with TERrain Contour Matching (TERCOM) and Digital Scene Matching Area Correlation (DSMAC) features and hits targets on land and sea with pin-point accuracy. The missile can carry both conventional and nuclear weapons. An earlier assessment,[32] carried out at NIAS, had highlighted the dimensions and performance of the missile. The report had concluded that the missile diameter was 560 mm and not suitable for fitment in the Pakistani licence manufactured

Agosta 90B (Khalid-class) submarine. The report had also done an apportionment of the space required for different missile subsystems and had concluded that the missile was 6.6 m long and capable of carrying a payload of 400 kg. The schematic of the *Babur* missile as worked out in the NIAS report, is shown in Figure 13.12.

Figure 13.12: Cutaway view of Babur Cruise Missile

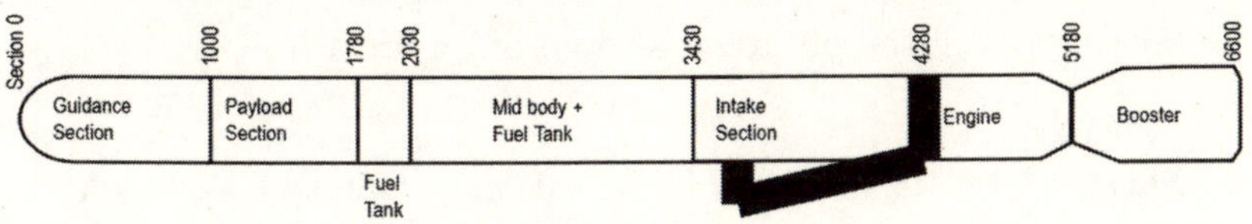

The range of the missile in the maiden flight was claimed to be 500 km and in test launches carried out in 2007, an increased range of 700 km was claimed. It was calculated that an additional fuel mass of 40 kg would be required, which can be accommodated with minor re-engineering of the fuel tanks. The increased-range *Babur* is referred to as *Babur-2* and can be fired from canisterised launchers. Pakistan has carried out a number of flight-tests of this system and the missile system is operational.

Ra'ad (Hatf-8) Air-Launched Cruise Missile

Two years later, in 2007, Pakistan unveiled its 350 km range, air-launched subsonic cruise missile, *Ra'ad*. This weapon system is not a variant of *Babur-2* but is rather a new design developed by NESCOM and the Air Weapons Complex of PAF. The Dassault Mirage III-Rose aircraft with the Pakistan Air Force has been modified to accommodate one *Ra'ad* missile in the centre-fuselage section. The missile is pictured in Figure 13.13.

Figure 13.13: Ra'ad ALCM (a) belly-mounted on Mirage aircraft, (b) release from aircraft and (c) in free flight

The *Ra'ad* missile fuselage has a square cross-section; the wings are placed low at the mid-body section; and twin vertical stabilisers are provided. The fuselage cross-section perhaps adds to the stealth capability of the missile. Like the *Babur*, *Ra'ad* possesses the terrain hugging, TERCOM and DSMAC features. The missile range is claimed to be 350 km and it is understood that Pakistan may be attempting to enhance the same. The missile was part of Pakistan's National Day Parade held on 23 March 2019 and a static image of the missile[33] from the parade is shown in Figure 13.14.

Figure 13.14: Ra'ad ALCM in the Pakistan National Day Parade, March 2019

Babur-3 Submarine-Launched Cruise Missile (SLCM)

Since the early development and launch of the *Babur* GLCM, Pakistan has viewed second-strike capability as an absolute must and has harboured the development of submarine-launch missile capability as an important prerequisite. In 2005, along with *Babur* GACM, Pakistan had viewed the SLCM[34] capability as priority over ALCM capability. Pakistan achieved this capability on 9 January 2017, when it successfully tested *Babur-3*[35] from an underwater mobile platform. The missile range was claimed to be 450 km and

Babur-3 was termed as a sea-based variant of GLCM *Babur-2*. The image of the missile launch taken from the ISPR website, is shown in Figure 13.15.

The Pakistan Navy possesses the French Agosta 70 and Agosta 90B submarines in its fleet. The Agosta 90B is equipped with Air-Independent Propulsion and has the *Exocet SM-39* missile launched from its torpedo tube as standard armament. Details of *Exocet SM-39* are available adequately in open source documentation and this information as well as domain expertise has been used by the author and his colleagues in deducing the dimensions and performance of the *Babur-3* cruise missile.[36] The missile has to be encapsulated in a shell, to protect it from exposure to sea water in its journey from the submarine to the surface and the torpedo tube dimensions provide a clue to the missile diameter and length.

Figure 13.15: Babur-3 SLCM

With a state-of-the-art turbofan engine, the missile could be engineered to have a range of 450 km. However, the platform survivability is a major requirement and missiles like *Exocet SM-39* use an underwater propulsion system which ensures the missile breaks surface at a point quite removed from the platform. It is obvious that *Babur-3* would use such a feature, which in turn would reduce the length available for housing the missile. Reduced length will translate to reduction in the propellant tank volume with attendant loss in performance. The resulting performance is calculated to be in the region of only 250 km.

Taking cognizance of these parameters, the missile diameter has been surmised to be 510 mm and the missile length, including the solid propellant booster, is estimated as 6.74 m. The cutaway view of the author's assessment of the missile dimensions is shown in Figure 13.16.

Figure 13.16: Babur-3 Subsystems and Estimated Dimensions

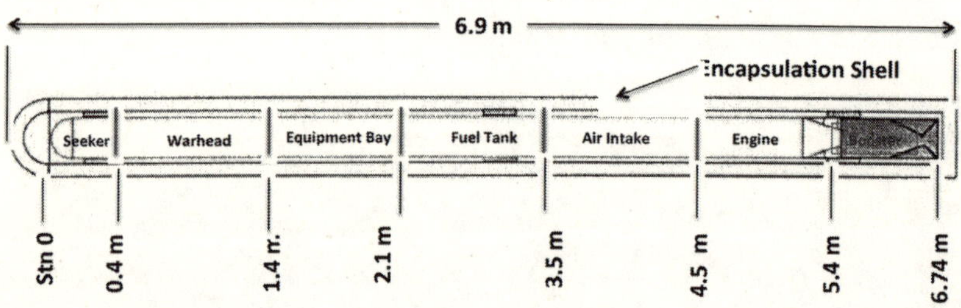

In the SLCM development, the critical parameter is the release from the platform, underwater passage, sensing the clearing of the water surface followed by ignition of the booster and control. The safety of the platform and its crew is paramount. Keeping the safety and reliability in mind, a number of tests to qualify the system are required and from this angle, the deployment of the missile may be some time away.

Pakistan finalised a deal with China in July 2015 for the procurement of eight Type 039B Yuan[37] Class submarines. The export version of the submarine is designated S20. The submarines will be built by Wuchang Shipbuilding located at Wuhan. The deal was valued between $4-5 billion, with supply of four ships by 2023 and the balance by 2028. These submarines have six torpedo tubes, and one of these could be engineered for use with *Babur-3*. These submarines equipped with *Babur-3* even with its 'claimed' range of 450 km can hardly provide a credible second-strike capability. This is because the Indian coast and territorial waters are heavily patrolled by the Navy and Coast Guard vessels. Further, the early warning systems and other surveillance systems will complicate a close approach. For an effective deterrence, missiles with longer ranges, capable of firing outside the well-defended zones would be essential.

Pakistan also has interest in acquiring nuclear submarine capability. If media reports are to be believed, Pakistan is negotiating with China for lease of *Han*-class attack submarines and some indigenous[38] efforts may have also been taken up. The *Han*-class of submarine has provision for torpedo-launched cruise missiles—C 801 with a range of 40 km and will not add value to Pakistani capability in this sphere, though it may help Pakistan to get the required familiarization of operating SSNs.

For effective second-strike capability, Pakistan will work towards developing long-range sea-based second-strike. This will call for submarines with vertical launch systems (VLS) and *Shaheen II/III* or *Ababeel*-class of ballistic missiles. That goal appears to be sometime in the distance.

Cruise Missile Reach

Based on the discussion on the preceding lines, Pakistan has cruise missiles employing nuclear warheads with different levels of reach into Indian territory. Also, as stated earlier, this range is the direct 'as the crow flies' distance. As the missile will deviate from this ideal path to avoid known air defence sites as also Air Force fighter aircraft bases, its penetration capability will be less than the design range. For the GLCM, as the missile is road-mobile, it could be fired from any location; for the ALCM, the penetration will be maximum if the missile is fired close to the border and without entering into adversary air space in normal times. In times of hostility, this precondition may not apply but will be conditioned by the concentration and capacity of the detection and neutralisation capability of the adversary country.

Figure 13.17: 'As the Crow Flies' Reach of Babur-2 and Ra'ad Cruise Missiles

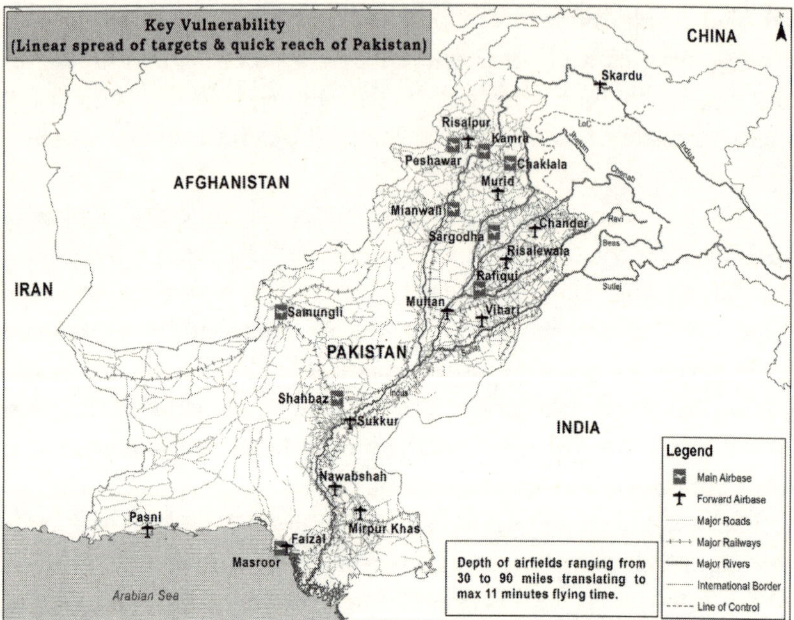

© GIS Section, Manohar Parrikar Institute for Defence Studies & Analyses (MP-IDSA). Map not to scale.

As the 'crow flies' reach of *Ra'ad* and *Babur-2* into Indian territory is shown in Figure 16. For the purpose of this sketch, *Ra'ad's* release is taken close to the border. Further, *Ra'ad* could be launched from other locations also, and from this consideration, locations within 300 km of the coast are also vulnerable. For *Babur-3*, the range of 250 km is not fully realisable depending upon how close to the coast the platform can come. These waters will be heavily patrolled and coastline protection will also be of a high order and hence, the efficacy of *Babur-3* is questionable.

Discussion

- It is claimed that all Pakistani cruise missiles are equipped with TERCOM and DSMAC capability. While it is possible to buy high-resolution commercial imagery (or obtain from China) for the purpose of creating the terrain maps, integrating this into a system with inputs of other onboard sensors is a challenging and complicated task.

- Pakistan may be dependent on foreign markets for the inertial navigation system and other onboard sensors. These may be available freely, as they are also used in commercial aircraft.
- Pakistan does not manufacture the turbofan engine required for powering the cruise missiles. Pakistan uses an imported system sourced either from China or Ukraine.
- Pakistan will have to use a plutonium-based miniaturised weapon in the cruise missile. The mass of the missile subsystems and the missile range requirement will put a limitation of 400-500 kg on the payload mass, and this in turn, will necessitate the use of a plutonium-based weapon system.
- The fact that Pakistan has not tested a plutonium-based system may impose penalties on mass of weapon and reliability. In addition, Pakistan has limited uranium reserves which influences the quantity of fissile material and the number of weapon it can stockpile. In an in-depth study, Lalitha Sundaresan[39] and Kaveri Ashok have estimated that, as of 2014, Pakistan may have 34-52 plutonium-based weapons with limited annual addition.
- The following missile platforms of Pakistan will need to use miniaturised Pu-based weapon systems:
    - *Babur-2* GLCM
    - *Ra'ad* ALCM
    - *Babur-3* SLCM
    - *Nasr* TNW (may require higher quantity of Pu if a linear implosion device is used)
    - *Ababeel* IRBM (MIRV) [each missile may carry 3-4 MIRV]

  With the limitations in the arsenal mentioned in the cited article above, either availability for each of the platforms will be sub-critical or some platforms may need to be equipped with conventional weapons only.
- *Babur-3* may be more useful as an anti-ship cruise missile and may not serve the purpose of land-attack. In the well-patrolled and watched space of India's territorial and nearby waters, it is imperative, from platform-safety considerations, to maintain a safe distance between the missile release platform and the location where the missiles emerge from the sea. This necessitates

the use of an underwater propulsion module (similar to *Exocet*). This in turn will eat into the fuel that can be taken on board and the range of the missile will be as low as 250 km (55 per cent of the claimed range of 450 km). This range is inadequate for a credible second-strike claim.

- From the above consideration, Pakistan appears to be some distance away from achieving credible second-strike capability.

Conclusion

Pakistan has developed and fielded an array of nuclear-capable ballistic and cruise missiles. The range of these missiles varies from tactical to short and medium-range. Pakistan benefitted in the early years from design and technology acquisition from China and North Korea. Pakistan can be said to have internalised the learning and is in a position to design and develop new systems. Some kinks still seem to be there, especially relating to design reliability, as evidenced from long delays between launches and other missing factors. These are however, normal technology development-related issues. The road-mobility of the missiles is also catered to.

The fielding of the *Nasr* tactical nuclear weapon weakens the robustness of deterrence between India and Pakistan. As has been stated in an earlier NIAS report on *Nasr*, the fielding of the weapon poses issues of: (a) credibility (untested weapon system), (b) possible doctrinal shift for Pakistan from 'first-use' policy to 'first-strike' policy; the absence of a change in India's nuclear doctrine denies Pakistan the doctrinal flexibility it may be aiming for; and (c) operational issues like fielding of the weapon system close to the border and extent of control/pre-delegation.

The submarine-launched cruise missile *Babur-3* has provided Pakistan with sea-based deterrence. However, the short range of the missile in heavily-patrolled and shallow territorial waters does not add much to a credible deterrence.

Pakistani nuclear forces are India-centric and the tendency in Pakistan's missile development will be to match/counter Indian capabilities. Consequently, based on India's missile and Anti-Ballistic Missile (ABM) developments, it is to be expected that Pakistan would develop matching capabilities and MIRV capability, as well as second-strike capability. The overall trajectory of Pakistan's missile development is on expected lines.

Disclaimer: The figures, charts and tables in the chapter are from the author's previous work on the subject.

Notes

1. Computed from information, at http://www.astronautix.com/s/sonmiani.html. Accessed on 3 March 2019.
2. Feroz Hassan Khan, *Eating Grass: The Making of the Pakistani Bomb*, Stanford University Press, 2012, p. 175.
3. "From Belier to Eridan", at http://www.sat-net.com/serra/sudav_e.htm. Accessed on 30 April 2019.
4. The SUPARCO management structure has seen frequent changes. Perusal of the SUPARCO, at http://www.suparco.gov.pk/pages/history.asp. Accessed on 30 April 2019 shows that the SUPARCO was under the charge of PAEC when it was formed in September 1961; it came directly under the charge of the President of Pakistan in 1964; in September 1966 the SUPARCO was constituted as a separate organization under the administrative control Scientific and Technological Research Division of the Government of Pakistan; in 1981 the SUPARCO was elevated to the status of a full-fledged commission with the Prime Minister as the President of Space Research Council; The SUPARCO was finally transferred to function under the National Command Authority (NCA) in December 2000. The SUPARCO's Space Research Council and its Executive Committee were dissolved and replaced by the Development Control Committee of NCA.
5. The development of Hatf-1/2 appears to be a hurried response to India's test of the Prithvi a few months earlier.
   Pakistan developed *Hatf-1* and *Hatf-2* based on sounding rocket technology obtained from France. The Sud Aviation sounding rockets had fins of rectangular platform and the *Hatf-1* and 2 missiles sport similar geometry for the fins. Sud Aviation also had given the technology of composite PVC plastisol-based propellant and related rocket technologies. Pakistan had re-engineered *Hatf-1* and *Hatf-2* based on these technologies. Refer to the test at "Pakistan Missile Chronology", Nuclear Threat Initiative, at https://media.nti.org/pdfs/pakistan_missile_1.pdf. Accessed on 7 May 2019.
6. Details derived from the article From "Belier to Eridan" (main text: Rockets in Europe), at http://www.sat-net.com/serra/sudav_e.htm. Accessed on 11 May 2019.

7. India also had a technology transfer agreement with Sud Aviation for Centaure IIB sounding rocket. The author had observed first-hand the setting up of the facilities and the implementation of the technology transfer. Based on this, the assessment of technologies Pakistan would have acquired from France is fairly correct.
8. The Centaure launch history from Somniani is analysed from the launch list provided at http://www.astronautix.com/s/sonmiani.html. Accessed on 11 May 2019.
9. The similarity in the fins is evident; the wire tunnel running from cylindrical region on top to the base shroud is also common; and the plume of smoke near the left fin is due to firing of the spin rocket—another feature of Sud Aviation sounding rockets.
10. "Pakistan Derives its First 'Hatf' Missiles from Foreign Space Rockets", Wisconsin Project on Nuclear Arms Control, 1 October 1995, at https://www.wisconsinproject.org/pakistan-derives-its-first-hatf-missiles-from-foreign-space-rockets/. Accessed on 12 May 2019.
11. According to the Nuclear Threat Initiative (NTI), Pakistan took Chinese assistance for developing *Hatf-2*. See https://fas.org/nuke/guide/pakistan/missile/hatf-2.htm. Accessed on 12 May 2019.
12. *Missile Technology Control Regime (MTCR) Annex Handbook-2017*. MTCR category I items include complete rocket systems, ballistic missiles, space launch vehicle vehicles, sounding rockets and unmanned air vehicles including cruise missiles. The category II items include production facilities for such missile systems, rocket stages, rocket engines, re-entry vehicles, guidance systems and warhead mechanisms.
13. Feroze Hassan Khan, n. 2, p. 236.
14. Nuclear Threat Initiative (NTI) quoting Joseph Bermudez in *Jane's Defense Weekly* of 20 May 1998 states: 'Benazir Bhutto becomes prime minister of Pakistan and supports the acquisition of missiles from China and extending bilateral ties between Pakistan and North Korea in the nuclear and missile fields'. Available in *Pakistan Missile Chronology*, at https://media.nti.org/pdfs/pakistan_missile_1.pdf. Accessed on 17 May 2019.
15. https://media.nti.org/pdfs/pakistan_missile_1.pdf. Accessed on 18 May 2019 provides a chronological list of missile technology transfer from China to Pakistan, Chinese denials and assurances, differences in interpretation of MTCR guidelines on pp. 100-116.
16. Ibid.; Also see, S. Chandrashekhar, Arvind Kumar and Rajaram Nagappa, 'An Assessment of Pakistan's Ballistic Missile Progeamme', NIAS Report No. R5-06, National Institute of Advanced Studies, Bengaluru.
17. Ibid.
18. http://www.b14643.de/Spacerockets_1/Diverse/Dong-Feng/. Accessed on 18 May 2019.
19. The post-separation-attitude control (PSAC) system uses common tanks for the propellants which feed into banks of thrusters mounted to provide stability to the re-entry vehicle (RV). The thrusters provide correction in the

three directions (pitch, yaw and roll) and prevent the RV from tumbling. Reference to PSAC can be seen under the caption, 'Ballistic missile *Hatf IV* test fired', *Dawn*, 25 April 2012, at http://beta.dawn.com/news/713388/ballistic-missile-hatf-iv-test-fired. Accessed on 19 May 2019.

20. As per www.astronautix.com/lvs/shaheen1.htm. Accessed on 13 May 2019.
21. Image sourced from http://info-browse.blogspot.in/2011/12/state-of-art-missile-technology-of.html. Accessed on 30 November 2013.
22. 'Ballistic missile *Hatf-IV* test fired', n. 19.
23. Rajaram Nagappa, 'Pakistan's *Ghauri* November 2012 Missile Test', at http://isssp.in/wp-content/uploads/2013/05/Ghauri-Missile-Test-of-28-December-2012.pdf. Accessed on 21 May 2019.
24. 'Pakistan tests its longest-range missile', *Dawn*, 10 March 2004. The paper quoting Dr Samar Mubarakmand, Chairman of National Engineering and Science Commission (NESCOM) states that the missile is capable of 2500 km range but was restricted to 2000 km so as not to cross Pakistan's declared territorial sea limit. See https://www.dawn.com/news/392423. Accessed on 23 May 2019.
25. '*Shaheen-2* missile test fired', *Dawn,* 14 November 2014. See https://www.dawn.com/news/1144418. Accessed on 23 May 2019.
26. Riffath Kazi, 'Possibly failed Pakistani ballistic missile test raises doubts about overall capability', *Delhi Defence Review*, 10 December 2018, at http://delhidefencereview.com/2018/12/10/possibly-failed-pakistani-ballistic-missile-test-raises-doubts-about-overall-capability/. Accessed on 24 May 2019.
27. 'Pakistan conducted successful training launch of surface to surface ballistic missile *Shaheen-2*', ISPR Press Release No. 104-2019, 23 May 2019, at https://ispr.gov.pk/press-release-detail.php?id=5308. Accessed on 24 May 2019.
28. ISPR Press Release No. PR 94/2011-ISPR, Rawalpindi, dated 11 April 2011, at https://ispr.gov.pk/press-release-detail.php?id=1721. Accessed on 25 May 2019.
29. Gen. Qamar Javed Bawa, COAS, after watching the launch of enhanced-range *Nasr* expressed confidence in the "effective command, control, safety and security of all strategic assets and measures being taken toaugment these". He is believed to have remarked that "*Nasr* has put cold water on cold start", ISPR Press Release No. PR-344/2017-ISPR dated 5 July 2017.
30. Feroze Hassan Khan, n. 2.
31. ISPR Press Release, n. 29.
32. Rajaram Nagappa, Arun Vishwanathan and Aditi Malhotra, '*Hatf-IX/NASR*—Pakistan's Tactical Nuclear Weapon: Implications for Indo-Pak Deterrence', Report No. R17-2013, National Institute of Advanced Studies, July 2013.

33. NTI in its Pakistan Missile Chronology entry dated 24 August 1998 states, "an unidentified unexploded US cruise missile was found on 22 August 1998 in Pakistan. Pakistani officials said that the missile was found approximately 10 km from Kharam near the site where Pakistan conducted its nuclear tests in May". Entry of 31 August 1998 talks of finding a second unexploded US *Tomahawk* missile. Quoting Christopher Farce of *Jane's Defense Weekly*, the NTI entry of 1 September 1998 indicates, Christopher Farce, editor of *Jane's Defense Weekly*, told BBC reporters that having two unexploded US *Tomahawk* cruise missiles land on Pakistani territory "could well be good news for Pakistan." Farce said that although Pakistan may not have the complete technical ability to reverse-engineer the missile, it could strip down the missile and probably find out some things about the missile. He said that Pakistan has a fairly well-established anti-tank and air defence industry and have a good base in anti-tank and surface-to-air missiles, but are just now moving into ballistic missiles. Even if Pakistan cannot fully utilize the US cruise missile, it could sell the missile to China. Farce said that Pakistan and China are working closely together and a lot of trading occurs across borders. He said there is an obvious possibility that "the missile or parts could go across to China and that would be a great assistance for the Chinese missile industry ..." (*emphasis added by the author*).
34. Rajaram Nagappa and S. Chandrashekar, 'An Assessment of *Babur-Hatf* 7 Cruise Missile', Report No. R5-07, NIAS Study-2007, National Institute of Advanced Studies, Bangalore. In this study based on *Tomahawk* details and domain engineering judgement, the authors have carried out a layout analysis of the missile subsystems, determined the mass of the subsystems and worked out the performance of the missile.
35. 'In pictures: Pakistan shows off its military might at annual parade', *Dawn,* 23 March 2019, at https://www.dawn.com/news/1471416. Accessed on 27 May 2019.
36. In an interview to *Jane's Defense Weekly* ('Pakistan tests cruise missile', *Jane's Defense Weekly,* 17 August 2005), a Pakistan official is quoted to have said, "ultimately, the *Babur* is being developed for land and submarine-launched applications, with a longer term goal of making it suitable for airborne launch". The Pakistani source is further quoted: "the intention is to have the *Babur* deployable on the country's French Agosta 90B-class attack submarines, although (he noted) it does not appear that the (*Babur*) missile is small enough to fit into the 533 mm torpedo tubes in its current configuration".

    This statement confirms that *Babur* LACM diameter is larger than 533 mm and for submarine deployment a new missile has to be configured.
37. See Inter-Services Press Release No. PR-10/2017-ISPR, 9 January 2017.
38. Detailed derivation of dimension and performance parameters of *Babur-3* are available in the publication: Rajaram Nagappa, Riffath Khaji and Suba Chandran, 'Pakistan's *Babur-3* Submarine-Launched Cruise Missile

(SLCM): An Assessment', Report R59-2017, National Institute of Advanced Studies, Bengaluru.

39. 'Type 039A Yuan-class exports', at https://www.globalsecurity.org/military/world/china/yuan-export.htm. Accessed on 30 May 2019.
40. 'Pakistan to build nuclear submarines?', at http://www.riazhaq.com/2012/02/pakistan-to-build-nuclear-submarine.html. Accessed on 30 May 2019.
41. Lalitha Sundaresan and Kaveri Ashok, 'Uranium constraints in Pakistan: How Many Nuclear Weapons Does Pakistan Have?', *Current Science*, 115 (6), 25 September 2018. In this article, the authors have carried out an estimate of Pakistan's HEU and Pu-based weapons using data on Pakistan's uranium reserves and annual output. Their estimates, which are based on the approach they have taken, is logically different from the figures projected by H.M. Kristensen and R. S. Norris, 'Pakistani Nuclear Forces', *Bulletin of Atomic Scientists*, 72(6), 2016, pp. 368-376.

14. Pakistan's TNWs: The Signal and How it Should be Received

Manpreet Sethi

It is now a decade since Pakistan first tested a very short-range ballistic missile, the *Nasr*, on 19 April 2011 and declared it as nuclear-capable. The Inter-Services Public Relations Directorate (ISPR) of Pakistan explained this development as necessary to "add deterrence value to Pakistan's strategic weapons development programme at shorter ranges" and described it as a "quick response system", capable of carrying "nuclear warheads of appropriate yield with high accuracy".[1] The Director General, Strategic Plans Division, witnessed the test and claimed that it had "consolidated Pakistan's nuclear deterrence at all levels of [the] threat spectrum."[2]

The idea of a low-yield nuclear weapon for possible use against targets in the battlefield appears to fit in perfectly with Pakistan's carefully crafted nuclear strategy. Since Pakistan believes in the merits of using terror to keep India unsettled, the primary role for its nuclear weapons is to avoid having to engage with the Indian military. Through the suggestion of an inevitability of nuclear use in case of an Indian retaliation to an act of terrorism, the presence of 'tactical nuclear weapons' is perceived to add another layer as cover to this insurance policy.

A signal is, thus, being transmitted by Pakistan through the projection of a capability to use low-yield nuclear weapons on military targets. This message is meant as much for India as for the international community. What is this signal and how should it be received? This chapter closely examines Pakistan's purported objectives with Tactical Nuclear Weapons (TNWs). How does it intend to use them? Is it looking for a battlefield advantage by actually detonating them or is it merely seeking to deter conventional conflict through the projection of this capability? Will it build a large arsenal of such weapons? Can it?

Answers to these questions are important to prudently determine India's own response to this development. With this in view, the chapter addresses the relevant issues over four sections. The first two examine the role of TNWs and the assumptions underlying their development from a Pakistani perspective. The last two sections explain why India's doctrine of nuclear deterrence continues to be valid and effective even in the face of TNWs and suggest how to make Pakistani TNWs redundant to conventional military responses that India may want to take to deter/punish continued acts of Pakistan-supported terror.

TNWs in Pakistan's Nuclear Strategy—Where and How do they Fit

There is no universally-accepted definition of TNWs. Differences in geographical distance between adversaries, densities of population and technological capabilities of nations possessing nuclear weapons can lead to variations in whether one defines missiles of different ranges or yields as tactical or not. For instance, in the case of the Cold War, in the European battlefield, short-range (less than 500 km) nuclear-tipped ballistic missiles or bombers carrying gravity bombs of up to 200 kilotons or even artillery shells, depth charges or land mines, were described as tactical. Pakistan, meanwhile, has claimed *Nasr* with a range of just 60 km and a sub-kiloton yield to be tactical. Apparently then, the description of tactical is used more with reference to the target of the missile and the purpose (which supposedly in the case of both Europe and Pakistan is to halt the conventional offensive by projecting a threat of nuclear escalation).

During the Cold War, NATO firmly believed in the value of TNWs. The argument was that "deploying nuclear weapons near the front makes their use virtually automatic and therefore denies the opponent the option of conventional war. He is left with the choice between not attacking or setting off a nuclear war that would be likely to get out of hand."[3] By magnifying the risk of an uncontrollable nuclear war in case use of TNWs became necessary owing to how conventional war proceeded, NATO signaled greater deterrence against Russia's conventional superiority. The projected use of TNWs was meant to dissuade conventional responses.

Pakistan's nuclear strategy is operating with the same logic. The idea behind this development is to raise the spectre of nuclear escalation, thereby scaring India from using force at the conventional level. In fact, Lt. Gen. Khalid Kidwai, the longstanding Head of the Strategic Plans Division, the Pakistani body tasked with construction, maintenance and execution of the country's nuclear assets and strategy, provided a rather graphic description of the purpose of his TNW when he described it as Pakistan's effort to "pour cold water on Cold Start".[4]

Cold Start, as it may be recalled, was announced as an Indian military doctrine that envisaged a rapid military offensive through the constitution of pre-positioned integrated battle groups (IBGs) that could quickly take limited offensive action in response to terrorist activities. India came up with the idea of Cold Start after its experience of *Operation Parakram*, when in response to the attack on the Indian Parliament in December 2001, the Indian Army followed the conventional pattern of mobilisation that was long-drawn and which did not prove to be effective since it allowed time for Pakistan to simultaneously mobilise too. A need was then felt to develop a capability for rapid reaction in order to punish acts of cross-border terror. The idea of Cold Start then took root.[5] This obviously caused concern to Rawalpindi and the idea of TNWs was adopted as a counter to deny India space for punitive action by suggesting that such a step would invite use of low-yield nuclear weapons against military targets, including Indian troops or tanks in Pakistani territory.

The logic to use TNWs has since been widely propagated by many strategic thinkers in Pakistan and beyond. Of course, it cannot be overlooked that some references by the Pakistani Army to the need for TNWs even predate the 1998 nuclear tests.[6] However, most scholarship of the period immediately after 1998 did not seem to be inclined towards the concept. Surprisingly, even Shireen Mazari, a nuclear strategist turned politician, had articulated in 2002 that "Pakistan, with a lack of spatial depth, cannot afford the luxury of tactical, battlefield nuclear weapons since, in terms of nuclear weapons it cannot distinguish between the tactical battlefield arena and the strategic war area."[7] But in just about a decade after that Pakistan found it prudent to test the *Nasr* and embarked on its journey to deploy TNWs.

Dr Adil Sultan, who was once with the Strategic Plans Division (SPD), has explained this development as part of a "strategy of assured deterrence" since "in response to limited military incursions by the Indian forces, the threat to destroy New Delhi or Mumbai seemed incredible and disproportionate".[8] Maleeha Lodhi, a former ambassador of Pakistan to the US, articulated in an article of November 2012 that the purpose of Pakistan's TNW is to "counterbalance India's move to bring conventional military offensives to a tactical level".[9] Mazari too had changed her earlier position by 2014 and described TNWs as necessary to "plug the perceived deterrence gap created by India's missile defence capability and Cold War conventional military doctrine."[10] Some other keen Western Pakistan-watchers also subscribe to the same view. Michael Krepon, co-founder of Stimson Center, has interpreted TNW as Pakistan's "perceived need to counter adventurous Indian military doctrine, and by inference, the lack of utility of longer-range missile systems to address localized threats". And in this schema, "their advertised possession of tactical nuclear weapons will further dissuade Indian leaders from authorizing limited incursions into Pakistani territory."[11]

So, the apparent objective of Pakistan's nuclear weapons is to deter a limited conventional offensive from India. As part of this strategy, the *threat of use of TNWs* is deemed to be more important than the actual use of the weapon. In fact, Pakistan has no illusions about the military effectiveness of the weapon on the battlefield. As admitted by Pakistani strategists themselves, "The ability of low yield nuclear weapons to destroy Indian tanks is limited to the extent of being inconsequential because to cause substantial damage to a well-dispersed attacking armoured formation a large number of 15-20 kiloton yield weapons would be required."[12] They well understand that the loss of a few troops or tanks would matter little in the overall battle scenario. Naeem Salik also makes the same point when he states that, "low-yield weapons envisaged to be mounted atop *Nasr* are not likely to make much physical impact unless used in large numbers. Their psychological impact may be out of proportion to their capability...."[13] Indeed, it is the novelty of the act and the resolve thereby indicated of the readiness to accept escalation of the conflict, that is believed to serve as a deterrent to the very first step towards military action.

Through its embrace of TNWs, Pakistan is signaling that since it cannot withstand an Indian conventional onslaught, it would be forced to use nuclear weapons. And in its perception, a suggestion to use low-yield versions against military targets would appear more credible to India and more condonable by the rest of the world. Hence, Rawalpindi perceives the threat of use of TNWs as being more effective than relying solely on large-scale, long-range nuclear strikes. A Pakistani analyst similarly articulates that, "a weapon that is small and usable possesses more deterrent value than a weapon which is big and has strategic value."[14] This is a belief akin to that held by the Superpowers during the Cold War when their TNWs were seen to be "more credible than the threat to escalate directly from a conventional conflict to an attack on a major target in the other state".[15]

In fact, in the case of South Asia, Pakistan's propensity for projection of this threat is likely to increase if its conventional military balance with India continues to be adverse. In such a situation, the threat of use of TNWs will be utilised even more vociferously to constrain India's military actions by playing up the fear of nuclear escalation. So, for Pakistan, its TNW is not essentially a military weapon, but a political projection capability to deter conflict by holding up the threat of escalation. Maj. Gen. Qasim Qureshi, a retired officer of the Pakistan Army, accepted this logic when he stated "It is precisely this danger [that something goes wrong resulting in a nuclear exchange] and uncertainty that from

Pakistan's point of view will ensure stability of deterrence in the conventional domain".[16]

The idea of TNWs, therefore, is meant to send a political signal of resolve. The intention is not to use the weapon for winning on the battlefield or redressing an adverse situation. It has certainly not escaped Pakistan's attention that in order to prevail in a tactical situation, it would need a large arsenal of TNWs, which may be beyond its capacity of fissile material production and safe storage. A Pakistani nuclear analyst pointed this out when he expressed that battlefield nuclear weapons as part of a deterrence by denial strategy pose "very different demands in terms of size of arsenals, command and control and battlefield management."[17] He does not see Pakistan fulfilling any of these requirements and in fact laments that Pakistani strategic planners have not clarified the "apparent dichotomy in the declaratory doctrine and actual force posture". For observers viewing the developments from the outside, therefore, all that Pakistan appears to be doing can best be described as playing out an escalate to de-escalate strategy or using nuclear brinksmanship to restrain India's response.

Pakistan's Assumptions about India's Response to use of TNWs—A Gamble that could Prove Costly

Pakistan appears to be basing its TNW strategy on a few assumptions. The first of these is that the threat of use of low-yield weapons on military targets is *more credible* than that of using larger-yield weapons in counter-value mode. Therefore, Pakistan believes it can deter India better by threatening use of 'small' nuclear weapons because the fear of imminent escalation would stop India in its tracks. Two other related assumptions follow from here: One, that such a threat would also get the international community rushing in to mount pressure on India to refrain from any conventional use of force against Pakistan. The fear of a nuclear exchange in the region would ensure that they do not allow India to respond to any action of terror, which Pakistan would deny in any case. Thus, the threat of use of TNWs would be seen as real enough by everyone to seek immediate de-escalation of the situation.

Several Western writings have encouraged this perception by placing greater emphasis on 'rational' India to resolve bilateral issues of discord with 'irrational' Pakistan so that it does not have any pretext to push the region over the nuclear brink. The onus for maintaining stability is squarely placed at India's doorstep without realising that there is great rationality in Pakistan's irrationality.[18] The development of a TNW is thus a manifestation of this approach of causing international concern to harness India's space for maneuverability in retaliation in case of a Pakistan-sponsored act of terror.

The next assumption inherent in Pakistan's TNW is that such a use would cause such little damage of military significance that India would rather absorb it than escalate the situation through a nuclear retaliation that would only beget more nuclear attacks. In any case, Pakistan appears to perceive the nature of Indian domestic politics and its predominantly economic focus as factors that would incline New Delhi towards war termination over the possibility of uncontrolled escalation. Pakistan's understanding appears to be that India would try to avert a nuclear war at all costs. So, if Pakistan raises the prospect of such a war by threatening the use of more usable TNWs, then India would never muster enough political will to start a military crisis that could run out of control. The premise here is that *Pakistan's willingness to suffer death and destruction is more than India's willingness to inflict death and destruction because of the nature of the Indian polity and the psycho-social attributes of the nation.* So, while Pakistan is sure about India's capability, it seriously doubts its willingness to use that capability.

As is evident in both the above beliefs, political and moral constraints are expected to stop India from responding to the Pakistani act of using TNW. In Rawalpindi's view, its own threat of use of TNWs is credible but the possibility of Indian retaliation is unlikely—owing to international pressure and India's own political nature and focus on the economic trajectory. Therefore, for Pakistan, even its threat of use of TNWs would create conditions that would make it impracticable for India to execute/continue military operations for fear of getting into a situation that would divert it from its economic growth and development. Rawalpindi safely assumes, therefore, that its TNW strategy adds a further deterrence dimension to its overall nuclear strategy.

Are these assumptions true? Is the threat of use of TNWs more credible than that of larger-yield weapons in counter-value mode? Would Pakistan find it at all easy to use them early in a conflict? At what stage of conflict would it seem useful to hold out this threat? Would India really be deterred by the threat of their use? Deterred enough not to take conventional action? Deterred once the conventional conflict was underway? If Pakistan was actually to use the weapon, would India's offensive come to a halt? Would India find it difficult to retaliate with its nuclear weapons even after taking a nuclear hit?

An examination of the recent developments as they unfolded in the wake of the Pulwama attack on Indian para-military forces, offers some answers to these questions and some pointers for the assumptions that are made by Pakistan on its TNWs. For instance, as regards Pakistan's belief that international pressure would mount on India not to take military action, the exact opposite scenario played out in February 2019. Most major powers empathised with India's longstanding suffering of cross-border terror. President Trump offered full support to India to combat terror and reprimanded Pakistan for continuing to offer safe havens to terrorists. Former US National Security Advisor John Bolton even accepted India's right to act in self-defence.[19] France decided to bring a Resolution at the UN Security Council in support of India's efforts to declare Masood Azhar as a global terrorist. Others too made statements in support of India and condemning Pakistan for not being able to control terror emanating from its territory.

Meanwhile, as regards Pakistan's perception about India's unwillingness to use force, it was proven wrong yet again. The Prime Minister showed steadfast resolve and a willingness to take unprecedented air action much deeper inside Pakistani territory than has ever been done or even contemplated in war games played at several Track-II initiatives.

The air strikes at Balakot exposed the limits of Pakistan's nuclear brinkmanship strategy with TNWs. Not only did India demonstrate there was room for a conventional response, it also rather uncharacteristically, did not shy away from manipulating the risk of war. Meanwhile, except for announcing a meeting of the National Command Authority or the Pakistan Prime Minister's reminder of possession of certain weapons by both countries, Pakistan refrained from overt nuclear signaling. Wanting to appear responsible and to deflect the negative attention it was already getting for Pulwama, Pakistan chose not to overplay its nuclear card and did not even mention TNWs. India's military action, therefore, exposed the non-usability of nuclear weapons, even the low-yield ones that Pakistan has held out as ready for early and easy use. They are clearly not. All through the Cold War, even as hundreds of TNWs were deployed by both sides in Europe, it was not a capability that either side found easy to use.

With all the assumptions underlying Pakistan's TNWs disproved by recent developments, it becomes incumbent to address Pakistan's assumptions about the credibility of India's massive retaliation doctrine. Can it safely assume that it could get away with the use of TNWs?

Do Pakistan's TNWs have Implications for India's Doctrine of Massive Retaliation?

Many writings that have emerged after Pakistan threw in the idea of 'tactical nuclear weapons' into the nuclear rink, opine that India will not have the willingness or the courage to undertake *massive retaliation* if Pakistan were to use a low-yield nuclear warhead on Indian military targets. According to some Indian strategic analysts, the possibility of Pakistan's use of TNWs would raise a "serious decision dilemma" for India since "it could make it hard for Indian leaders to find justification for infliction of disproportionate damage to avenge against what limited damage the TNWs could inflict."[20] It is argued that the Indian leadership would find it difficult to "react by wiping out a few cities in Pakistan—besides opening up the escalatory ladder of nuclear exchange culminating into mutual destruction".[21] It is even argued that this dilemma created by India's doctrine of massive retaliation actually emboldens Pakistan to engage in nuclear brinkmanship.

Across the border, Pakistan certainly assumes that the damage caused by its use of TNWs would be too low to provoke India into undertaking massive retaliation. For one, it is assumed that it is not in India's nature to inflict large-scale civilian casualties. And second, even if India was so inclined, the international community would restrain India from doing so. Thus, the asymmetry between the use of tactical nuclear weapons and a response in the form of massive retaliation is supposed to have made India's deterrence posture less than credible. Nuclear strategists are also quick to point that the US, a proponent of the idea of massive retaliation, itself gave it up because it was seen as not credible.

All of the above arguments require some unpacking. First, the reason that the US found its MR suffering from a credibility problem was because it was supposed to be in response to any provocation, anywhere, including a conventional attack far away from the US mainland. This certainly did not look credible to execute and neither did it appeal to the domestic constituency or American allies. In contrast, India professes MR with a no-first-use (NFU) doctrine.[22] It clearly states that "nuclear retaliation to a first strike will be massive..." Two things are worth highlighting in this statement. First, in nuclear parlance first use is different from first strike. As typically understood, first strike would be a large, coordinated strike from the adversary hitting out at Indian counter-force and counter-value targets. It is unthinkable that retaliation to such a strike could be anything less than massive. The second aspect relates to the fact that India's action of massive retaliation would be in response to a situation in which its own territory or troops would have first suffered a nuclear attack. Retaliation to cause punishment in such a case certainly sounds more credible and legitimate to execute than the US threat of MR to any kind of provocation, even at the conventional level and irrespective of its scale.

India has maintained that the only purpose of nuclear weapons is deterrence, and it seeks to project deterrence through the threat of punishment. Hence, it has eschewed nuclear war-fighting doctrines, including the concept of 'limited nuclear war' with low-yield nuclear weapons. India believes that it would be difficult, if not impossible, to contain a situation once any kind of nuclear weapons have come into play. Moreover, in the case of India-Pakistan conflict, even a so-called limited war would be fought on own and geographically contiguous territories and spell huge human, financial and environmental costs.

This understanding, therefore, refuses to put nuclear weapons in different categories. As put by a former NSAB chairman, "for India the label on the weapon, tactical or strategic, is irrelevant since the use of either would constitute a nuclear attack against India.... This would invite a massive retaliatory strike. For Pakistan to think that a counter-force nuclear strike against military targets would enable it to escape a counter-value strike against its cities and population centres is a dangerous illusion."[23] This statement echoes India's belief that the best use of its nuclear weapons is to deter through the promise of a disproportionate response as spelt out in the massive retaliation strategy. By maximising the fear of extreme nuclear escalation, or in other words, by promising the worst, India's nuclear strategy seeks to make the possibility of use of nuclear weapons as remote as possible. Just as Pakistan claims it has only a *one-rung escalation ladder* which it will be compelled to climb in case of an Indian conventional attack, India's MR signals a *one-rung nuclear escalation ladder*.

Therefore, even when Pakistan expresses doubts about India's response to its use of TNWs, it can never be really sure that India would not respond with massive retaliation. Can it find it prudent to test India with use of one or a few TNWs? As succinctly put by a former National Security Advisor to Government of India:

> "If Pakistan were to use tactical nuclear weapons against India, even against Indian forces in Pakistan, it would effectively be opening the door to a massive Indian first strike, having crossed India's declared red lines. There would be little incentive, once Pakistan had taken hostilities to the nuclear level, for India to limit its response, since that would only invite further escalation

> by Pakistan.... Pakistani tactical nuclear weapon use would effectively free India to undertake a comprehensive first strike against Pakistan."[24]

Indeed, India maintains the approach that deterrence can best be established by clearly indicating that any use of nuclear weapons—and for India they all fall in the same category—would lead to an expansion of the nuclear combat zone and cause disproportionate loss. As pointed out by Freedman, "Tactical nuclear war, by the very nature of the weapons, has a built in escalation mechanism. It is hardly consistent to argue that nuclear weapons will inevitably be introduced because they are more efficient than conventional weapons and then assume that, once nuclear combat begins, both sides will be content to employ only the least efficient nuclear weapons."[25] TNWs hope to achieve minimum destruction. But their use would certainly engender an unstable situation with a potential for enormous destruction. As Therese Delpech wrote, "limited wars without escalation may look attractive, but the guarantee that they will remain so is limited as well."[26]

Recommendations for India

The objective of the development of TNWs by Pakistan, which is quintessentially a battlefield weapon, is to convey a political message to India. It threatens to create circumstances that would constrain political decision-making from executing military action owing to the fear of escalation of conflict.

Pakistan military planners would like to have India and the world believe that any use of force by India could provoke Pakistan's use of TNWs. But had this been true, Pakistan would not be investing as much as it is on modernising its conventional military. It well realises that the war would have to be executed in the conventional realm if the country has to survive after the conflict. Therefore, it is Pakistan's compulsion to brandish its TNWs to deter India, so long as it continues to use terror. This must not lead India to make the wrong inference that, "space left for prosecution of conventional offensive had purportedly shrunk to inconsequential levels, and therefore [it] is left with no option but to sequester India's conventional power and continue to stoically suffer the consequences of Pakistan's proxy war".[27] Pakistan's projection of TNW use need not deter India's requirement, if it so arises, to use conventional force to punish Pakistan's use of terrorism. This was visibly demonstrated through the air strikes at Balakot, where India exhibited the resolve to go to war to punish the Pakistan-supported terrorist strike at Pulwama. Meanwhile, across the border, Pakistan did not make any nuclear noises.

It is strange that analysts in India are taken in by the threat of Pakistan's use of nuclear weapons in the battlefield but they find it incredible that an India, even after being struck by nuclear weapons—a use which would have breached a huge psychological threshold—will not be able to carry out MR! In following massive retaliation, India has signaled that it refuses to play the game of tactical/limited nuclear war. Even if the adversary is threatening the use of 'clean, counter-force, low-yield weapons', India should express that it would have no option but to respond with its 'dirty, counter-value weapons'. This makes for credible deterrence.

Robert Jervis wrote in 1984 that, "states may be able to increase the chance of peace only by increasing the chance that war, if it comes, will be total. To decrease the probability of enormous destruction may increase the probability of aggression and limited wars."[28] India's MR is seeking the same. It refuses to decrease the horrors of nuclear war in order to avoid any temptation to use nuclear weapons under the mistaken assumption that the costs of the resulting war would be tolerable. Where the use of nuclear weapons is involved, it cannot be so, and India's massive retaliation is only underlining the obvious.

The test of *Nasr* and its eventual deployment in Pakistan's nuclear arsenal is obviously a move that the country has made in keeping with its own threat perceptions and its consideration of how it can best address them. It seeks to deter India from launching even limited conventional action by the suggestion of an inevitable escalation up the nuclear ladder. Therefore, in Pakistan's perception, by holding out the prospect of use of TNWs, it is actually enhancing its deterrence and thereby meeting the objective of its nuclear strategy, which is to obviate the possibility of a conventional war with India.

From India's perspective, however, nuclear weapons are all the same and Pakistan's use of what it describes as TNWs would not earn any concessions on India's doctrine of massive retaliation. In response to the Pakistani signal, therefore, there is no need for India to either make any material changes in its arsenal by way of developing tactical nuclear weapons itself, nor any changes to its doctrine of massive retaliation. At the same time, India need not be constrained from taking punitive military action in response to Pakistan-supported terrorist activity. The projection of TNWs cannot hope to guarantee protection to Pakistan's policy of using terrorism.

Notes

1. ISPR Press Release No. PR94/2011, 19 April 2011, at http://www.ispr.gov.pk/front/main.asp?o=t-press_release&id=1721. Accessed on 21 January 2019.
2. Ibid.
3. Thornton Read, 'Limited Strategic War and Tactical Nuclear War', in Klaus Knorr and Thornton Read (eds.), *Limited Strategic War,* Pall Mall Press, London, 1962, p. 96.
4. Feroz Hassan Khan, *Eating Grass: The Making of the Pakistani Bomb,* Stanford University Press, Stanford, 2012, p. 396.
5. It is a different matter that contradictory statements by Indian military officials have since created ambiguity about the existence of Cold Start strategy. It has also been referred to as the Proactive Strategy.
6. For instance see M. Iqbal, 'Deterrence Brings Peace', *NDC Journal* IX, 1996, as cited in Sadia Tasleem and Toby Dalton, 'Nuclear Emulation: Pakistan's Nuclear Trajectory', *Washington Quarterly*, vol. 41, No. 4, p. 140.
7. Shireen Mazari, 'Comment: Nature of Future Pakistan-India Wars', *Strategic Studies*, vol. 22, No. 3, Summer 2002, p. 4, as cited in Sadia Tasleem and Toby Dalton, n. 6.
8. Adil Sultan, 'Pakistan's Emerging Nuclear Posture: Impact of Drivers and Technology on Nuclear Doctrine', *Strategic Studies* (ISSI), vol. 32-33, Winter 2011 and Spring 2012, no. 4 and 1, at http://www.issi.org.pk/publication-files/1340000409_ 86108059.pdf. Accessed on 29 March 2020.

9. Maleeha Lodhi, 'Pakistan's Nuclear Compulsions', *The Jang*, 6 November 2012.
10. Shireen Mazari, 'Time to Target Nuclear Pakistan Again', *The Nation*, 13 February 2014, at https://nation.come.pk/13-Feb-2014/time-to-target-nuclear-pakistan-again. Accessed on 12 January 2018.
11. Michael Krepon, 'Pak Strategy: Deny India Nuclear Victory', *Tribune*, 3 January 2013.
12. A.H. Nayyar and Zia Mian, 'The Limited Military Utility of Pakistan's Battlefield Use of Nuclear Weapons in Response to Large-Scale Indian Conventional Attack', Pakistan Security Research Unit Brief, No. 61, University of Bradford, 11 November 2010.
13. Naeem Salik, *Learning to Live with the Bomb: Pakistan: 1998-2016,* Oxford University Press, London, 2017, p. 122.
14 Rabia Akhtar, 'NASR and Pakistan's Nuclear Deterrence—Analysis', *Eurasia Review*, 2 May 2011, at https://www.eurasiareview.com/02052011-nasr-and-pakistans-nuclear-deterrence-analysis/. Accessed on 4 June 2019.
15. A.H. Nayyar and Zia Mian, n. 12.
16. Qasim Qureshi, 'Deterrence Stability in South Asia', in Feroz H. Khan and Nick M. Masellis, *US-Pakistan Strategic Partnership: A Track II Dialogue*, sixth iteration, Phuket, Centre for Contemporary Conflict, US Naval Postgraduate School, Monterey, CA, January 2012, p. 10.
17. Naeem Salik, n. 13, p. 116.
18. For more on this see Manpreet Sethi, 'Defeating Pakistan's Nuclear Strategy', *Air Power Journal*, vol. 6, No. 1, Spring 2011, pp. 105-122.
19. 'Trump describes Pulwama Attack as "Horrible", State department asks Pakistan to Punish the Responsible', *Economic Times*, 20 February 2019.
20. Gen. N.C. Vij, 'Strengthening India's Nuclear Deterrence', in *Securing India*, VIF Perspective: Issues and Trends, Wisdom Tree, New Delhi, 2017, p. 7. Similar views may be found in Ajai Shukla, 'After a Pakistani TNW Strike, India Can Go for Pakistan's Nuclear Arsenal: Former NSA Shivshankar Menon', *Broadsword*, , 18 March 2017, at http://ajaishukla.blogspot.in/2017/03/after-pakistani-tnw-strike-india-will.html. Accessed on 15 May 2018 and Arka Biswas, 'Incredibility of India's Massive Retaliation: An Appraisal on Capability, Cost and Intention', *Comparative Strategy*, vol. 36, No. 5, pp. 445-456.
21. Ibid., p. 7.
22. The following paragraphs draw upon an earlier article by the author. For more see Manpreet Sethi, 'Massive Retaliation: Is the Threat Less than Credible?', *Air Power Journal*, vol. 13 , No. 2, Summer 2018, pp. 1-20.
23. Shyam Saran, 'Dealing with Pakistan's Brinkmanship', *The Hindu*, 7 December 2012.
24. Shivshankar Menon, *Choices: Inside the Making of India's Foreign Policy,* Penguin Random House India Pvt Ltd, Gurugram, 2016, p. 174.

25. Lawrence Freedman, *The Evolution of Nuclear Strategy,* Palgrave Macmillan, New York, 2003, p. 77.
26. Therese Delpech, *Nuclear Deterrence in the 21st Century: Lessons from the Cold War for a New Era of Strategic Piracy,* RAND, Santa Monica CA, 2012, p. 50.
27. Gen. N.C. Vij, n. 20, p. 8.
28. Robert Jervis, *The Illogic of American Nuclear Strategy,* Cornell University Press, Ithaca, 1984.

15. The Curious Case of Pakistan's Nuclear Proliferation

Arjun Anand and *Aarushi Vikram*

Introduction

The objective of this chapter is to highlight the past and future trends of the Pakistani proliferation network. After realising the asymmetry in conventional capabilities vis-à-vis India, Pakistan hoped to unconventionally increase its military capabilities. Contrary to the perception within a section of the global policy community that its participation in the nuclear world commenced with the arrival of A.Q. Khan, Pakistan had a plan to develop nuclear weapons ever since its inception. This plan thrived under Prime Minister Z.A. Bhutto who groomed A.Q. Khan and his Khan Research Laboratories (KRL) to find an alternate route to develop nuclear weapons. The Pakistan Atomic Energy Commission (PAEC) was the institution that first was supposed to develop plutonium-based nuclear weapons. A.Q. Khan, as the senior scientist at KRL (previously known as Engineering Research Laboratories), focused on the production of Highly-Enriched Uranium, using gas centrifuge technological methods. KRL became the cornerstone of Pakistan's atomic bomb project.

Pakistan initially imported technology and materials from various countries across Europe, the United States (US) (via Canada, South Africa and UAE), Japan, and China. Pakistan's nuclear weapons development programme with Chinese assistance has been a cause of concern for the international community for long. China was one of the leading exporters to Pakistan and continues to cooperate with it to date. The import network operated without complications and using techniques such as falsifying end users and paying more than the market premium, which ensured results without raising any suspicions. Critical nuclear weapons technology, including warhead design information, was shared by Beijing with a number of countries, including Pakistan.

In recent years, China projects its willingness to engage in nonproliferation efforts, including the adoption of export controls and the imposition of sanctions on proliferators, notwithstanding that it has continued to supply nuclear power reactors to Pakistan. China signed an agreement to build the Chashma-3 reactor in 2013. In 2015, a Chinese official confirmed that China had offered assistance in building six nuclear reactors in Pakistan. Recently declassified Central Intelligence Agency files have also highlighted Beijing's willingness to risk its own nuclear cooperation with the US to boost Pakistan's ambitions. The China National Nuclear Corporation (CNNC) had signed a framework agreement with the Pakistan Atomic Energy Commission for technical cooperation and development of uranium resources (July 2017). The civil nuclear energy cooperation provides an excellent cover to supply nuclear goods to Pakistan's nuclear weapons development programme.

The cooperation between China and Pakistan has also been extended in the realm of missiles. The Chinese missile system has a wide range of ballistic, cruise, air-to-air and surface-to-air missiles. It has also been a continuous provider of technology and missile components to Pakistan. In the past, China had exported Dong Feng-11 (DF-11) to Pakistan which served as basis for the *Shaheen I* and *Shaheen II* missiles.

Greed often contributed to suppliers turning a blind eye to Pakistan's purchase of goods for more than the sale price. Greed also led to Pakistan transitioning from an importer to an exporter of nuclear technology and materials. A weak economic state, Pakistan sought a lucrative business opportunity in proliferating to other states in the nuclear black market such as Iran, Saudi Arabia, North Korea. Apart from the economic opportunity, there were also political and ideological motivations that led to this transition.

The infamous A.Q. Khan network worked with few obstacles and excessive autonomy within the state until it was finally exposed in 2001.

The success of the Pakistani nuclear proliferation network has played a pivotal role in identifying the debilitating effects of the lack of control of the state when individual actors act on behalf of the same. The A.Q. Khan network not only managed to escape suspicion for over three decades but also changed the military capabilities of all states involved in the "Nuclear Walmart" and ignited the fear of technology falling into hands of non-state actors at the right price.

This chapter begins by looking into Pakistan's proliferation network and the clandestine measures it uses. It will then go on to examine the motivations of proliferation, both by the state and the individual actors involved. Further, this chapter will examine the current motivations for continued proliferation and its implications.

'Nuclear' Khan and Pakistan's Proliferation Network

Before proceeding to discuss Pakistan's proliferation motivations, it is necessary to understand the A.Q. Khan Network. Abdul Qadeer Khan was instrumental in setting up a proliferation network that made Pakistan a prominent entity in the nuclear black market. Providing buyers with not only material but also technical expertise, Khan did not just ignite the strategic importance of Pakistan but also fed into his own commercial greed. Seen as a criminal worldwide and a hero domestically, as the 'founder of Pakistan's uranium enrichment programme', A.Q. Khan was given immense importance within Pakistan, the benefits of which he reaped all his life. Even writings sponsored by the Pakistani establishment have underlined the operation of the network, and acknowledged A.Q. Khan's illicit collaborations.

A person who served in the nuclear establishment pointed to the CHIC-4 design and Highly-Enriched Uranium (HeU) from China[1] maintains that the National Defence Complex or National Engineering and Science Commission[2] had merely replicated the design in making the bomb which was tested in 1998. Apparently, the same design was seized by American officials when it was being secretly transferred to Libya. The A.Q. Khan network was unravelled during his attempt at assisting Libya in a nuclear effort.

Another very important work on the subject informs that "... Khan had not in fact fired a *Ghauri* on 6 April 1998 but a real North Korean *No-dong*. KRL technicians had been unable to perfect the technology, so Khan had simply ordered his men to repaint the North Korean weapon in the livery of the Pakistani military. 'The paint was barely dry, but nobody noticed, such was the excitement'...."[3] Quite interestingly, using air sample analysis of the US Los Alamos nuclear laboratory, this work also sheds light on the fact that one of Pakistan's 1998 tests was the plutonium bomb.[4] In fact, in the past, a section of the Western media had also informed of the plutonium-based bomb test in 1998. The conclusion of the US Government apparently was that Pakistan had conducted one of its tests—that of the North Korean plutonium bomb—for North Korea in 1998. It seems North Korea was hesitant to conduct tests and Pakistan had an opportunity to do so. This reveals the extent of the network's operation and coordination among the proliferators, including Pakistan. British intelligence had informed that Khan used "North Korean connections to purchase materials for Kahuta—rare metals, magnets and other difficult-to-source items—which were being used to amass an export stock, a store room of nuclear equipment for Pakistan to hawk."[5]

The Pakistani Government made available enormous resources for the operations of the clandestine proliferation network so that the its nuclear weapons project benefitted. A.Q. Khan had the privilege of taking a chartered plane from not only Pakistan but also from any other country, to transact items. Special planes were flown in to bring foreign scientists from any part of the world to assist the project. Similarly, special planes were sent in the name of carrying coffins but actually nuclear items, especially centrifuges were sent to the countries within the network. The network set up coordination centres not only in the countries developing nuclear weapons but also in some transit hubs like Dubai and the prominent former Soviet states in Central Asia.

Pakistan also sought help from the Al-Qaeda network and Osama bin Laden. In return, the concerned authorities in Pakistan indicated to have an interactive relationship with Jihadis. Osama bin Laden's men searched for uranium to build the Jihadi bomb. Several writings and reports document the Jihadi desire to acquire its own nuclear weapons. It seems they found an ally in Pakistan to receive a finished product. In 1996, the Lithuanian Government arrested some people who had links with Sunni extremists and Osama bin Laden. These people were selling 100 kg of uranium to the Pakistan-Al-Qaeda nexus, though these arrested persons mentioned that a Pakistani national was their client.[6] A general understanding also emerged that Al-Qaeda was basically focused on the making of the dirty bomb; possibly, it realised the difficulty in making the regular fission or fusion-based nuclear bomb.

The Pakistani military, scientific and political leadership coordinated with Jihadists regarding nuclear weapons. Some prominent military officials such as Lieutenant General Jamshed Gulzar and Muhammed Aziz were coordinating with Pakistani intelligence agencies and the global nuclear black market. Jihadis facilitated import of required nuclear items from Pakistan as well.

The end of the A.Q. Khan network is a myth. There is continued suspicion over Pakistan's involvement in nuclear proliferation even in the Western strategic community. After A.Q. Khan was exposed, the state denied knowledge over his actions. However, given the incessant control and complete autonomy given to Khan, many believe that to be untrue. While the state's and Khan's motivations for proliferation were different, it cannot be denied that nuclear proliferation basically served state interests. It is widely believed that Pakistan has continued to develop and test ballistic and cruise missile capabilities and is suspected of maintaining an illicit procurement network for goods and technologies related to its nuclear and missile programmes, although the extent to which the state participates directly in these activities may be a matter of speculation.

Before looking into the state's motivations, it is necessary to understand that the military establishment has been behind the true origin of any kind of political power in Pakistan for the past few decades and plays an active role in clandestine nuclear proliferation. Pakistan believes that the possession of nuclear weapons could serve to dissuade potential conventional aggression.

The inability of the international intelligence community to detect the extent of A.Q. Khan's illicit network for so long contributes to its consistent growth. One author highlights: "... the U.S. intelligence community experienced massive cuts in human intelligence collection post-Cold War, which played a critical role in the disruption of illicit smuggling networks. The intelligence agencies also did not have experience with the illicit transnational non-state networks", which were beginning to emerge. Unfortunately, even when the intelligence community procures information about Pakistan's illicit nuclear weapons acquisition activities, the US establishment overlooks it possibly because of its geopolitical considerations. Also, the weakness of export controls and the fatalism of Western suppliers caused primarily by greed helped in abetting Pakistan's import network.

The network used several deceptive tactics. At times, foreign governments like Sri Lanka were provided with wrong facts to ensure smooth transactions or secure benefits. The network was able to secure benefits because of the complicity of the Pakistani state. One of the commentators on the subject rightly maintains that the proliferation network was immensely aided by the process of globalisation.[7] The network falsely provided innocuous objectives through government and private companies. A number of state actors alongside Pakistan, such as Iran and North Korea got entangled with the steel industry to global high technology companies. Some knew the objectives but many were completely in the dark about the motives.

Pakistan would continue to proliferate for various reasons. First, in the past couple of decades, the true origin of any kind of nuclear ambition has been the military establishment. The Pakistani military has been a major cause of concern while discussing nuclear proliferation. Maintaining the armed forces in Pakistan costs an inordinately large sum despite the slow economic growth of the state. There is a possibility that proliferation is used as rogue-funding to maintain the military costs. The cost also has to be justified to the people, who must believe that the military is dominant. Public sentiment is an important driver in this containment of power. It could also be for ideological reasons, to build a relationship of cooperation with other Islamic countries, such as Saudi Arabia. It also gives Pakistan a sense of geopolitical security and political prestige.

While state motivations could have economic determinants, such as rogue-funding to maintain military capabilities, they were more strategic in nature. The state's tacit support to A.Q. Khan due to its dependence on his sophisticated proliferation network provided him with ample opportunities to proliferate with states (such as Iran).

It is difficult to believe that Khan exceeded whatever mandate he received from the Pakistani leadership. Khan's cooperation with states had continued in the form of cooperation with Iran, or bartering sensitive nuclear technologies for decades-old liquid-fuel missile technology, or Libyan trade. He defied the global non-proliferation and Western order while establishing himself as a powerful force domestically and in the nuclear black market. There was also an underlying ideological motivation where Khan claims his actions were nationalist and meant to benefit the Islamic states. However, his dealings with North Korea or Iran (which is primarily a Shia state) were contradictory to his "nationalist beliefs".

The Pakistani state often claims to be unaware of the extent of Khan's dealings but is significantly responsible for his nuclear enterprise. The Pakistani government granted Khan unquestionable authority, had minimal nuclear oversight and ignored warning signs, perhaps, due to the presence of a powerful "deep state"[8] within Pakistan. Khan was given complete control and broad financial autonomy which allowed for him to grow his nuclear network by giving him flexibility in the operation of his procurement network.

Pakistan's Proliferation Network: Current Trends

The nuclear policy of Pakistan in the past has been a crucial element of its foreign and security policy. Pakistan's desire to unconventionally increase their military capabilities can be attributed to countering

India's military dominance and nuclear policy. The A.Q. Khan Nuclear Proliferation Network changed the nuclear black market and the sophistication of the network ensured that it went undetected for more than three decades until it finally unraveled in 2004. However, the question of global nuclear proliferation currently emanating from Pakistan still ensues.

Apart from restructuring the contours of the geopolitics of a region with the proliferation of nuclear weapons to state actors, the current instability and existence of the radical "deep state" within Pakistan risks the proliferation of nuclear weapons in the hands of non-state actors or even terrorist organisations. Many terrorist organisations, targeted against India and Afghanistan, are based in Pakistan and garner support from various elements based within the Pakistani intelligence community or military establishment.

Thus, it is not unwise to suggest that the Pakistani state can proliferate these weapons to non-state actors poised against countries like India or even, Israel. In this era of mass-casualty terrorism, a nuclear dirty bomb is an ultimate weapon in the hands of terrorists. Furthermore, the development of Tactical Nuclear Weapons (*Nasr* or *Hatf-9*) by Pakistan is said to be susceptible to ill use at the hands of terrorists.[9] The gnawing presence of a deep state within Pakistan was instrumental in orchestrating the proliferation of nuclear weapons and technology (both outflow and inflow) across Libya, Iran, Iraq and North Korea.

To explain the future of Pakistan's nuclear weapons proliferation, we must take into account the current situation with regard to its own economic and political woes in the context of the current geopolitical scenario. Turning to the Middle East, it is important to note the current power struggle between Iran and Saudi Arabia to establish its own rule over the Islamic realm. The Sunni Kingdom of Saudi Arabia and Shia Iran are fighting a battle of hegemony in the Middle East, be it through strengthening their economic positions or by investing in increasing their respective military prowess.

However, we saw the dawn of a great game being played out in the Middle East with the arrival of the Trump administration in January 2017 and the renewed importance of the US-Israel Alliance.

As the *New York Times* revealed, the Trump administration pursued a deal with Saudi Arabia to develop its nuclear energy sector. "By ramming through the sale of as much as $80 billion in nuclear power plants, the Trump administration [provided] sensitive know-how and materials to a government whose *de facto* leader, Crown Prince Mohammed bin Salman, suggested that he may eventually want a nuclear weapon as a hedge against Iran and [showed] little concern for what the rest of the world thinks."[10]

Muhammed bin Salman's visit to Pakistan raised questions of potential proliferation as well. The purpose of this visit was economic discussions where $1 billion was deposited out of the $3 billion cash pledge for the Gulf's financial assistance. However, behind these economic discussions lay the potential new developments in Saudi-Pakistani understanding on nuclear weapons and missiles. In the past, Saudi oil was understood to have financed the development of Pakistan's uranium enrichment plant and Riyadh has been believed to view Islamabad as a potential source of atomic bombs if it feels sufficiently threatened. In the current scenario of increasing tensions between Saudi Arabia and Iran, it is possible that Saudi Arabia has finally turned to Pakistan for nuclear assistance. If we are to find truth in these speculations, we may see a reactivation of the Pakistani Proliferation Network in the Middle East. The US may use Pakistan as a conduit to supply nuclear knowledge to Saudi Arabia, so as to delicately balance expectations in the Middle East and with Western allies. Since Pakistan is a 'usual suspect' in many proliferation cases, the US will seek to keep this status quo intact. It frequently sensitized the international community that Pakistan is in dire straits, due to domestic instability and economic challenges. Pressure from Saudi Arabia and the US will force Pakistan's hand in proliferating nuclear weapons to the Saudis.

The Waltzian theory of "security through increased horizontal spread of nuclear weapons" or the principle of "... possession of nuclear weapons may slow arms races down, rather than speed them up ..."[11] are challenged by the security threats posed by Pakistan. Pakistan has been increasing the size of its nuclear stockpile in terms of nuclear warheads, according to the *SIPRI Yearbook 2018*, making

Pakistan the sixth-largest Nuclear Weapons State. As per Ashley Tellis' deposition before the Subcommittee on Strategic Forces of the Committee on Armed Services, United States Senate "In contrast to both China and India, [who] view their nuclear weapons primarily as second-strike systems, Pakistan's nuclear doctrine conceives of its weapons as being used first, mainly in response to a conventional attack by India. Hence, Pakistan has invested heavily in developing a diverse set of capabilities ranging from the strategic to the tactical."[12] It has surpassed India, Israel and North Korea. This is once again in direct conflict with Waltzian theory on spread of nuclear weapons, since Pakistan is a state dependent on its military for administration, marred at the same time, by domestic instability and conflicts.

The aim here is to prove that Pakistani nuclear proliferation and development is a dangerous trend, since the nuclear weapons may end up in the hands of non-state actors giving rise to nuclear terrorism in South Asia and neighbouring regions.

Pakistani nuclear weapons have always been a concern for global security. Michael Krepon, co-founder of the Henry L. Stimson Center, has argued that "a prolonged period of turbulence and infighting among the country's President, Prime Minister, and Army Chief" could jeopardise the army's unity of command, which "is essential for nuclear security."[13]

The US military officials also expressed concern about the security of Pakistan's nuclear weapons. Experts also worry that nuclear weapons could be sold by insiders during a worsened crisis.[14] This shows the inherent nuclear insecurity that persists in Pakistan. Another concern regarding the security of nuclear weapons is the presence of radical groups within government agencies and the presence of a 'deep state' within Pakistan, which can use nuclear weapons to further their own fiendish agendas. Nuclear weapons have garnered support from the ruling elites, Islamic clerics and military leaders for the sole purpose of serving as a tool against India, since the Indian intervention in Bangladesh in 1971.

There are two possible scenarios as to how nuclear weapons being developed in Pakistan may end up in the hands of a non-state actor/terrorist organisation:

1. The insecurity of nuclear weapons establishments—Time and again, countries around the world have expressed concern over the security of Pakistani nuclear establishments. With the growing number of nuclear weapons and deployable battlefield warheads, security of these nuclear weapons remains a lingering concern. Theft of nuclear weapons is a real threat, if a state of nuclear insecurity increases in the country. As more and more nuclear warheads are being built, the security of these warheads may be too much to handle for the National Command Authority of Pakistan. One possible scenario will be to delegate nuclear weapons security to the military. With the dominance of the military in Pakistan, any sort of the excessive delegation of nuclear weapons to the military undermines the practice of civilian command and control.
2. Collusion—The nature of covert operations undertaken by the ISI in the Af-Pak, PoK regions through proxy; the existence of a "deep state" in Pakistan, borne out of disgruntled ruling elites, radical clerics and the independent military establishment, are no secret within the international community. This strategy of asymmetric warfare (here, asymmetric denotes unconventional or proxy warfare) has been an unspoken part of Pakistan's military discourse.

   Even if we are to believe, in a possible scenario, that a terror organisation acquired fissile materials through theft, it would be a folly to overlook the fact that a crude Radiological Dispersion Device (RDD) dirty bomb is beyond the expertise of terror groups. This theft and the subsequent dispersal of nuclear technology and fissile material, is not an impossible scenario, considering the A.Q. Khan Network's spread across West Asia and East Asia, eluding intelligence agencies all over the world. Moreover, to advance vested Pakistani interests, smuggling of nuclear crude bombs to any target country through covert means is not an improbable situation. The current instability and ambitions of various factions in Pakistan is a troubling threat.

Why will Pakistan proliferate weapons to non-state actors, with regard to India? In an attempt to answer it simply—because it does not have the will to follow its own doctrinal guidelines of first use, fearing massive nuclear retaliation from India. Firstly, a dirty bomb detonation is untraceable to the perpetrator. Pakistan may use this as an option when pushed back through continuous pressure from India, without giving enough grounds for any massive nuclear retaliation against its own. Conventional options will result in a military conflict, attracting the attention of an already divided world community. A vigilant focus on South Asia by the international community is undesirable to India's interests.

Theatre Nuclear Weapons proliferation is a threat, but will not involve government agencies since a Tactical Nuclear Weapon (TNW) strike against India will be met with massive nuclear retaliation—albeit the perpetrator is a rogue or has been bought off. A TNW has clear Pakistani signature, even though the fear of its proliferation by rogue elements (due to the delegated command given to Brigadier-level field officers) to non-state actors remains high. But the very nature of the second-strike option that India may adopt, serves as a counter to this sort of proliferation.

Implications

Pakistan has developed nuclear weapons and capabilities in a clandestine manner through acquisitions of nuclear and weapons technology. However, the problem is not of the clandestine inflow of these technologies to Pakistan but lies in the outflow or proliferation of these technologies to third countries. The highly unregulated and rogue nature of its own proliferation has calamitous implications for the geostrategic environment. As suggested by many international as well as US congressional reports, Pakistani nuclear weapons exist in a state of high instability and irregularity. This is further evidenced by the excessive delegated Command and Control (C2) of its own TNWs (local commanders exert full control over the deployment of TNWs). The country's internal instability, poor economic conditions, complemented with a false sense of regional superiority renders it the 'usual suspect' for rogue proliferation.

Proliferation to states

The Pakistani proliferation network covers states such as Saudi Arabia, North Korea, and Iran. At the moment, it is well known that Iran and Saudi Arabia are involved in a regional power struggle (the civil war in Yemen, which has turned into a power struggle between the Saudi-backed Yemen State and the Iran-backed Houthi rebels). Saudi Arabia, as the recent reports suggest, is an "all-weather ally" of Pakistan and maybe the client for Pakistani nuclear weapons. Pakistan has time and again extended "reliable" military assistance to Saudi Arabia. In exchange, Riyadh has maintained high-profile economic assistance to Pakistan, with the US$ 20 billion potential investment bequeathed by Crown Prince Mohammed Bin Salman. We also know of the assistance extended by Pakistan to facilitate weapons transfer between China and Saudi Arabia, as mentioned above.

The implication of such a close relationship is the role that nuclear weapons would play. On Saudi Arabia's "request", Pakistan may proliferate nuclear weapons to the Saudis. Nuclear weapons in the Middle East, in the current scenario, will be a game- changer and would further destabilise the situation in the region. If the Saudis are to garner a nuclear edge, the entire Iran Nuclear Deal may be struck down, which may consequently herald the beginning of an arms race and nuclear one-upmanship in the region. A nuclear Iran is unacceptable to Israel and will be met with fierce resistance resulting in possible military conflicts between the two countries. Israel has showcased its boldness and adopted aggressive military tactics to deny nuclear proliferation in the region (the famed Osiraq pre-emptive strike by Israeli F-16s; the 2007 Israeli attack carried out against Syria to destroy a nuclear reactor being built with North Korean assistance). It will not be prudent to rule out further such steps that by Israel to safeguard its own interest.

India will be caught in an awkward position if nuclear weapons are proliferated in the Middle East by Pakistan. India shares warm relations with Iran, Saudi Arabia and Israel. How will India manage its relations with these countries in the scenario of nuclear weapons being proliferated in the Middle East? How will India manage the rise of a potential arms race and military brinkmanship in the Middle East? These scenarios will require a check on Pakistan's proliferation network, to avoid nuclear radicalism in the Middle East.

Proliferation to Non-state actors

It is no secret that Pakistan has indulged in the policy of arming and training non-state actors/terrorists to advance its own agenda. Pakistan's Inter-Services Intelligence has sponsored several terrorist groups in the region. There is a varied level of cooperation between the Pakistani army, Pakistani intelligence, and radical organisations. There is cooperation and collaboration between government agencies within the "deep state" of Pakistan and terror organisations; the presence of radical organisations is a highly dangerous situation. It would not be prudent to turn our attention away from Pakistani nuclear weapons ending up as dirty bombs in the hands of terrorists due to help from this "deep state".

In this era of mass-casualty terrorism, nuclear weapons are the ultimate weapon in the hands of a terror organisation, given the context of India's and Pakistan's strained and challenging relationship. A nuclear detonation on India's counter-value targets by a terrorist organisation is a high possibility. We have already seen the military riposte India adopted after the recent Pulwama attacks through military aggression, albeit against non-military targets. But it does not discount the heavy mobilisation and alertness that the Indian defence establishments adopted post the Pulwama attacks. It is unimaginable to comprehend the nuclear Armageddon that would ensue, post a dirty bomb detonation on Indian soil by a Pakistan-based terror organisation.

Conclusion

The arrest and confession of Pakistani nuclear weapons scientist, Dr A.Q. Khan, revealed an extensive global nuclear proliferation network, which provided nuclear technology and expertise to clients like Iran, North Korea and Libya. The alarming aspect of this revelation was the nature and intensity of the clandestine operation of the Khan Network, which eluded both the national and international intelligence communities. But the discovery highlighted the fact that nuclear technology is no longer the monopoly of industrialised countries, and can be purchased by both state and non-state actors.

In current geopolitics, the renewed importance of nuclear weapons—has once again put the focus back on the proliferation network that may emanate out of Pakistan. The illicit nature of nuclear technology and knowledge transfer that borne out of Pakistan has made it the centre of the current discourse on the dangers of horizontal proliferation among the Middle Eastern state and non-state actors. Pakistan is finding itself being pushed to the wall, with economic woes and domestic instability. There is distrust between the military and the democratically-elected government, with the military establishment being wary of Imran Khan wielding control over the nuclear button.

The clandestine nature of Pakistani "deep state" is unnerving, given the current backlash and mistrust Pakistan faces over its nuclear security from the international community. Pakistan's motivations to proliferate nuclear weapons to terror organisations against countries like India is not a case that can be overlooked. Similarly, an economically weak but militarily powerful Pakistan will find it lucrative to trade nuclear weapons with countries like Saudi Arabia, which is ready with its financial might to "assist its an all-weather ally".

The international community must take note of and ensure that nuclear motivations are left out of the purview of power politics in any region. The proliferation of nuclear weapons to any Non-Nuclear Weapons State (NNWS) is an irresponsible act, especially in the volatile Middle East. Although Pakistan has time and again tried to reassure the international community of its nuclear commitments, it is high time that the state of Pakistan is made to accede to international counter-proliferation regimes. The nature of clandestine nuclear trade must be tackled through cooperation within the international intelligence community, so as to prevent the prop-up of another Khan Network.

Notes

1. Feroz Hassan Khan, *Eating the Grass: the Making of the Pakistani Bomb*, Foundation Books, Delhi, p. 188.
2. Ibid., p. 190.
3. Adrian Levy and Catherine Scott-Clark, *Deception: Pakistan, the United States and the Global Nuclear Weapons Conspiracy*, Penguin Books, New Delhi, p. 268.
4. Ibid., p. 278.
5. Ibid., p. 279.
6. Ibid., p. 261.
7. Feroz Hassan Khan, n. 1, p. 365.
8. A deep state is a form of clandestine government made up of hidden or covert networks of power operating independently of a nation's political leadership, in pursuit of their own agenda and goals. Examples include organs of state, such as the armed forces or public authorities (intelligence agencies, police, secret police, administrative agencies, and government bureaucracy). A deep state can also take the form of entrenched, career civil servants acting in a non-conspiratorial manner, to further their own interests. The intent of a deep state can include continuity of the state itself, job security for its members, enhanced power and authority, and the pursuit of ideological objectives.
9. Given that the *Nasr* TNW has pre-delegated command and control to local commanders, there is a danger of the actual weapon system falling into the hands of jehadi groups with or without insider help (Nagappa, Viswanathan and Malhotra, 2013).
10. Hamid Dabashi, *Opinion/Al Jazeera*. 7 March 2019. https://www.aljazeera.com/indepth/opinion/making-nuclear-mbs-190307135114759.html. Accessed on 8 March 2019.
11. Kenneth Waltz, 'The Spread of Nuclear Weapons: More May Better.' *International Institute for Strategic Studies*, 1981, pp. 1-35.
12. Committee on Armed Services, 'Hearing before the Subcommittee on Strategic Forces of the Committee on Armed Services United States Senate.' Washington DC, US Government Publishing Office, 2015, pp. 27-29.
13. Michael Krepon, 'U.S.-Pakistan Strategic Relations,' Statement before the Committee on Senate Homeland Security and Governmental Affairs Subcommittee on Federal Financial Management, Government Information, Federal Services, and International Security, 12 June 2008.
14. Paul K. Kerr and Mary Beth Nitkin, *Pakistan's Nuclear Weapons*. Research Report, Washington DC, Congressional Research Service, 2016.

References

Bahgat, Gawdat. 2006. 'Nuclear Proliferation: The Case of Saudi Arabia.' *The Middle East Journal*, pp. 421-443.

Braun, Chaim and Christopher F. Chyba. 2004. 'Proliferation Rings: New Challenges To The Nuclear Nonproliferation Regime.' *International Security,* International Security 29 (2): 5-49.

Carnegie Endowment for International Peace. 2016. 'Pakistan's Nuclear Use Doctrine.'

Clary, Christopher. 2005. *The A. Q. Khan Network: Causes And Implications.* PG Thesis, Monterey: Naval Postgraduate School.

Dabashi, Hamid. 2019. *Opinion/Al Jazeera.* 7 March, at https://www.aljazeera.com/indepth/opinion/making-nuclear-mbs-190307135114759.html. Accessed on 8 March 2019.

Felbab-Brown, Vanda. 2018. 'Why Pakistan Supports Terrorist Groups, And Why The US Finds It So Hard To Induce Change', at https://www.brookings.edu/blog/order-from-chaos/2018/01/05/why-pakistan-supports-terrorist-groups-and-why-the-us-finds-it-so-hard-to-induce-change/.

Gupta, Arvind and K.D. Kapur. 2012. *Emerging Asian Nuclear Environment: Implications for India.* The Indian Pugwash Society Publication, New Delhi.

Hastings, Justin V. 2012. 'Geography of Nuclear Proliferation Networks.' *Nonproliferation Review,* p. 429-450.

Kerr, Paul. K. and Mary Beth Nitkin. 2016. *Pakistan's Nuclear Weapons* Research Report, Congressional Research Service, Washington DC.

MacCalman, Molly. 2016. 'A.Q. Khan Nuclear Smuggling Network.' *Journal Of Strategic Security,* pp. 104-118.

Maerli, Bremer Morten and Lodgaard Sverre 2007. *Nuclear Proliferation and International Security.* Routledge, Oxon.

Michael Krepon, 'U.S. Pakistan Strategic Relations,' Statement before the Committee on Senate Homeland Security and Governmental Affairs Subcommittee on Federal Financial Management, Government Information, Federal Services, and International Security, 12 June 2008.

Nabil, Rahmatullah. 2017. 'The World Must Secure Pakistan's Nuclear Weapons'. *New York Times*, 20 April 2017.

Nagappa, Rajaram, Arun Viswanathan and Aditi Malhotra. 2013. *Hatf-IX/NASR- Pakistan's Tactical Nuclear Weapon: Implications for Indo-Pak Deterrence.* NIAS Report, National Institute of Advanced Studies, Bengaluru.

Nelson, Dean and Tom Hussain. 2012. *Militants Attack Pakistan Nuclear Air Base,* 6 August, at https://www.telegraph.co.uk/news/worldnews/asia/pakistan/9479041/Militants-attack-Pakistan-nuclear-air-base.html. Accessed on 13 March 2019.

New York Times. 2015. 'The Pakistan Nuclear Nightmare', 7 November 2015.

Philipp, Elizabeth and Kelsey Davenport. 2016. 'Assessing Progress On Nuclear Nonproliferation And Disarmament'. An Arms Control Association Report.

Raina, Puneet. 2015. *Nuclear Terrorism: Threat Perception and Response in South Asia*. Gaurav Book Centre Pvt Ltd, New Delhi.

The International Institute For Strategic Studies. 2007. *Nuclear Black Markets: Pakistan, A.Q. Khan and the Rise of Proliferation Networks*. IISS, London.

Virmani, Arvind. 2006. *Trilateral Nuclear Proliferation: Pakistan's Euro-Chinese Bomb*. IDSA, New Delhi.

Walker, William and Wheeler, Nicholas J. 2013. 'Problem of Weak Nuclear States.' *Nonproliferation Review*, pp. 411-431.

Waltz, Kenneth. 1981. 'The Spread of Nuclear Weapons: More May Better.' *International Institute for Strategic Studies*, pp. 1-35.

16. Conclusion

Shalini Chawla and *Rajiv Nayan*

History of strained India-Pakistan relations which have experienced multiple crises indicate that nuclear dynamics play a critical role in the relationship. Statements made by senior Pakistani leaders signify Pakistan's inclination to use the threat of nuclear weapons directly or indirectly to deal with India's robust positioning or a probable threat of an Indian retaliation (to Pakistan's sub-conventional provocations!). The intensity and frequency of the threat of use of nuclear weapons are varied given the sensitivity of the geopolitical environment, Pakistan's strategic compulsions and its economic vulnerabilities, which have made it extremely dependent on external assistance over the decades. Pakistan's nuclear arsenal build-up is taking place at an accelerated pace with consistent Chinese assistance, and Pakistan reportedly has approximately 165 nuclear warheads. Pakistan's nuclear doctrine has evolved over the decades, and there have been critical developments in the last decade impacting Pakistan's thinking, position, and strategic posture. Pakistan's nuclear behaviour is shaped largely by its perceived threat perceptions; its desire to match India's conventional edge; yearning to obtain an ultimate weapon of survivability; project itself as a leader of the Islamic world, and most importantly, to successfully conduct cross border terrorism targeting India to pursue its objectives in Jammu and Kashmir without the fear of a possible Indian military retaliation.

For Pakistan, nuclear weapons are aimed towards 'war prevention', and possibly deny India any space for a conventional war. This stands in complete contrast with India's nuclear doctrine which talks about *no first use* and aims at using nuclear weapons to deter adversary's use of nuclear weapons. New Delhi's stance on a possibility of a 'limited conventional war' under the nuclear shadow did trigger alterations in Pakistan's nuclear posturing and build-up. India's former Defence Minister George Fernandes, at a National Seminar on "The Challenges of Limited War: Parameters and Options", after few months of the Kargil war, said: "Nuclear weapons did not make war obsolete, they simply imposed another dimension on the way warfare was conducted ... conventional war remained feasible, though with definite limitations, if escalation across the nuclear threshold was to be avoided."[1]

Although the objectives of the nuclear weapons for Pakistan have remained unchanged, the nuclear doctrine has evolved, and its nuclear behaviour has witnessed interesting shifts in the last decade. Pakistan's messaging in the overall nuclear position has not been very different from the time Pakistan started building its weapons in the early 1970s. Post its defeat in the 1971 war against India and the disintegration of the country Pakistan was convinced about the indispensability of the nuclear weapons and wanted to acquire the bomb at any cost. Then Pakistani Prime Minister Zulfikar Ali Bhutto, confidently announced that Pakistan is willing to compromise its economic development and 'will eat grass' but build the bomb. Indeed, the military led nation did divert a significant chunk of the national resources and contribution from the 'friendly' countries to acquire nuclear weapons, which it portrayed as an answer to its insecurities.

Nuclear weapons were to provide the ultimate guarantee of security to the nation and Pakistan raised money for weapon build-up from the Muslim nations (in 1970s and 1980s) in the name of an *Islamic Bomb*. Religion became an important factor in the strategic thinking and not only the nuclear weapon build up was facilitated by the religious fervor, but radical extremism also started to gain firm ground within the social, political and military dynamics of Pakistan. Jihad became the official motto of the Pakistan military and *Islamisation of the Army* was proudly embraced under General Zia's regime.

Pakistan's effort has been to maintain ambiguity in its nuclear posture with an element of 'uncertainty'. It has relied extensively on the 'first use' doctrine based on the assumption that India's responsible posture and its strategic culture, which dwells on 'restrain', would restrict New Delhi's willingness and ability to retaliate to Pakistan's first use of nuclear weapons. Pakistan has issued statements highlighting its low nuclear threshold very often to deal with the crisis vis-à-vis India. In 2002, during Operation Parakaram, Pakistan's SPD head, Lt Gen Khalid Kidwai talked about the red lines and tried to draw rather indefinite and vague boundaries which could potentially consider any possible punitive action by India (against Pakistan) as a provocation for Pakistan to use nuclear weapons. It is interesting to note that Pakistan talked about 'first use', projected a low nuclear threshold, and at the same time tried to project itself as a restraint and responsible nuclear weapon state which would use nuclear weapon as a *last resort*. In 2012, Pakistan proudly announced NASR—a short range nuclear missile which falls under the *Tactical Nuclear Weapons* with an assumption that it would close India's options of a limited conventional war. It expanded and developed its nuclear capability and claims to have developed a nuclear triad achieving the "*Full Spectrum Deterrence*".

Pakistan today possesses a significant number of warheads, is confident to have achieved a full spectrum deterrence, and claims that it has the capability to launch nuclear weapons from all three platforms- land, air and sea. The big question today is if Pakistan actually feels secure with the nuclear weapons, and how do we see its nuclear posture shaping in future?

Pakistan is struggling with multiple challenges internally and externally. Pakistan struggled to manage its insecurities from the time of its inception. While some insecurities emerged from its small size, complex geography, and rebellion it faced on its frontier borders, majority of the insecurities were perceived and highlighted to build up and maintain the stature of the all-powerful military.

The civil-military relations have been strained, and the historical evidence suggests a traditional pattern of events in Pakistan's democratic landscape. A democratic leadership comes into power with the support of the men in Khaki. The leader of the opposition party is targeted and charged with corruption, and responsibility of the Pakistan's economic woes is passed to the outgoing civilian regime. The civil-military cordial relations usually don't last long and the ruling party struggles to complete its tenure. Prime Minister Imran Khan won the 2018 elections with the military's overwhelming support and the elections were termed "Selection 2018". Imran Khan failed to keep up his commitments of *Naya Pakistan*. Troubles between Khan and the military started to brew on the issues of governance, but perhaps the most significant development denting the relationship was Imran Khan's resistance to give the official approval to the appointment of the new ISI chief—Lt Gen Nadeem Ahmed Anjum and his keenness to retain former DG ISI Lt Gen Faiz Hameed. Imran Khan undoubtedly went beyond the established limits of the civilian leadership in Pakistan, challenging the military's position. There is clearly a trust deficit between the power holders in Pakistan making the political situation (once again) highly unstable in the country. This has been a usual cycle in Pakistan reminding us of the dominance of the military.

Pakistan's economic figures are alarming. The inflation rate at consumer prices is estimated at 11.2 per cent (2022)[2] and the debt burden is a prime concern. Total debt and liabilities stand at 89.2 per cent of the GDP.[3] Total external debt and liabilities stand at 39.7 per cent of the nation's GDP.[4] It is estimated that a significant percentage in the liabilities has been added during the PTI's tenure starting in 2018. Reports suggest that Pakistan requires gross external financing of close to US$ 51.6 billion within a two-year period (2021-2023) to be able to meet its requirements. There is growing resentment within the masses and according to a consumer confidence survey conducted by *Ipsos*, a Paris based market research and consulting firm, majority of the Pakistan hold an opinion that the nation is moving in the wrong direction.[5]

Pakistan has faced consistent financial challenges due to the lack of prudent fiscal policies leading to high dependence on external aid and assistance. Military's desire to match India's conventional military capability did result in a sustained high defence budget and led to the neglect of development expenditure in Pakistan for decades. The critical social sectors (health and education) remain deprived of the much-needed national resources as compared to the spending on defence. Although Pakistan has a breather with the recent US$ 6 billion IMF package, it's unlikely that it will cut down is defence spending. The IMF package entails increase in taxes which implies an additional burden for the people.[6]

Balochistan remains highly troubled and has witnessed a series of attacks by the Baloch separatists against the Chinese workers. The attacks have alarmed the Chinese working in the country. Gwadar in Balochistan is extremely crucial to Beijing's geostrategic and geoeconomic interests. There have been major protests in Gwadar by the locals demanding access to basic facilities from the authorities. Despite the Chinese investing billions of dollars in CPEC, the Baloch have not been a beneficiary in any form. On the other hand, the local economy in Gwadar has been in shambles and the locals have been bearing a heavy cost of the high Chinese presence in the region. Baloch protestors are demanding access to drinking water, uninterrupted access to the seawater for fishing, and action against unnecessary checkpoints and illegal fishing. The protests seem to be gathering momentum and the Chinese projects have been impacted adversely. The CPEC is facing challenges and Chinese workers in Pakistan have been targeted in the past few years. There have been apprehensions about how these developments would impact the Sino-Pak alliance. Pakistan and China seem to be committed to the strategic alliance and the overall dynamics are unlikely to alter anytime soon. On the hand, Pakistan is unsure about its future relationship with the United States. Washington seems to be evaluating its options with Pakistan and there is less clarity on how the relationship will shape up in future. The US needs Pakistan's support in its counter-terrorism efforts/initiatives and Pakistan certainly cannot afford to stand against the US given its financial crisis and strategic constraints which require international support.

Pakistan sees the Taliban's takeover in Kabul on 14 August 2021, as its strategic victory and its long-cherished dream of seeking strategic depth has been fulfilled. While Pakistan did rejoice the defeat of the democratic institutions in Afghanistan, there are serious challenges of running the country (Afghanistan) without international aid and assistance. Pakistan has been struggling to deal with the massive influx of Afghan migrants and is also, appealing on various platforms for the Taliban's recognition and humanitarian assistance for Kabul. The ideological fallouts of the Taliban's coming into power in Afghanistan cannot be ruled out. The Tehrik-e-Taliban Pakistan (TTP) is actively conducting terror attacks and asserting itself as a potent force.

While the internal and external dynamics of Pakistan pose serious challenges to the policymakers adding to the state's insecurity, the nuclear dynamics in Pakistan remain unchanged. Pakistan has maintained a build-up of a significant nuclear arsenal and believes in a projection of a low nuclear threshold. It would be interesting to assess Pakistan's nuclear posture in the future:

1. Pakistan's reliance on nuclear weapons is likely to grow given the insecurities it is facing. Pakistan's fault lines are unlikely to settle down anytime soon.
2. The nuclear arsenal is expected to continue to grow. It would expand its options of delivery systems with consistent Chinese support.
3. The basic objectives of nuclear weapons remain unchanged for Pakistan and thus, the nuclear posture is likely to convey uncertainty with a low nuclear threshold, which Pakistan feels works towards its strategic advantage.
4. Pakistan will continue to highlight the dangers of a probable nuclear war in the region.

Notes

1. George Fernandes, 'The Challenges of Limited War: Parameters and Options', inaugural address at the National Seminar organised by IDSA, 5 January 2000, at http://www.idsa-india.org/defmin5-2000.html. Accessed on 2 January 2022.

2. International Monetary Fund, Country Data, Pakistan, imf.org/en/Countries/PAK. Accessed on June 25, 2022.
3. State Bank of Pakistan, https://www.sbp.org.pk/ecodata/Summary.pdf. Accessed on August 11, 2022.
4. Ibid.
5. 'Most Pakistanis believe country is headed in wrong direction', *Dawn*, 25 November 2021. Accessed on 30 November 2021.
6. Shahbaz Rana, 'Islamabad swallows bitter IMF pills', *The Express Tribune*, 22 November 2021, at https://tribune.com.pk/story/2330507/pakistan-imf-agree-on-measures-to-revive-stalled-programme. Accessed on 25 November 2021.

Index